WAY TO WATER

WAY to WATER
A Theopoetics Primer

L. Callid Keefe-Perry

With a Foreword by Terry A. Veling

and poems by Dave Harrity

CASCADE *Books* · Eugene, Oregon

WAY TO WATER
A Theopoetics Primer

Copyright © 2014 L. Callid Keefe-Perry. All rights reserved. Except for brief quotations in critical publications or reviews, no part of this book may be reproduced in any manner without prior written permission from the publisher. Write: Permissions, Wipf and Stock Publishers, 199 W. 8th Ave., Suite 3, Eugene, OR 97401.

Cascade Books
An Imprint of Wipf and Stock Publishers
199 W. 8th Ave., Suite 3
Eugene, OR 97401

www.wipfandstock.com

ISBN 13: 978-1-62564-520-3

Cataloging-in-Publication data:

Keefe-Perry, L. Callid.

Way to water : a theopoetics primer / L. Callid Keefe-Perry ; foreword by Terry A. Veling ; poems by Dave Harrity.

xx + 220 p. ; 23 cm. Includes bibliographical references and indexes.

ISBN 13: 978-1-62564-520-3

1. Human body—Religious aspects—Christianity. 2. Aesthetics—Religious aspects—Christianity. 3. Religion and Poetry—Christianity. 4. Hopper, Stanley Romaine, 1907–. I. Veling, Terry A. II. Harrity, David. III. Title

PN49 K223 2014

Manufactured in the U.S.A.

For Rubem Alves:
his verve has been contagious

Contents

Illustrations

Poems

Acknowledgments

The writing of *Way to Water* may well not have occurred at all were it not for the support of my friend and mentor Scott Holland, my MDiv advisor and inspiration Melanie Duguid-May, and my brilliant and compassionate wife Kristina Keefe-Perry. I am grateful to each of them for the personal encouragement to continue on my path, and for the criticism and direction that has helped this text be realized. I am similarly grateful to all those who read through various drafts of this work and provided valuable feedback and support.

I am also indebted to both Catherine Keller and Roland Faber, each of whom has extended a gracious hospitality to me, inviting me to participate in conferences and conversations that were fruitful in the development of my thinking. I owe thanks as well to all those who have shared work and time with the Theopoetics Working Group at the Annual Meetings of the American Academy of Religion. Having conversation partners there has helped to bring clarity to a great number of issues taken up in the course of this project. Among that group I have been particularly honored to think and work alongside Blake Huggins, a brilliant mind and a generous soul.

Finally, and perhaps most importantly, I would like to acknowledge the profound impact of my parents and—quite separately—the Religious Society of Friends. I am grateful to God for a childhood full of wonder and creativity and for calling forth a denomination that encourages the same. I am who I am in large part because of the time I have spent with those who have lived and loved faithfully, following their passions and striving to do what is right.

Foreword

In his book, *On the Way to Language*, Martin Heidegger says that "thinking goes its way in the neighborhood of poetry." Callid Keefe-Perry's *Way to Water: A Theopoetics Primer*, is a text infused with poetic sensibility while at the same time insisting that theopoetics is not simply a hybrid of theology and poetry. Rather, it is an attempt to show the close proximity or "neighborhood" of poetry and thought—and, moreover, of poetry and embodied living.

> **Incarnation**
> For every lofty idea
> You need a lowly idea.
> For every hope and aspiration
> You need a circumstance and situation.
> For every spirit that rises
> You need a spirit made flesh.

Theopoetics is a difficult topic to write "about." Callid is aware of this. He worries that his book may be too much "writing about theopoetics" rather than an exercise in theopoetics itself, the very topic he is passionate about. Yet my estimation is that Callid achieves the purpose he set himself—to offer a primer—and that he accomplishes this in a way that is elegant, humble, and creative in its own right.

Callid does a great service in bringing together a range of theopoetic writers/thinkers/artists/practitioners who have each, in their own distinctive way, contributed to the development of the theopoetic way. His "travelogue" is both fascinating and helpful. It is a theopoetic "Route 66" but it will also give you "kicks!"

Callid often notes that theopoetics is meant to "rough things up." It isn't interested in smooth or pat answers, whether these come from the political right or the political left, or from the religiously conservative or the religiously progressive. It is interested in the questions and doubts we all feel, the goodness and guilt we all bear, and the hope and the future we all share.

Theopoetics has a universal dimension because it taps into concrete and particular longings. The relation to God is more akin to "desire" than to "knowledge." Theopoetics recognizes that each and every person—from the most successful to the most destitute—is a person who desires. Desires what? Many things. Yet ultimately, desires to love and be loved, to name and affirm others and to be named and affirmed oneself, to support and lift up others and to be supported and lifted up oneself. This is what poets and artists ultimately "show" us. They show us our need for each other and our own uniqueness, dignity, and creativity.

> **Something Important**
> Amidst all the things that require my attention
> I nevertheless have this urge to write poetry.
> Why bother?
> What purpose can poetry possibly achieve?
> Then I think,
> In what way would anything matter or
> Anything count
> Without art and poetry?
> Society would be reduced to dry bones.

A society without art and culture, without creativity and commitment, is a society of "dry bones." That poetics should be linked to God—"the poetry of God"—strikes me as entirely resonant and essential to any spiritual discourse. God rarely comes to us propositionally or purely rationally. Callid cites Amos Wilder: "When imagination fails doctrines become ossified, witness and proclamation wooden, doxologies and litanies empty, consolations hollow, and ethics legalistic."

At the beginning of *God in Search of Man*, Jewish philosopher, Abraham Heschel notes that religion can sometimes be its own worst enemy. Rather than blame "secularism" for the demise of religion, Heschel says we need to look at the lack of creativity and relevance of our own faith traditions:

> It is customary to blame secular science and anti-religious philosophy for the eclipse of religion in modern society. It would

be more honest to blame religion for its own defeats. Religion declined not because it was refuted, but because it became irrelevant, dull, oppressive, insipid. When faith is completely replaced by creed, worship by discipline, love by habit; when faith becomes an heirloom rather than a living fountain; when religion speaks only in the name of authority rather than with the voice of compassion—its message becomes meaningless.

Similarly, in his book, *Creative Fidelity*, Catholic philosopher Gabriel Marcel links creativity intrinsically to fidelity. The best way to be faithful to a religious tradition (or to a partner, a community, a "work") is to be creative—continually renewing and revitalizing one's commitments rather than relying on fixed or stale bonds.

The ill health of religion in the world is attributable to its dearth of creativity. Non-creative religious traditions lead to fundamentalism, irrationalism, and dogmatism—upon which the sources of war and conflict feed.

Healthy religious traditions are attributable to the richness of creativity. Creative religious traditions lead to peace, healing, newfound wisdom—they draw on the sources of love and beauty.

As Callid notes: "It is possible to ask whether much of our Western Christian failings have arisen not from a lack of reason, but from too much of it, especially when we think that our reason is clearly reflective of some absolute Divine Reason of which we are the arbiters." Theopoetics suggests that God is encountered as much in the theo-poetical as in the theo-logical. "Encouraging a poetic sensibility within theological discourse allows for the continuing interpretation of God, God's word, and God's action, without any proclamation that these things can be fully known and entirely named."

> **Thanksgiving**
> When I thank you,
> I become more aware of the need
> For your love in the world
> And I try to be on your side.

Humility and hospitality are key words running throughout Callid's text. Theopoetics clearly means at least these two things. There is no grandiosity in theopoetics, no hubris, no clearly identified and assured "system," no overt power and hierarchy. Rather there is hospitality, receptivity, attention, teaching, learning, sharing, solidarity—and living with as large a heart as possible. Theopoetics is large-heartedness rather than narrow-mindedness. "Why theopoetics?" Callid asks. "Because I believe we owe it to ourselves and to the hope of our God to live and write and pray as if the world was a gift and each Other a reminder of that which gives."

My fear is that theopoetics will be relegated to a marginal and eso-teric realm. Marginal, because there are only a few to whom it appeals, and esoteric, because it is too often misunderstood. In this book, Callid endeavors to be both an advocate for theopoetics—so that it is not rel-egated to a marginal realm—and a defender of theopoetics as a practi-cal discipline that has effects, so that it is not relegated to an esoteric or impracticable realm.

Nurturing theopoetic sensibilities means nurturing spiritual and pastoral sensibilities, and fostering a socially engaged stance. Theopoetics encourages voices that might not otherwise be given space, "acknowledg-ing and lifting up voices that do not occupy seats of worldly power." We can't get a million and one truths all wrapped-up into One. We cannot find a "single, smooth, systematic articulation of reality and God, but a rough, textured, polyphony of cries, songs, and praises." Callid writes:

> The theopoetic invitation is a challenge for others to begin to speak their truth and to test it with others, making space for marginalized voices to safely enter the discourse. Theopoet-ics discourages a gate-keeping mentality wherein people must learn to speak and think in a certain way to have their voices heard. Conversely, it engenders dialogue from many voices and perspectives. More writing, more narrative, more metaphor, more confession, and more conversation. More invitation into the Kingdom of God realized such that a place is made here on earth for every voice and body.

Callid concludes his travelogue with an epilogue that exemplifies theopoetic engagement. A question is put to him: "Are you a poet?" He answers *sic et non*—"yes and no." Can one be a poet in a world of so much pain? On the other hand, isn't the poetic soul required even more so in the midst of human suffering? Moreover, Callid shows that poetic intuition and creativity is at work in a great variety of human disciplines—psychology, art, writing, ornithology, science, geometry, chemistry, magic, marriage, and parenthood—all of which respond to the beauty and mystery of our world, the "divine milieu," to use a favorite image from poet-scientist, Tielhard de Chardin. Poetry is a secret labor that is at work in all of humanity's intellectual and spiritual gifts.

While reading Callid's text, I found myself coming back to his title, *Way to Water*. A strange title, yet I noted his desire to find an "oasis" within the "desert of criticism" (Ricoeur). Amen to that. Ezekiel's image of bleached "dry bones" (Ezek 37) kept coming back to me, and then this verse from the poet-prophet, Isaiah (58:10–11):

> If you do away with the yoke of oppression,
>> with the pointing finger and malicious talk,
> and if you spend yourselves in behalf of the hungry
>> and satisfy the needs of the oppressed,
> then your light will rise in the darkness,
>> and your night will become like the noonday . . .
> You will be like a well-watered garden,
>> like a spring whose waters never fail.

Reading Callid Keefe-Perry's text has been a pleasure, a learning, and an encouragement. I hope that you too, dear reader, may be able to find your "way to water" in the pages that follow.

Terry A. Veling
Faculty of Theology and Philosophy,
Australian Catholic University

Introduction

It is in the age when our language has become more precise,
more univocal, more technical . . . that we want to recharge our language,
that we want to start again from the fullness of language. . . .
Beyond the desert of criticism we wish to be called again . . .

In every way, something has been lost, irremediably lost: immediacy of belief.
But if we can no longer live the great symbolisms of the sacred in accordance
with the original belief in them, we can, we modern peoples,
aim at a second naïveté . . .

—PAUL RICŒUR[1]

THIS BOOK IS AN academic travelogue of sorts, a (re)collection of the various authors and articles that have been formational in my own search for a way over and out of the academic "desert of criticism" toward an encounter with the Living Water of Christ. It is also the genealogy and history of a path called theopoetics that I've found, which has—on occasion—led me out of that same desert.

In early 2006 I was exposed to the concept of theopoetics as a part-time auditing student of Scott Holland's at the Church of the Brethren's Bethany Theological Seminary. There, as part of a course in postmodern theology, it was addressed in passing via a number of specific references to the philosopher John Caputo and even greater allusions to David Tracy and the power of metaphor and language to shape our perceived realities. Whether it was because I had been an undergraduate student of Marshall McLuhan's communication theory, or because of my own filled

1. Ricœur, *The Symbolism of Evil*, 349, 351.

notebooks of poetry, a term that was a very minor part of the course's syllabus, became the object of great focus for me. I began to look into who was using the word, what they thought it meant, where it had come from, and why it was not more widely used. While there are many nuances left out in J. Denny Weaver's articulation of theopoetics, I find that what it *does* say I agree with:

> A non-poet's definition of theopoetics might be that it is a hybrid of poetry and theology. But to call it that misses the mark. It is an entire way of thinking. From the side of poetry, it shows that ideas are more than abstractions. They have form—verbal, visual, sensual—and are thus experienced as least as much as they are thought. . . . What one learns from the theology side of theopoetics has at least as much importance. One observes that theology is more than an abstraction. It is a way of thinking, visualizing, and sensing images of God. And at that juncture, theologians should become aware that traditional theology . . . is a way to think about the divine, but is only one of multiple ways to consider God.[2]

The task of much of the rest of this book is to flesh out the detail and nuance that Weaver does not address and to provide the historical and theological context from which contemporary discussion of theopoetics emerges.

Way to Water traces the origins of the contemporary idea of "theopoetics" to Stanley Hopper and a speech entitled "The Literary Imagination and the Doing of Theology."[3] The talk was delivered at the 1971 Annual Meeting of the American Academy of Religion,[4] and David Miller, who had been Hopper's student, offers an articulate assessment of Hopper's stance. He writes that theopoetics is not "an artful, imaginative,

2. Weaver, "Series Editor's Forward," 13.

3. Historically "theopoiesis" was used by a number of early Christian writers (Justin Martyr, Theophilus of Antioch, Irenaeus, Hippolytus, and Clement of Alexandria) as a term meaning "deification," "making God," or "making divine" (Miller, "Introduction," 3). It often functioned as a description of what they believed to happen to faithful Christians after they died. In formulations such as Athanasius's "God became man so that man might be made God," *theopoieo* (θεοποιέω) is used as "made God." It functions similarly for Clement of Alexandria, such as in "the Word divinizes man by His heavenly teaching," where "divinizes" is the action of theopoeisis. While this historical trajectory of the term is briefly picked back up with Catherine Keller's comments in chapter 4, I generally engage with the usage beginning with Hopper, which is not the same as the early church's theopoiesis.

4. Miller, "Introduction," 3.

creative, beautiful, and rhetorically compelling manner of speaking and thinking concerning a theological knowledge that is and always has been in our possession and a part of our faith," but rather, "strategies of human signification in the absence of fixed and ultimate meanings accessible to knowledge or faith."[5] That is, theopoetics is not merely the "poetizing of an extant religious faith or theological knowledge," but "a reflection on poiesis, a formal thinking about the nature of the making of meaning, which subverts the -ology, the nature of the logic, of theology."[6] Hopper was interested in ways of subverting lifeless theology and metaphysics with beauty and a poetic sensibility. Given his cultural context his interests seem quite apt: he wrote and thought in the midst of the throes of the media fascination with the "Death of God" movement.

At the end of the 1960s, scholars working with "Radical Theology" contributed to a broader national concern that Christianity might be on its way out. It was in that context that both Hopper and, later, Amos Wilder, wrote about theopoetics. For early theopoetics thinkers, theopoetics was primarily about Christian renewal. While there was some interest in the idea at first, the 1970s and eighties saw the successful rise of a more conservative evangelicalism, so there was a decline in both the concern that American Christianity might be ending and the possible utility of theopoetics as a way to help people be engaged in Christianity again. It was not until the 1990s that there was any more concentrated focus on the concept of theopoetics. I believe that this re-emergence of focus came about as the result of two major factors.

First was the questioning of what had previously been at times presented as the monolithic quality of American evangelicalism. With the very public scrutiny of celebrity televangelists Jim and Tammy Faye Bakker, the Bakkers's PTL Ministries corruption trial, and the intersession of Jerry Falwell, much of what had seemed to be the inevitable thrust of American evangelicalism and political conservatism began to be questioned. Issues of power, faith, and trust began to come to the forefront of public *and* academic theological discourse.[7] Second was the maturation of the first generation of theologians and philosophers of religion who were students of, and conversant with, the work of continental philosophers such as Michel Foucault, Jean-François Lyotard, Jacques Derrida,

5. Miller, "Theopoetry or Theopoetics?" 14.

6. Ibid.

7. Ostling, "Religion."

and Paul Ricœur. Thus, as thinkers such as Melanie Duguid-May, Scott Holland, Catherine Keller, and Richard Kearney came to teaching positions, their work reflected a concern *with religion* and how discourse *on religion* might both be tied up in issues of power, bodies, representation, and self. Furthermore, the 1980s drew theological focus to methodology in general, and liberation, pragmaticism, and identity-politics in particular. By the 1990s, Duguid-May, Holland, Miller, and Keller had each lifted up theopoetics as worth considering again.

As the topic then began to be explicitly referenced again in theological institutions (Bethany Theological Seminary, Colgate Rochester Crozer Divinity School, Claremont School of Theology, and Drew University), a number of younger scholars entered into the discourse as well. I write as a member of this younger cohort, the convener of the Theopoetics Working Group, which meets at the American Academy of Religion; one of the managing editors of the journal *Theopoetics*; and the webmaster of Theopoetics.net, a resource entirely devoted to cataloging and promoting work in theopoetics. It is through my work on that site that I have come to realize the impact and potential importance that theopoetics has for the contemporary Christian: I often receive a emails from people who have happened upon the term somewhere and—directed by Google— ended up reading my work.

Beginning with contact from North American post-evangelicals and stretching from newly emerging Christians in China to Spanish teenagers trying to find their own way, I found my web traffic moving from the hundreds to an audience of tens of thousands within two years. Through a potent combination of word-of-mouth, forwarded emails, and Google's decision that my website was second only to the Wikipedia entry on the subject, I suddenly found that a personal passion had turned into something in which others had significant interest. As of the spring semester of 2014, classes and seminars devoted specifically to theopoetics have now been taught at Harvard, Drew, Boston University, Claremont School of Theology, Bethany Theological Seminary, Seminary of the Southwest, Lynn University, and University of Warwick. None of those schools had done so prior to 2005.

In early 2009 I was asked to write an introduction to theopoetics for a special issue of *Christianity and Literature* concerned with contemporary poetry. That was followed by invitations to address theopoetics in the Association for Religion and Intellectual Life's *CrossCurrents*, the journal on process theology and faith's *Creative Transformation,* a number of working groups at the American Academy of Religion, one of Drew University's Transdisciplinary Theological Colloquia, a Claremont School of Theology conference on "Theopoetics and the Divine Method," and the University of London's Heythrop College theology conference "The Power of the Word." Also during this time my wife and I were welcoming our firstborn into this world and we were both continuing to travel in the ministry within our denominational home, The Religious Society of Friends. Things have been busy.

That is all to say that as I sit to write this I find I am filled with a mix of joy, perseverance, and trepidation: as yet there is no single text which encompasses the full history, arc, and possible future of theopoetics, and I intend for this book to do exactly that. I am grateful for the opportunity to embark on such a task, and am yet nervous that in attempting to "explain exactly what it is that theopoetics is," I am setting off to press and dry a rare fragile flower so as to preserve its wild, living beauty. In spite of this fear—or perhaps because of it—I move ahead with a very particular method: as a primer I intend for this book to (1) serve as a means of reference to the vast majority of the writing done on theopoetics prior to 2013, (2) develop a robust functional definition of theopoetics, (3) provide an argument as to the theological importance of encouraging the development of a poetic sensibility in theological discourse, and (4) sketch out some of the possible concrete implications and manifestations of a theopoetic stance for Christian practices.

I write both as an academic that finds this material endlessly captivating and as a minister convinced that the holy power of God is ever inviting us all toward a greater and more holistic relationship with Christ. I write as an archivist of the formal discourse on theopoetics and as a poet who cringes whenever he sees that Cliff Notes has published another summary of a collection of poetry. I write as a frustrated scholar who sometimes feels the theological academy has forgotten that the church is the *body* of believers, and as a father who hopes that his daughter finds words with which she can cry out to God in her pain and her joy. I write as a hopeful, clumsy, white, married, bisexual, Quaker man and father. I write fully-fleshed.

Intent

This book takes as its foundation the possibility that theopoetics is a viable method for encountering what Ricœur referred to as a "second naïveté." I believe that there is a transformative power in the creative articulation of embodied experiences of God and faith, and I believe that this power is a way that can lead beyond the "desert of criticism," connecting us as contemporary people of faith to a transformative experience—however ephemeral—of the Living Water. Upon this foundation I trace the development of the discourse surrounding the term "theopoetics" and address some of the reasons why creative, embodied experience is related to encouraging a more poetic sensibility within theological discourse and academic theology.

I believe that a re-enfleshment of theological discourse is called for and that a turn to the flesh will simultaneously bring with it a turn to the poetic rather than the prosaic, to a surplus of meaning rather than a linguistic mechanicalism, and to the Christian imagination rather than ossified doctrine. I believe that if Christians accept the articulations and explanations of God that have come before simply *because* they have come before, then what is being practiced is not some kind of reverence for tradition, but a form of idolatrous traditional*ism*. At the heart of this book is the belief that how we articulate our experiences of the Divine can alter our experiences of the Divine. I also take as a given that God still moves in the world and that we are constantly being given the opportunity to come to know God more fully.

What theopoetics suggests is that talking to one another about how God has come to be known might be better suited to a form of discourse that acknowledges and values the multiplicity of experience rather than one which tends to reify experiences of God into an absolute and rigid theology. Crudely put, theopoetics asserts that we humans often find God easier to encounter in the (theo)poetic rather than the (theo)logical. As such, this work is also a sideways inquiry into the theological legitimacy of my belief that creative, individual expressions of the Divine have a place in faithful personal and congregation formation and within the rigor of academic theological discourse.

I am primarily concerned that the revivifying power of the Holy Spirit be more fully encouraged and known, and I believe that a movement toward a theopoetic perspective will engender exactly such a thing.

I have egalitarian commitments as well, believing that by virtue of our Baptism, each Christian has been plunged into the stream of Living Water, allowing for each of us to articulate our personal experience of God in the world without needing formal ecclesial or academic endorsement as a "theologian." While it is indeed the case that there is a tradition and a language to which theological discourse is indebted, God is not so insignificant as to be invisible except in that which has come before. Some of our articulations will fall far short of the truth, but others will be closer, and in the effort to discover how God is working in the particulars of each life we will all be enriched in a way that is hard to come by in solely systematized and propositional thinking. I stand fully with Amos Wilder:

> Imagination is a necessary component of all profound knowing and celebration; all remembering, realizing, and anticipating; all faith, hope, and love. When imagination fails doctrines become ossified, witness and proclamation wooden, doxologies and litanies empty, consolations hollow, and ethics legalistic. . . . When this happens doctrine becomes a caricature of itself. Then that which once gave life begins to lull and finally to suffocate us.[8]

When we encounter practices, beliefs, and communities which we believe ought to be life-giving, and discover them to be suffocating instead, then it behooves us to ask how it is that God is at work: to explore for ourselves whether that which we have encountered is a faithful, hope-filled, and loving manifestation of God's movement, or if it rings false, hollow, and wooden. To paraphrase Jerome Bruner: "since lived life rarely conforms to anything resembling a cookbook of recipes or formulas, we ought not think that when we look into cookbooks we'll see life as it is."[9]

I contend that a movement toward the theopoetic is both a means of clearing away the flotsam that clutters access to the Living Water and a method for moving more deeply into a whole and renewed life wherein that which is articulated about God more closely resembles the way things are actually experienced. Encouraging a poetic sensibility within theological discourse allows for the continuing interpretation of God, God's word, and God's action, without any proclamation that these things can be fully known and entirely uttered.

It is my intent that none of the work contained herein descend too long into the depths of technical theological and philosophical language,

8. Wilder, *Theopoetic*, 2.

9. Bruner, "The Narrative Construction of Reality," 14.

and I must acknowledge that insofar as I intend for this book to serve as a primer on the subject, I must occasionally touch down upon work that is challenging and sometimes obscure. In each and every instance where technical language is a necessity to communicate the objective of the original author, I attempt to walk the line between providing sufficient context such that the content is coherent and writing with the assumption that readers are intelligent and thoughtful: I hope to make this work accessible, not watered down such that it loses the flavor and verve that interested me in the first place.

Organization and Method

It is a matter of how you begin: if you begin with theory, then one way or another your research winds up geared to making the case for or against the truth of the theory. Begin with theory, you begin with the answer; begin with observation, you begin with questions. A theory always turns into a scientist's point of view and a way of seeing the job at hand. Begin with observation and your task is to look at things and to look at what happens. To see.

—ERIC McLUHAN[10]

In method, this book's exploration of theopoetics is modeled after Marshall McLuhan's enjoinder—when investigating a form of media—to begin by cataloging its effects, working backwards to arrive upon its nature only after observation. Thus, the first six chapters take up the question of what theopoetics is primarily by lifting up the work of writers who have themselves claimed to be engaging with theopoetics, trying to tease out some of the effects and consequences of that engagement. The book begins in the next chapter with theoretical work about *what* theopoetics has been, and spirals further and further out until chapter 6, when a culminating, synthetic claim is made on *how* theopoetics can be understood and why it ought to be considered for use in life-giving practices within the church. Throughout the text, my attempt is to allow the authors to speak for themselves. The effect is somewhat like bricolage until chapter 6, when I take a step back to reflect upon the various effects inventoried, and attempt an articulation of a series of definitions of theopoetics which are reflective of each of the effects encountered.

10. McLuhan, "Marshall McLuhan's Theory," 26.

Very reductively put, my claim is that theopoetics can be best understood as a resonant oscillation between cataphatic and apophatic theologies, honoring both God's mystery and our desire to proclaim God's word. Chapters 7 and 8 are reflections on some of the practical theological implications of the material presented in the previous six chapters. The epilogue is an homage to the writers with whom I have danced, a *poeisis*, a God-naming with theologian, poet, and educator Rubem Alves in view. It is an attempt to embody the intent of the whole in such a way that it is both written *about* theopoetics and *as* theopoetics. Some readers may find it beneficial to begin there before turning to the material that emphasizes more technical, historical, and bibliographical aspects.

Chapter 1 surveys the theological ground explored during the "Death of God" movement(s) of the 1960s and discusses how it inspired the pioneering theopoetic work of Stanley Hopper. In particular, a connection is made between Altizer and Hamilton's *Radical Theology and the Death of God* and the ways in which early theopoetic articulations can be seen as a response to the challenges laid out in that text. It also addresses the theoretical origins of theopoetics in Heidegger's phenomenological hermeneutics and a literarily-minded biblical criticism. Consequently, I'll briefly address those topics in such a way so as to be accessible without the reader needing expertise in those fields. Hopper works with theopoetics in a way that is primarily focused on the production of a "new theopoetic," where "theopoetic" is used as a noun to refer to new ways of talking about God that speak more readily to present day people. Given the influence that the early theopoetics writers have played upon all that follows, this chapter and the one that follows pay particular attention to the contexts from which the authors write. A number of biographical details seem highly relevant to the investigation of theopoetics, and as such, they are included.

Chapter 2 takes up both Amos Wilder and Rubem Alves, the two authors cited most often when theopoetics is referenced in contemporary scholarship. Wilder follows Hopper's work in that he also had a vision for a radically renewed theological discourse, but presented that vision in a rather traditional academic genre. Alves breaks with this pattern. He writes *about* theopoetics *in* theopoetics. Because he and Wilder have such drastically different biographies and methodologies, insight is given by triangulation, revealing what theopoetics does that is so important to both of them.

Whereas Wilder played international champion tennis at Wimbledon and was, academically speaking, a Bible scholar, Alves is a Brazilian theologian exiled from his homeland as a result of a military coup d'état. Wilder's work is presented in tension with, and having to resist, the trajectories found within Rudolf Bultmann's concept of "de-mythologizing." Conversely, Alves is situated as the first Brazilian liberation theologian and a psychoanalyst, exploring the relationship between the body and belief. Indeed, Alves's insistence on the primacy of materiality and embodiedness in both method and point is a hallmark of his work. His emphasis on the body is carried forward in the next generation of theopoetics writers, which are considered in the following chapter.

Chapter 3 takes up the work of both Melanie Duguid-May and Scott Holland, Church of the Brethren theologians in the second wave of writers to take up theopoetics work. In both Duguid-May's *A Body Knows* and Holland's *How Do Stories Save Us?* theology is construed in such a way so as to maintain that faith must be fleshly and imaginative before it becomes propositional and dogmatic. Both are concerned with the ways in which "academic theology" can too readily be pressed into the service of oppressive powers due to cultural and institutional mores regarding "proper" voice, style, and diction. Indeed, Holland writes that "even we constructive theologians who have become skilled in redeeming the pleasures of Babel in the task of public theology need to be reminded not to neglect the voices from the margins. The sexy ones are becoming easier for most of us to hear, but the suffering ones still speak."[11] Both he and Duguid-May see in theopoetics an affirmation of the body, which functions as a means of radical egalitarianism, allowing voices to speak and be encouraged that might otherwise be kept pressed into silence.

Chapter 4 considers the contributions of process theology to the theopoetics conversation, and the uneasy relationship between the process vision of the theopoetic and one that is closer to the vision as embodied in Hopper and Alves. Process theology here is represented by the two scholars who have most significantly taken up theopoetics in their writing and teaching: Catherine Keller and Roland Faber. Both have been central to the rise of theopoetic discourse taking place among process thinkers, and this chapter attempts to capture their related perspectives. Keller is overtly committed to theology with flesh and to maintaining a place for pluralism. She writes, "to put it bluntly; if God is immaterial, God doesn't

11. Holland, *How do Stories Save Us?* 37.

matter."[12] Keller's perspective leads to another process theologian, Roland Faber, who, similar to Hopper and Wilder, works in a relatively traditional —albeit brilliant—academic manner. Method aside however, Faber's emphasis is on the ongoing, creative work of God and the relationship between God, humanity, and creation. He pointedly argues not only that "God is the Poet of the World," but that "process theology *is* theopoetics."[13] Faber and Keller insist that theopoetics must *not* remove the capacity of theological discourse to argue with oppressive structures, and suggest that if the inclusion of a poetic sensibility interferes with their ability to attack oppressive stances, then the poetic must be abandoned.

Chapter 5 explores two thinkers—Peter Rollins and John Caputo— who more readily identify as philosophers than theologians, exploring how they each conceive of the relationship between the poetic and theological discourse. In a co-authored essay with Keller, and books *The Weakness of God, The Insistence of God,* and *What Would Jesus Deconstruct?,* Caputo addresses the topic of theopoetics specifically. For him, the emphasis is an interpretation of Jesus as "the centerpiece of a 'poetics' of the 'kingdom of God' found in the New Testament, of a kind of theopoetics . . . in which the task of converting that poetics into reality falls squarely on our shoulders."[14] The importance of God working in the poetic, for Caputo, is that it more readily resists being employed for coercive purposes and is always in a state of calling faithful people forward into "the symbolic space one obtains in the kingdom," and into "the dynamics of a desire beyond reason and beyond what is reasonably possible, a desire to know what we cannot know, or to love what we dare not love, like a beggar in love with a princess, whose desire is not extinguished by the impossible."[15] This kind of language—of the hope and longing for the "impossible" future driving us to action in the present—is also found in the work of Peter Rollins, an Irish philosopher of religion, and a friend of Caputo. Rollins's work is considered in both *How (Not) To Speak of God* and *The Idolatry of God.* His methodology of "pyrotheology" is examined as a possible manifestation of theopoetic exploration as fused with Derrida's sense of deconstruction. The chapter closes with a critique of deconstructive methods for Christian theology, using the work of

12. Keller, "The Flesh of God," 91.
13. Faber, *God as Poet of the World,* 15.
14. Caputo, *The Weakness of God,* 134.
15. Ibid., 104.

Jeffery Hocking to suggest that what can be accomplished for the church by means of employing deconstruction can also be done—perhaps more successfully so—by theopoetics.

Chapter 6 is a culmination of sorts, a co-opting of insights from Richard Kearney's concept of "anatheism" and Karmen MacKendrick's interpretation of theology as a form of seduction. Their work is used to put forth an experiential articulation of theopoetics that incorporates all the effects noted in the work of previous authors. Kearney's development of "anatheism" is examined, beginning with his *Poetics of Imagining* and moving on to essays "The God Who May Be" and "Epiphanies of the Everyday," in which he asserts both that we can "touch the sacred enfolded in the seeds of ordinary things"[16] and that God "is a God who puns and tautologizes, flares up and withdraws . . ."[17] The tension of an experience that is both "in ordinary things" and that which is "not yet for us," is then considered specifically in an exploration of Kearney's book *Anatheism*. Theopoetics is then re-articulated as an encounter with an anatheistic moment, and the question is asked "Why would anyone want theopoetics if its God is 'flaring up and withdrawing'? Isn't the Christian God certain and fixed?" An answer comes by means of Karmen MacKendrick and her brilliant book *Divine Enticement*. The chapter closes with a framing of theopoetics as a faithful response to our finite nature, using both MacKendrick and Kearney to weave together the various effects inventoried throughout the previous chapters. As the end of the theoretical and historical analysis of theopoetics, chapter 6 contains an offering of three definitions that—when taken together—are intended to address all of the extant material presented.

Following the culminating articulation of *what* theopoetics is, chapters 7 and 8 take up the question of *how* it is that theopoetics might be relevant to a community other than the academy. A number of implications are considered, including recommendations for the sermon, pastoral care, communal worship, spiritual formation, and social action. Using philosophical insights from both Paul Ricœur, Hans-Georg Gadamer, and M. Craig Barnes's text *The Pastor as Minor Poet*, chapter 7 describes how the sermon can be conceived of as a possible site for the in-breaking of the kingdom of God, not merely a means of instruction, edification, or condemnation. Attention is paid to the shifts in expectation needed to

16. Kearney, "Epiphanies of the Everyday," 3.
17. Kearney, "The God Who May Be," 85.

develop the theopoetic perspective for a sermon, and challenges to both the preacher and the congregation are considered. Next is a re-envisioning of the pastoral care encounter cast in a theopoetic frame, based on Phil Zylla's "Disorientation-Recalibration Model." Working from Zylla, additional perspectives are brought in from Donald Capps's book *The Poet's Gift: Toward the Renewal of Pastoral Care,* Viktor Frankl's "logotherapy," and from the expressive arts discipline of "Poetry Therapy." Balancing the attention paid to the individual throughout the section on pastoral care, the next chapter moves on to consider the possible role of theopoetics in the more communal activities of liturgy, and the interaction of social action and spiritual formation.

Chapter 8 opens using Travis Poling's "Poetic Worship Model" as a guide for a possible theopoetic liturgy, considering the implications of the work of liturgical theologian Richard McCall. Then, the influence of theopoetics on spiritual formation is considered via Roberto Goizueta and Matthew Guynn. Goizueta's work on the "theopoetic-praxis" is explored, wherein theology becomes grounded in an engagement with the political and social world by means of aesthetics. Guynn's contributions come through his piece "Theopoetics and Social Change," which includes some of his reflections as a trainer for non-violent activists. Chapter 8 closes with my hopes and vision for future work with theopoetics and my own version of Wilder's "plea for a theopoetic" that does justice *to* the imagination and *for* God's people and creation.

The closing epilogue is an experiment in belief and profession, stylistically composed in homage to the work of Rubem Alves and crafted as a reflection on Paul Ricœur's notions of the desert of criticism and the second naïveté. I intend for it to function as a series of aphoristic essays, intended to be taken together as a verbal bricolage, a playing around without playing pretend. They are an attempt to enact theopoetics theopoetically: in form, content, and method. After the epilogue there is an appendix that contains a variety of short quotations from different authors' perspectives on what theopoetics is. I have included it for the sake of reference; however, while I believe that each definition has its merit, none—including my own—addresses the fullness of what theopoetics is, or might become.

In closing this section on method, it should be noted that each of the first six chapters of this book—the ones engaging the history and theory of theopoetics—closes with a poem. These pieces were written by the poet

Dave Harrity specifically for this project. Dave is an author and teacher from Louisville where he lives with his wife and children, and his most recent book, *Making Manifest*, is a meditative guide of creative exercises to foster contemplative living, peacemaking, and community building. It is a very fine book and he is a very gifted poet. We have been in contact for years and he is quite familiar with the ideas surrounding theopoetics. When it became clear that I wanted to include original poetry in the text, I could not think of a better person with whom to collaborate.

Each chapter's closing poem was written to be in thematic resonance with the material that precedes it. We invite you to enter into each of the poems more slowly that you might were they prose. I have included these pieces as opportunities to reflect and take in what has just been read. I encourage you to allow the poetry in this text to function as the readerly equivalent of a slow traffic zone. Consider reading them aloud. Consider reading them more than once. They are an invitation to become more attentive and to sink into the kind of reading that poetry requests of us: sensual, evocative, and rich, both for what it says and how it has been said.

PART ONE

Early Articulations

1

Orbits and the Ineffable

An Investigation of Stanley Hopper

The primary calling of the theologian is to name God,
and to name that God who can actually be named by us.

—THOMAS J. J. ALTIZER[1]

WHILE THE FIRST PUBLISHED mention of "theopoetics" as such is
in Stanley Hopper's 1971 American Academy of Religion address
"The Literary Imagination and the Doing of Theology,"[2] the phrase did
not spring forth from nothing. Given this, prior to exploring Hopper's
explicit reference to the word, and so as to contextualize the environment
in which Hopper was writing, I will address three circles of dialogue
in which Hopper was a participant, tracing his thought as a trajectory
around these significant pulls: The Society for the Arts, Religion, and
Contemporary Culture; Drew University's Consultations on Hermeneutics; and The Radical Theology movement. Once these orbits have been
traced, I will follow Hopper's path as influenced by these conversations,
concluding with perspectives from his own writing in which theopoetics
is either discussed explicitly or alluded to by means of suggested method.

1. Altizer, *Living the Death of God*, 177.
2. Miller, "Introduction," 3.

Three Circles

The Society for the Arts, Religion and Contemporary Culture (SARCC), was founded in late 1961 by three men: Alfred Barr Jr., the art critic and founder of the Museum of Modern Art, and the theologians Paul Tillich and Marvin Halverson. Its first board of directors included these three as well as Unitarian Universalist theologian and parish minister James Luther Adams; mythologist Joseph Campbell; principle developer of the merger forming the United Church of Christ, Truman B. Douglass; Congregationalist parish minister and theologian, Amos Wilder; and Stanley Hopper.[3] It was a predominantly left-leaning organization, with aims "based on the deep and complex relationship between religion and the arts."[4] SARCC board members and fellows were engaged in a variety of professions, spanning from theology to law, with poets, architects, clergy, therapists, and violinists in the midst as well.[5]

Throughout the 1960s, SARCC sponsored numerous gatherings focused around the intersection of faith and art, with a greater emphasis being placed on the art than on any particular religion or creed. Bill Conklin, an early member of SARCC's board, recalls that all three founders "thought that the religions of the world were noble in intentions, but were far out of touch with the current world."[6] As a consequence of this position, the primary thrust of the organization was not to be theological, but toward the artistic, which could more powerfully "address the Universal in contemporary society."[7] Indeed, although Tillich was one of the founding members, and his significant influence was already beginning to be noted, both he and fellow theologian Halverson mutually agreed that Barr ought to serve as SARCC's first President, believing that "the artists should be in charge."[8]

As Hopper came to serve on SARCC's board, they were in the midst of developing plans for SARCC centers in the major cities of the world, "devoted to their common hopes concerning the coalescing and penetrating capabilities of religious thought, of great art, and of the immense

3. Meyer, *The ARC Story*, 4.
4. Conklin, Email Correspondence.
5. ARC, "ARC Fellows."
6. Conklin, Email Correspondence.
7. Ibid.
8. Ibid.

importance of human conversation."[9] For Hopper, this would have all been familiar and well within his areas of interest.

From 1948 to 1950 Hopper chaired the Commission on Literature at the National Council of Churches, and was the sole delegate from the United States at the First Conference on Religion and the Arts at the Ecumenical Institute in Celigny, Switzerland. In 1958, at Drew University, he founded the first graduate program in Theology and Literature in the United States. Throughout his life he had a profound personal predilection toward the arts, was a published poet himself, and was close friends with both Cleanth Brooks and T. S. Eliot.[10] Hopper's interest in art was paralleled by an interest in interpretation, which is exemplified by his work with Drew University's Consultations on Hermeneutics.

According to David Miller, a student of Hopper's, the "consultations were located intellectually at the intersection of left-wing Bultmannian Biblical interpretation, the thought of the late period of Heidegger's existential philosophy, and the Religion and Literature movement."[11] As the "Religion and Literature movement" was closely associated with the work of SARCC, the following sections will clarify "the late period of Heidegger's existential philosophy," and "left-wing Bultmannian Biblical interpretation."

Broadly speaking, hermeneutics is the study of interpretation, the study of *how* humanity makes sense out of things, most often texts. The Drew Consultations were interested in this same type of investigation, and were particularly interested in the work of Martin Heidegger, a twentieth-century German philosopher whose work in the philosophical sub-discipline of "phenomenology" is relevant to nearly all work done today in that field. At its most basic, phenomenology focuses on the study of experience, or how things are experienced by people, rather than the study of metaphysics, or the attempt to study the essential nature of things and being. Heidegger's position, as pertains to the Consultations, is well-framed by the three questions he asked to be considered[12] at the

9. Ibid.

10. Miller, "Stanley Hopper and Mythopoetics," 1–2.

11. Miller, "Theopoetry or Theopoetics?," 9.

12. Prior to the Third Consultation, Hopper and Karfried Froelich had visited with Heidegger and invited him to be in attendance. He had agreed, but then because of later illness, could not attend. In place of his presence he sent a letter in which he asked that three particular questions be taken up by those in attendance. The letter can be found in Martin Heidegger, *The Piety of Thinking: Essays by Martin Heidegger*.

Third Consultation in 1966. These questions—and my explanatory commentary—are as follows.

What is the nature of the referent of theological utterance?

That is, when we make theological assertions (about the nature of God, salvation, end times, etc.), what are we actually talking about? Presuming—for the sake of this philosophical line of questioning—that there is a God, is there a know-able, grasp-able nature to that God, or is it beyond our human capacity to understand?

What is the nature of thinking that is objectifying?

That is, Heidegger presumed that there was some quality of thinking—thinking here means using language, even if it is not spoken—that somehow could diminish the totality of that which was spoken of. By naming something, or thinking about it in such a way that it becomes readily categorized and able to be discussed, we are setting ourselves up for the possibility that we would not actually talk about the thing itself, but only about our thoughts/words for the thing. Put another way, the target of our interest becomes objectified so that when believe we are speaking/thinking of it, we are only speaking/thinking of the representation/interpretation we have assigned to it. Here, Heidegger was asking what it was about the nature of thinking that makes this objectification happen.

Is a non-objectivizing thinking and speaking possible?

That is, even given that we know about the content of the second question, might it be possible to circumvent that set up, and somehow actually engage in dialogue such that when we think/speak we actually are referencing the thing itself, not just our thoughts about the thing?[13]

Given the relatively abstract and highly philosophical tone of these questions, it is important to know that though Heidegger was a detailed and technical philosopher, he also had a firm appreciation for the poetic. He often cited the German poet Hölderlin when discussing the nature of humanity, writing that "poetically human beings dwell upon the earth."[14]

13. Heidegger, *The Piety of Thinking*, 27–32.
14. Heidegger, *Poetry, Language, Thought*, 217.

While Heidegger's methods were thoroughly philosophical, his focus was such that his thinking was appealing to artists and those whose focus was on interpretation. Similar interests also point to the reason that "left-wing Bultmannian Biblical interpretation," was key to the Drew Consultations.

Rudolf Bultmann was a contemporary and friend of Heidegger as well as a Lutheran theologian who taught New Testament Studies at the University of Marburg, where Heidegger also taught. Influenced significantly by Heidegger's phenomenological existentialism, he too kept his focus on the importance of the present moment and an individual's experience of that moment, rather than doctrinal or metaphysical claims that were presumed *a priori*. Most famously, Bultmann is remembered for what in English is called "demythologization," an unfortunate translation from the German, as his concern was not an utter removal of myth, but "rather a reinterpretation of the cosmological categories of the Bible . . . [understood as] anthropological or, better, existential and personal."[15] Wanting to do away with literalist interpretive strategies and universal claims, Bultmann favored arguments that emphasized the context in which the interpretation was being done.

Similar to Heidegger's assertion that language objectified the object of interest, and therefore speech/thought about that object was not actually about the object itself, but about our interpretation of that object, Bultmann argued that "no exegesis is without presuppositions, because the exegete is not a *tabula rasa*, but approaches the text with a specific way of asking questions and has a certain idea of the subject matter with which the text is concerned."[16] Since Bultmann thought it was impossible to engage the text without *some* interpretive predisposition, he then argued that the most useful disposition—for contemporary society—was one of existentialism and our experience of things in the present. Given how hard it is to maintain strictly literal biblical understandings of things in the face of critical and scientific advancements, Bultmann encouraged readers not to discard Scripture, nor to demythologize it into non-existence or irrelevance, but instead to discard the myths they *think* Scripture means, to bracket off the objectifying speech/thought *they* have traditionally put *on* the text, and to "abandon the mythological conceptions precisely *because* we want to retain their deeper meaning."[17] Bultmann

15. Borchert, "Demythologization," 334.

16. Mead, *Biblical Theology*, 152.

17. Ibid., 152. Emphasis added.

wanted Scripture to remain a possible source of transformation and engagement for contemporary readers, and he felt that "demythologizing" it contributed to this desire.

At the heart of the Third Consultation—at which Hopper was present, and at which he had prepared Heidegger himself to be present—was an acceptance that while it may be true that any manner of thinking/speaking could reify/objectify its subject in some manner, it also *might* be possible for us to think/speak in such a way that this does not happen. A way was held open for the possibility that some method of communication might be available that allowed for the transmission of knowledge without utterly tainting it with human preconceptions. To use Heideggerian phenomenological terms, it might be possible "to bring Being to appearance, to allow the unveiling of Truth, and to let that which is *appear as* that which it is."[18] As Miller recalls it, events of the Third Consultation revealed that "the 'as' is crucial," since those in attendance began to move from Heidegger's claims in *Being and Time* that all language has an as-structure to the "implication that theology is not a theo-logy, but is ineluctably theo-poetic, where poetry is interpreted as radical metaphor."[19] Construed loosely, the insight here is that if language itself is inherently metaphorical and based on "as-structures," then language pertaining to God and ultimacy must be all the more so metaphoric.

What was being suggested was not that theology ought to be glibly poetic or rhyming in form, but that it might be better if it possessed some of the radical quality of *poeisis*, of a "formal thinking about the nature of the making of meaning, which subverts the -ology, the nature of the logic, of theology."[20] Just as Bultmann sought to demythologize and discard myth, not for nihilistic purposes, but for "deeper meaning," so too did the Consultations consider radical subversions of the tradition of theology and theological language. By giving greater credence to the power of the poetic and more significant consideration to the ways in which theology too is an inventive and created type of language, theologians were standing on the cusp of a new era in American religious thought. Ultimately, it was exactly this kind of thinking that led to the movement often referred to as Radical Theology.

18. Miller, "Theopoetry or Theopoetics?," 9.

19. Ibid., 10.

20. Ibid., 8.

On Easter Monday, April 8, 1966, *Time* published the first ever issue which had no picture or photograph on the cover. Instead, there was a fully black background with three bold red words: "Is God Dead?" This launched a media campaign wherein enormous amounts of national coverage in various markets focused on a theological issue that was perhaps too complex to be pinned down by a mainstream media that did not always capture all of the nuances of the conversation.

Broadly speaking, at least three strong streams of "Death of God Theology" can be articulated: (1) Thomas J. J. Altizer's "extreme kenosis" theological argument, in which he posits "God had become fully human in Christ, so as to lose his divine attributes and therefore his divine existence"; (2) William Hamilton's sociological argument "that modern people were unable any more to believe in God, and the church ought, therefore, to seek to do without him as well"; and (3) Paul Van Buren's social-linguistic claim that "the concept of God was 'cognitively meaningless,' since God's existence and nature were not verifiable or falsifiable by the methods of science."[21] Given that there were more perspectives than even these three, and that these three themselves are far from equivalent, when Altizer and Hamilton published *Radical Theology and the Death of God* in 1968 they did so into a murky scene of vague understanding. As such, the preface to that book contains the following, edited here for length:

> The phrase "death of God" has quite properly become a watchword, a stumbling-block, and . . . Radical Theology thus best interprets itself when it begins to say what it means by that phrase . . . It might mean:
>
> 1. That there is no God and that there never has been.
>
> 2. That there once was a God to whom adoration, praise and trust were appropriate, possible, and even necessary, but that now there is no such God.
>
> 3. That the idea of God and the word God itself are in need of radical reformulation.
>
> 4. That our traditional liturgical and theological language needs a thorough overhaul; the reality abides, but classical modes of thought and forms of language may well have had it.

21. Frame, "Death of God Theology," 194.

5. That the Christian story is no longer a saving or a healing story. It may manage to stay on as merely illuminating or instructing or guiding, but it no longer performs its classical functions of salvation.

6. That certain concepts of God, often in the past confused with the classical Christian doctrine of God, must be destroyed: for example, God as problem solver, absolute power, necessary being, the object of ultimate concern.

7. That [people] do not today experience God except as hidden, absent, silent. We live, so to speak, in the time of the death of God, though that time will doubtless pass.

8. That the gods [which people] make, in their thought and action (false gods or idols, in other words), must always die so that the true object of thought and action, the true God, might emerge, come to life, be born anew.

9. That of a mystical meaning: God must die in the world to be born in us.

10. Our language about God is always inadequate and imperfect.[22]

To explore a major perspective on what was at stake for the school of Radical Theology,[23] it is useful to consider Altizer's recent work, which clarifies some of his earlier thinking and allows for a perspective that has more depth than was perhaps possible in 1968.

I find that a useful touchstone for understanding Altizer is his quotation in this chapter's opening: "the primary calling of the theologian is to name God, and to name that God who can actually be named by us."[24] Altizer believes the task of Radical Theology is not to dismantle religion arbitrarily, but because the only "God who can actually be named by us in our time . . . is only nameable as unnameable—a God who is absent, or

22. Altizer and Hamilton, *Radical Theology*, 3–4.

23. Although the original writings that prompted much of the discussion about theopoetics arose out of published discourses in the late 1960s, for the purpose of succinctness, information from contemporary publications about the topic are used as they are slightly more accessible and clear. Readers interested in original material are encouraged to consider Charles N. Bent's *The Death of God Movement* or Bernard Murchland's (ed.) *The Meaning of the Death of God*.

24. Altizer, *Living the Death of God*, 177.

nameable only as a negative presence."[25] Altizer's vision of the fruition of
the Radical Theology of the Death of God is a bold undertaking of trying
to state things as they are, not how we might want them to be. He sees
traditional theological methods as nothing more than a facade against
which humanity projects its own simplistic desires, not an articulation of
"that God who can actually be named by us." For Altizer, God *can* be discussed, but not in traditional *theological* methods, which he says are too
bound up in tradition and presumption to be of any genuine theological
use to the contemporary thinker.

> We must be prepared to accept the paradox that modern philos-
> ophy has been more deeply theological than modern theology.
> . . . Ironically, it was Spinoza who initiated a truly modern un-
> derstanding of the Bible, just as it was Hegel who more fully in-
> corporated a biblical ground into his thinking than has any other
> philosopher, and Nietzsche and Heidegger who fully embodied
> an apocalyptic horizon in their thinking, one absent from all of
> our established theologies. . . . So it is that Nietzsche can genu-
> inely be known as a poetic philosopher, even as Kierkegaard can
> be known as a poetic religious thinker, and if here thinking and
> the imagination are truly united, this is a union that has been
> impervious to all of our theology. . . . Clearly [Radical Theol-
> ogy] cannot simply challenge the Church or challenge society,
> it must go far deeper than that, for it is inevitably a challenge to
> everything that we can know or name as God . . .[26]

What seems to emerge here is a use of the term "theology" that
subverts itself. If the primary calling of the theologian is "to name that
God who can actually be named by us," and yet Altizer envisions the
role of Radical Theology as one that challenges "everything that we can
know or name as God," we are left with the primary calling of a radical
theologian as something akin to "naming that God who can actually be
named by us in such a way so as to encompass the 'embodiment of an
apocalyptic horizon.'"[27] Put more simply, Altizer's hope for the Radical
Theology coming out of the Death of God would be one in which there
is an acknowledgement that there is a limit to the extent revelation can

25. Klemm, "Forward," ix.

26. Altizer, *The Call to Radical Theology*, 3–4.

27. Altizer's use of the phrase "apocalyptic horizon" is frequent in his later works,
and those interested in exploring this facet in particular are encouraged to see Laurence Paul Hemming's piece "Are We Still in Time to Know God?"

be revealed, that there is an edge to our sight after which there is only unknowing.

As an active participant in the SARCC and the Drew Consultations, and intimately aware of the content of the Death of God theologies, Hopper's contributions to the discourse of theopoetics can be seen as a response to Heidegger's question, "Is a non-objectivizing thinking and speaking possible?" His answer? "Yes." With a methodological movement away from abstraction toward experience, from mathematical propositionalizing to artistic expression, from cold universal statements to profound and personal ones that held open the space for mystery and unknowing. From a theo-logic to a theo-poetic.

Hopper Himself

Having traced the three orbits from which Hopper drew in the development of his idea of theopoetics, we are now in a position to more fully reflect on some of Hopper's own words.[28] As mentioned at the beginning of this chapter, Hopper's speech, "The Literary Imagination and the Doing of Theology," is the first published piece of scholarship to make direct use of the term "theopoetic."[29] In that piece, Hopper asserts that humanity is in the midst of a "radical revisioning of our way of seeing and thinking."[30] He suggests that the question is not how to develop a new, socially relevant theology, but "whether theology, insofar as it retains methodological fealty to traditional modes, is any longer viable at all."[31] Read in the context of the three orbits described previously, Hopper's methods are familiar. If theology is to remain a discipline worth practicing, Hopper suggests, Christians must reclaim the power of myth and imagination, moving toward a poetic perspective of the divine instead of a prosaic, theo-logical approach that results in the "progressive reification of doctrine, squeezing the myth out, trying to contain the symbolic in a science and to reduce mysteries to knowledge."[32] Hopper seeks to place more emphasis on the interpretive and literary aspects of theologi-

28. I am profoundly grateful for the work of David Miller, without which, much of my insight into Hopper would be markedly diminished.

29. Miller, "Introduction," 3–4.

30. Hopper, "The Literary Imagination," 207.

31. Ibid.

32. Ibid., 208.

cal discourse. He wants to remember that aesthetics and experience play a role in how we understand God.

Hopper's thinking often reminds me of Theodore Roszack's assertion that empiricism can become "empiricide, the murder of experience. Science uses the senses but does not enjoy them; finally buries them under theory, abstraction, mathematical generalization."[33] Hopper re-engages experience in a powerful way, freeing it from the weight of outmoded methods and mining it for glimpses of the possible presence of the living God hidden under years of stagnant human interpretation. Seen in the context of his work at the Drew Consultations, it becomes all the more clear that his approach is informed by Heidegger's phenomenology: he is trying to discuss things as they appear, not as we say they *should* be.

Hopper argues that interest in religious discourse is not what it once was because the vocabulary of theological conversation is so far removed from experience that it does not engage most people in a meaningful way. Here there is an echo of his work with SARCC and the founders' belief that "the religions of the world were noble in intentions, but were far out of touch with the current world." Hopper's position is that any successful attempt at reinvigorating a common religious dialogue would essentially abandon attempts to logically systematize religious thought. Instead, he advocates the shared expression of spiritual experiences that "evoke resonances and recognitions."[34] The shift away from theo-logic, which he characterizes as utilizing hollow language, would require first "the unlearning of symbolic forms" and then "the activation of a new archetypal image."[35] Drawing on *What is Called Thinking?*, Hopper cites Heidegger's statement that, "we moderns can learn only if we always unlearn at the same time[;] . . . we can learn thinking only if we radically unlearn what thinking has been traditionally."[36] Interestingly, while Hopper was indeed one of the first contemporary pioneers of theopoetics, his working method was actually fairly conventional: he never quite managed to move to a position that demonstrated that "unlearning what thinking has been," could also entail "unlearning *how* thinking has been done." That is, for all of his emphasis on the poetic, Hopper's theological writing is firmly in the academic genre of writing. This is not to discount

33. Roszack, *Where the Wasteland Ends*, 280.

34. Hopper, "The Literary Imagination," 218.

35. Ibid., 220.

36. Ibid., 221.

Hopper's contributions, but to be clear about his project and the extent of its realization.

For Hopper, the primary issue was not that the language of theology was merely stale and needed some sprucing up by means of rhetorical and poetic devices. He did not understand the turn to the poetic as merely a superficial stylistic preference, but rather as a deep aesthetic recalibration in which the terms of discussion would be reconfigured to shift from a kind of scientistic mechanicalism toward an organic and embodied surplus of meaning. Language—even, or perhaps *especially,* language about God—is not a black and white affair. Hopper posited that to the degree that modern theology has rigidly attempted to prove anything absolutely, the whole project had been a fool's errand.[37] In his words, any "theology founded upon the mathematical models of propositional logic is founded upon a profound metaphysical error."[38]

Trying to propositionalize God and God's action is like trying to summarize a symphony. There are words in the discipline of music theory and composition that might allow one to comment on the structure, form, and phrasing of a piece, but that language is of a different order of discourse than the symphony itself. The tools of the discipline might allow someone who has not experienced the piece to be able to communicate with another person about the structure, form, etc., and they would outwardly sound much the same as someone who *had,* but the fact remains that they would *not* have actually experienced it. Without sharing a common experience, the tools of the discipline of music theory allow for a situation in which whole conversations can be had *about* something without experience *of* that thing itself. The parallel then is to draw a comparison between music theory and theology: one must take care not to confuse discussion about something with the thing itself. In this way, Hopper's insights can be seen as a theological extension of Kant's epistemology in his First Critique.

Just as Kant says that the experience of a thing is not of the "*ding an sich*" (thing-in-itself), but rather only of our noumenal *perception*

37. While Hopper's position may seem overly aggressive to contemporary readers, almost as if theology is being set up as a straw man against which theopoetics can ride to victory, I believe that his position is understandable when historically contextualized in a period when it seemed that the church may be coming to an end. Perhaps—ironically—his argument was too black and white, but he felt he was writing at a time that merited such brazen aggression.

38. Hopper, "The Literary Imagination," 224.

of the thing, so too is it for Hopper that our experience of God is not the Godhead-itself, but our filtered, human intuition. For both thinkers though, even if individuals do not experience "pure" phenomenon directly, the fact that we experience anything at all suggests that something is out there, even if beyond our grasp. Or, in Kant's words, "though we cannot know these objects as things in themselves, we must yet be in a position at least to think of them as things in themselves; otherwise we should be landed in the absurd conclusion that there can be appearance without anything that appears."[39] This is a key insight, and with it we can see why Hopper's claims regarding the problem with religious language were even more significant than the music theory situation.

Though a group of music theorists could talk about a written symphony without the symphony ever having been played, it is likely that were they to experience the piece bodily and sensorily their understanding might change and the content of their discussion change some, shifting to include their experience of the performance. For the music theorists to have sat together and listened to the symphony come to fruition in a great hall and yet still only to talk of the ink of the page would be a failure to fully participate in the piece. Just as musicologist Christopher Small argues that "there is no such *thing* as music," because music is "an activity that people do,"[40] I believe that theology is better understood as the establishment of a set of relationships, experiences, and agreed upon linguistic conventions, rather than an articulation of a fixed thing or being that is called God. Unfortunately, this is precisely the failure Hopper claims that theologians regularly make when writing of God: there is too great of an emphasis on some argued notion of God's nature and not enough attention paid to the human experience of that nature.

Hopper argues that too many theologians write as if God is distant, distinct, and as observable as a printed score, even when what we call an experience of God rarely seems to manifest in ways that are as discrete and consistent as that. He suggests that the narrative of humanity is too closely held within the story of God for any theological claim of an objective, external conclusion to be accurate. Hopper explains this position by citing Meister Eckhart's statement that "God is nearer to me than I am to myself," going on to add that God's nearness compels us to accept that God is not "out there," not an object to acquire knowledge of, but . . .

39. Kant, *Critique of Pure Reason*, 23.
40. Small, *Musicking*, 2.

... something I must experience. ... That is why theopoetics would seem to be a more appropriate way of thinking about the ineffable. Theology tends to develop talk about God logically, where the logos is constrained within the model of Aristotelian propositional thinking; whereas theopoetics stresses the poem dimension, the creativity of God, his is-ness, if you wish to theologize it, so that I must move within his own creative nature and must construe him creatively, so that I would become co-creator with God, if you must speak theologically. If I am going to talk about God, I must recognize this mythopoetic, metaphorical nature of the language I use.[41]

Hopper closes his 1971 speech with an appeal for theologians to recognize that the true root of an engaged and relevant religious discourse belongs in "the realm of mytho-poetic utterance."[42] Framed in terms of an effect, Hopper's contribution is an assertion that theopoetics is that which leads us into a new language where theologies are not rigid, logical assertions, but ecstatic expressions that plunge us into an experience of mystery and a primal being; a theology that is "not theo-logic but theo-poiesis."[43] Not a conclusion or an enclosure, but an invitation to discover and reflect on how—or if—God is coming to be known.

41. Miller, "Stanley Hopper and Mythopoetics," 6.
42. Hopper, "The Literary Imagination," 225.
43. Ibid.

At Cave Hill Cemetery

Some say a beginning, others a conclusion—either way
it's a window into our earth, the starched slate quiet monuments,
or the eroded wool posture of each etched angel's worn face.

It's soul & silence; it's sun & silt—the gospel
of the body spread in the hope of how it ends—that it ends—
in each step we take forward in our bustled jars:

our bodies taking shape from earth; earth shaped from taking
our bodies. We walk the brink so well that we forget.
But here, each branch lends itself another arrow through.

& all the cages the body tries to dodge relax into groves,
coal pressed crystal beneath the lake, cloud caravan across
the blank, gray & white winnowed lisps to daggered blue.

All these leaves waxed out, shelling seeds incarnadine—
this twisting blonde exit of summer & lost
or buried clarities—I think, right now—I can't help but become.

2

Renewal and Nets

Amos Wilder and Rubem Alves

Poetry is the way we help give name to
the nameless so it can be thought.

—AUDRE LORDE[1]

BEYOND THE CONTRIBUTIONS OF Hopper there are two other writers whose work completes the initial foray into the discussion of
theopoetics. While others later take up the term and begin to make use
of it for their own work, it is Hopper, Amos Wilder, and Rubem Alves
that contemporary scholars tend to cite when beginning to enter the
conversation.[2] In fact, in comparison to Hopper, both Amos Wilder and
Rubem Alves contributed significantly more words to the specific topic

1. Lorde, "Poems are not Luxuries," 283.

2. This is shifting somewhat as a number of process theologians (Catherine Keller,
Roland Faber, John Thataminil et al.) have begun to explore theopoetic thought. These
authors tend not to engage with the conversation by means of citing Alves, Wilder, or
Hopper, but because the process emphasis on multiplicity and "becoming" maps well
onto the connotations of the term theopoetics. There is a significant increase in the
amount of work being done on theopoetics coming from the school of process theology, and while it is unquestionably related to the project(s) envisioned by Hopper, it
can not be construed as identical. The process perspective is taken up in chapter 4, and
readers are encouraged to also see Faber and Fackenthal, *Theopoetic Folds: Philosophizing Multifariousness.*

of theopoetics. Thus, to complete an exploration of the first wave of theo-poetic writers I will take up first Wilder and then Alves, considering the contexts from which they wrote and the claims of their respective work. I conclude with a brief comparison of their rationales and stated intentions for using theopoetics. Though both approached the topic from radically different contexts, there is nonetheless a unifying thread that binds them together—and to Hopper—such that their individual works can be considered together as a related body of literature.

Amos Wilder

Born in 1895, Amos Niven Wilder shared a life-long appreciation for the arts with his brother, Thornton Wilder, Pulitzer Prize-winning play-wright of *Our Town*. Amos Wilder began his formal collegiate education at Oberlin but that was interrupted by World War I, in which he served as a corporal in the U.S. Field Artillery.[3] His time in the service was profoundly influential and resulted in both a 1923 published book of poems, *Battle-Retrospect*, and, toward the end of his life, a memoir of the war in *Armageddon Revisited*. Both serve as evidence that the events of his military service continued to work on him throughout his life. I believe his experiences during war had a profound effect upon his theological methods and will later explore this idea in greater detail.

In 1926 he completed his ministry studies at Yale and was ordained, serving for several years in a Congregationalist church in New Hampshire. While continuing to serve as a pastor he eventually took his doctorate in New Testament studies from Yale in 1933. From there he worked at Chicago Theological Seminary and the Federated Theological Faculty at the University of Chicago until 1954.[4] After leaving Chicago he went to work at Harvard, being appointed in 1955 to the Hollis Chair of Divinity, the country's oldest endowed professorship, a position he took following the Bible Scholar, Henry Cadbury. It is from this post at Harvard that Wilder began to produce some of his most significant work.

3. *Encyclopedia of World Biography*, "Amos Niven Wilder."

4. It is interesting to note that Charles Hartshorne, innovator of process theology, was a professor of philosophy at the University of Chicago from 1928–55, and was a part of the University's Federated Theological Faculty from 1943–54. That Hartshorne and Wilder were colleagues adds another layer to the ways in which process philosophy and theopoetics may be seen to have mutually influenced one another.

Wilder's contributions are a particular and potent blend of poetic artistry, biblical scholarship, literary critique, and pastoral insight. Sallie McFague, much-lauded author of *Metaphorical Theology*, wrote in her review of Wilder's 1976 book, *Theopoetic*, "If I were to have to choose two mentors for my own work on theology and the imagination, they would be Amos Wilder and Paul Ricœur. Wilder has been and continues to be a seminal thinker for many of us who are trying to uncover the intricate network joining biblical literature, poetry, and theological reflection."[5] In biblical interpretation, Wilder's focus tended to be on eschatological texts. He was interested in reading Scripture that revealed something about the final events to occur in the history of the world so that it had implications for the present. His work was oriented toward considering how to read a genre about a time not-yet-come so that it has relevance for that which currently is.

He had a nearly equal number of publications spread among Bible commentary, his own poetry, and critical reflection upon the work of other scholars. However, rather than his diverse interests becoming an indistinct amalgam, Wilder's work was such that "the integrity of each vocation [was] fully respected, and each genre of his work [stood] on its own in its special function."[6] Though he kept them separate, to his poetic work he brought a clear vision adopted from his endless study of the New Testament, and to his scholarly pursuits he never rested in championing the importance of the poetic. In fact, more than merely a supporter of poetic sensibilities, he felt as if they were essential both for understanding Scripture and for ministering in the present. As Paul Minear put it, "not only does [Wilder] accuse exegetical colleagues of deficiencies in this type of imagination; he also asserts that the biblical authors are prime examples of theopoesis, and thus the contrast between biblical author and modern exegete becomes painful to contemplate."[7] For Wilder, an understanding of theopoetics was not a theological dalliance or curiosity, but an essential way to aid in our understanding of Scripture.

As early as 1955 Wilder had come upon the heart of the claims that would later be made more robustly. The key to Wilder's later "plea for a renewed theopoetic" is clearly stated in his *New Testament Faith for Today*, where he wrote that "the chief obstacle to the proper validation of

5. McFague, "Review of *Theopoetic*," 592.
6. Beardslee, "Amos Niven Wilder," 5.
7. Minear, "An Early Christian Theopoetic?" 201.

religious myth and all cognate mythopoetic portrayals of life and history is the stultifying axiom that genuine truth or insight or wisdom must be limited to that which can be stated in discursive prose, in denotative language stripped as far as possible of all connotative suggestions, in 'clear ideas,' in short, in statement or description of a scientific character."[8] Wilder emphatically rejected the notion that rigorous thinking and imagination were incompatible. Instead, he offered that the only full and captivating space for theological discourse was one in which critical scholarship was wed with an emphasis on experience and visceral knowing via creative articulation: by theopoesis. Wilder was acutely aware of the ways in which our capacity for novel thought and social movement is bound up in our capacity to employ language creatively. Moreover, he had a powerful belief in the capacity of new expression to catalyze new convictions and new action.

> Any human language represents a special kind of order superimposed upon existence. Generations live in it as a habitat in which they are born and die. Outside it is nescience. The language of a people is its fate. Thus the poets or seers who purify the language of the tribe are truly world-makers and the "unacknowledged legislators of the world." Perhaps one can say that nothing affects the significance of human existence more than the range and resource of our articulation, vocabulary, syntax, and discourse. Men awaken to a greater plenitude of being as they operate with more signs and names and media of communication, and so find themselves more aware of their world and its interrelationships.[9]

As Wilder expanded and clarified these ideas throughout the 1950s, he began to make use of the term "mythopoetic," employing it to discuss what he felt to be an essential quality of New Testament writings. In his 1956 Presidential Address to the Society of Biblical Literature, he said, "we are dealing with a mytho-poetic mentality and not with a prosaic or discursive one. We cannot apply to the imaginative representations in question our modern alternatives of literal versus symbolic. They were meant neither literally nor symbolically . . ."[10] I believe this is one of Wilder's most significant theological trajectories, and one he engaged with from as early as his Yale dissertation: "on the one hand we take [apocalyptic

8. Wilder, *New Testament Faith for Today*, 60.

9. Wilder, *Early Christian Rhetoric*, 5–6.

10. Wilder, "Scholars, Theologians, and Ancient Rhetoric," 11.

scriptural texts] too literally and ignore the poetical mentality of the race and the age. On the other hand we make a mistake if we think of them as merely symbol and poetry as a modern would understand them."[11] It was of the utmost importance to Wilder that religious texts not be flattened and read as manuals, but as works with depth, with poetic and mythic registers. In fact, it was precisely because of Wilder's frequent early use of "mythic" and the rising scholarship of Rudolf Bultmann's concept of "de-mythologizing" that Wilder was clear to explicitly note differences between his perspective and the Bultmannian school of thought.

While he united with Bultmann that a literal interpretation of es-chatological scriptural texts was no longer critically feasible, Wilder felt that Bultmann's approach "confined the saving work of God to the personal and individual sphere," something with which Wilder passion-ately disagreed.[12] Indeed, he even went so far as to state that Bultmann's "theology of the Word of God has a strange resemblance to an older indi-vidual pietism."[13] This was unacceptable to Wilder, who felt as if Scripture ought to be read in, and have effect upon, *communities* of believers. Con-sequently, "it is not enough to effect this translation in individualistic, pietistic or existentialist terms. What is represented in a naïve, uncritical, first-century mythology must be carried over into our thought-world in terms of a realistic Christian sociology."[14] In opposition to Bultmann's existentialist position, Wilder argued that the New Testament ought to be read such that its mythological language would directly address contem-porary ethics and social spheres, catalyzing action in the temporal and fleshly world as well as reordering our very language.

Ultimately, I believe that it was because of a desire to distance his work from that of Bultmann that Wilder decided to move ahead with his later book as *Theopoetic* and not *Mythopoetic*. While he addressed "mythopoetics" in the book itself, and his colleagues Stanley Hopper and David Miller continued to use myth as a guiding term, I believe that Wilder so clearly desired that he not be misconstrued with what he felt was Bultmann's overly individualistic proposals, that the mythic began to take a clear second seat to the poetic. This is not to say that the entirety of Wilder's decision was grounded in an anti-Bultmannian polemic, as

11. Wilder, "The Relation of Eschatology to Ethics," 7.
12. Wilder, "Kerygma, Eschatology and Social Ethics," 527.
13. Ibid., 517.
14. Ibid., 532.

he certainly had other reasons for its use, but I do think that it is important to note, especially given the influence of Bultmann on Hopper and the Drew Consultations on Hermeneutics as addressed in the previous chapter.

As Wilder retired from active regular teaching and began to write outside of the classroom, he came further into an emphasis on the theopoetic. By the time he published *Theopoetic: Theology and the Religious Imagination* in 1976 he had already been exploring some of the ideas it contained for nearly forty years, including a re-editing of some pieces that had appeared in the late 1960s and early 1970s in *Christianity Today*. As the most referenced text devoted to theopoetics, and the culmination of Wilder's work in this area, it is worth considering that book in some depth.

In the opening to *Theopoetic*, Wilder gives thanks to Hopper and the Consultations in Hermeneutics at Drew where he "picked up" the term theopoetics, immediately moving on to bemoan the pabulum quality of most theological discourse. He opens with a barrage of criticism, leading the way with an assertion that "religious communication generally must overcome a long addiction to the discursive, the rationalistic, and the prosaic. And the Christian imagination must go halfway to meet the new dreams, mystiques, and mythologies that are gestating in our time."[15] He categorized most modern theology as "wan and bloodless abstraction," and suggested that the state of Christian discourse is a large factor in the decline of interest in the church, claiming that most priests and pastors have, "widely lost—and all but forgotten—the experience of glory which lies at the heart of Christianity."[16] This theme of experience as essential to powerful theological communication is significant, and Wilder is explicit that in contemporary spirituality "the dimension too often missing is that of rooted-ness, creaturehood, embodied humanness."[17]

Wilder was consciously wary of the possibility that his plea for a theopoetic[18] would be heard merely as a call for a fresh coat of paint on

15. Wilder, *Theopoetic*, 1.

16. Ibid., 8.

17. Ibid., 14.

18. So as to avoid confusion, it should be noted that while I primarily use "theopoetic" as an adjective, Wilder more commonly uses it as a discrete noun to refer to something like "a creative, new way of talking about God and God's action that pays more attention to experience and therefore is more accessible to contemporary people of faith."

a rotting wall, and wanted to actively avoid this perspective. He asserted that what was called for was "not an irresponsible aesthetic-ism but the essential dynamics of the heart and soul."[19] If a theopoetic of this sort were available, Wilder suggested, people would have greater access to the redemptive power of Christianity, and society would be able to more fully "purge itself of its own complacencies."[20] In effect, Wilder argued that rather than functioning as an analgesic or means of promoting individualism, an authentic renewal of Christian discourse would engender a social movement that would eschew moral complacency in favor of a liberating ethic of action with social ramifications that would have paralleled shifts in theological language. Wilder suggested that it is precisely the lack of such an engaged theopoetic that "encourages an evangelical pietism or an ineffective liberalism."[21]

Wilder believed whole-heartedly that if Christians could manage to revitalize the gospel's message with a dynamic language that grew with the contemporary imagination, the result would be adaptive and rich and would fully address the principalities and powers, able to "overcome their bondage, exorcize their evil, and shape the human future."[22] Wilder's plea in *Theopoetic* culminates not simply in the call for reworded theologies: not only language, but *method* must change. At the heart of his work lies the idea that without religious language that fully engages the embodied experience of the modern world, Christians will never be able to reclaim a dynamic faith. Wilder did not think that the theopoetic perspective was a new thing, rather, he claimed that it was the native quality of discourse for much of the Gospels and for Paul's epistles. In spite of this, Wilder was clear that a plea for the theopoetic, or any plea in general for greater emphasis on religious imagination, would likely receive criticism on two fronts.

First, from "a pragmatic no-nonsense type of mentality, representing a kind of devastated area in a culture whose aesthetic and spiritual antennae have been blighted,"[23] and second, from those who are for "the cult of the imagination for itself alone: vision, fantasy, ecstasy for their own sakes; creativity, spontaneity on their own, without roots, without

19. Wilder, *Theopoetic*, 2.

20. Ibid., 23.

21. Ibid., 27.

22. Ibid.

23. Ibid., 101.

tradition, without discipline."[24] On the first front, for "rationalists and religious dogmatists for both of whom experience lacks its deeper creative registers,"[25] he presumed that a move toward a new theopoetic would appear to be frivolous aestheticism, and he challenged them to consider numerous concrete examples of Scripture and the manner in which various genres function to the contrary of a flat, "scientific" reading of the text. To the second he began with affirmation. He claimed that the rise of the undisciplined experience-seeking of the 1960s and 1970s was perfectly reasonable given that "we are heirs of a twofold tradition contributing to the stifling of the spirit and the emotions: on the one hand that sway of rationalism and on the other an inhibiting religious asceticism. It was inevitable that human nature would reassert the rights of spontaneity in explosive ways."[26] Those suspicious of Christianity, and therefore extremely uneager to re-engage with rooted tradition, are well within reason given the stifling cultures that have been normative within the church. If a robust and invitational theopoetic perspective was encouraged though, Wilder thought the stifling character of the traditions would fall away and this front of criticism would dwindle as well.

In both defenses, Wilder is striving toward a type of non-dualism that denies the ultimacy of either/or binaries.[27] Just as his early claim was that the interpretation of Scripture is rightly done "neither literally nor symbolically," and just as he rejected the notion that theology was most properly done in scientific "denotative language stripped as far as possible of all connotative suggestions," Wilder's work in theopoetics is a way toward that which bridges binaries, supplanting them not by the force of some unifying metaphysic or synthesis, but through language that attempts to promote resonances of experiential encounters with the Divine. Theopoetic language ought not be devoid of "rigorous thought," but neither will it map perfectly onto traditional models of proposition and proof. For Wilder, it was necessary that sometimes the language used to express God's nature and movement not adhere too firmly to the nor-

24. Ibid., 57.

25. Ibid., 101.

26. Ibid., 59.

27. It is interesting to note that while there is no direct connection, Wilder's opposition to an either/or hermeneutical formulation is remarkably similar in content to Jacques Derrida's later articulation of deconstruction in *Of Grammatology*, where what he is after is an "overturning" of "binary oppositions" (Derrida, *Positions*, 41–42). This parallel is taken up more fully in chapter 5.

mal linguistic register, but instead do "more justice . . . to the pre-rational in the way we deal with experience."[28] John Dominic Crossan, author of a career retrospective on Wilder, reflects on exactly this issue in the closing passage of that text: "it is surely unsafe to linger too long at the null point, the zero, the instant of unreason. From thence must come not only mysticism, apocalypticism, gnosticism, but also nihilism, that fearful drive to make one's suicide as social as possible. One must certainly insist, as Wilder so eloquently has done, that only with [Reason and Imagination] in conjunction is one fully human."[29] Ultimately, Crossan considers that the culmination of Wilder's work has made it possible to ask whether much of our Western Christian failings have arisen not from a lack of reason, but from too much of it, especially when we think that our reason is clearly reflective of some absolute Divine Reason of which we are the arbiters.

Rubem Alves

While Wilder's contributions culminate rather neatly in *Theopoetic*, the work of Rubem Alves, while no less important, does not track so easily. Born in Boa Esperança, Brazil, in 1933, Alves's career has spanned work as a theologian, psychoanalyst, popular educator, and now, in his eighties, author of children's books. Among those who have named him a close personal friend were James Cone, Walter Wink, and Paulo Freire. His life's history is rich and varied, and given that I believe his biography plays a significant role in his intellectual and theological formation, I feel it is worth exploring.[30]

Alves took his bachelors of theology at the Presbyterian Seminary of Campinas Brazil in 1957, his masters of theology at Union Theological Seminary in New York in 1964, and his doctorate in theology at Princeton in 1968. However, between his masters and doctoral degrees, the 1964 Brazilian *coup d'état* wrested control of the government from the elected leadership and placed it in the hands of a military regime that

28. Ibid., 2.

29. Crossan, *A Fragile Gift*, 67.

30. I am incredibly indebted to Bruno Linhares for the insight into Alves's life. His 2008 dissertation, "Nevertheless I Am Continually with You," has a number of passages from Alves never before published in English, and they have contributed powerfully to my understanding of the context in which Alves wrote.

lasted until 1985.[31] During that period Alves was home in Brazil for the first time since completing his work at Union, and as a result of the coup, rather than being reunited with wife and children, was forced into hiding. As the regime came into power, an attempt was made to purge the country of communist supporters and left-leaning thinkers and writers of all types. Wanting to escape further persecution, the Presbyterian Church of Brazil gave forward six names as scapegoats that the newly formed government could detain. Alves—who had not been living in Brazil for three years—was on that list.

According to the formal declaration, Alves and the others were charged with more than forty accusations that they "preached that Jesus had sexual relations with a prostitute, that [they] rejoiced when [their] children wrote hate phrases against Americans, . . . and that [they] were financed by funds from the Soviet Union."[32] Writing about the charges, Alves notes that "the positive side of the document was that it was so virulent, that not even the most obtuse could believe that we were guilty of so many crimes[;] . . . but that was the tragedy: the people in the church, brothers, pastors, and elders, did not have a minimum of ethical sense, and were so willing to denounce us."[33] Alves later discovered that there were also suggestions and insinuations that he had been directly involved in conspiracy against the government, and that the claims to this effect were made by the director of a Protestant secondary school built on land that Alves's own grandfather had donated to the Presbytery.[34] Plunged into fear and running from the government, Alves managed to escape Brazil only through an underground network of Brazilian Freemasons and the support of the Presbyterian Church U.S.A., who convinced the President of Princeton to invite Alves to work on his doctorate there. Thus, less that two months after returning home he was headed back toward the north and "the delicious euphoria of freedom."[35] His flight from

31. It is worth noting that there is some significant scholarly agreement (Skidmore, *Politics of Military Rule in Brazil*) that the coup and resulting military government was beneficial to, and supported by, American interests. That Alves was a Brazilian benefiting from American education while simultaneously his own country was being manipulated by those same forces would not have been lost on him.

32. Linhares, "Nevertheless I Am Continually with You," 261.

33. Ibid.

34. Ibid., 262.

35. Ibid.

Brazil, however euphoric, only brought temporary relief: Alves felt exiled and alone.

> The doctorate required that each one of us mastered the field of our chosen segment of learning: "to dominate the field," this was "scholarship." I was dreaming, however, of a world that I had lost. And I was amazed with the questions students had chosen, to which they would be dedicating four or five years of their lives. They were fantastic abstractions to me, which I was unable to connect with anything. I remember the famous colloquia with the doctoral students in ethics. The most painful questions, of life and death, were transformed into trapezes where intellectual virtuosities were performed. What was at stake was neither life nor politics, but analytical exercises in which an intellectual skill was exhibited. But I had no alternatives: it behooves the exiled to obey the rules of the country that receives him. I would have to learn how to play the game that everybody played.
>
> What I really wanted to think was about my own destiny.[36]

Alves was informed by his department chair that he could not write as he wanted nor use the methods he desired. Consequently, he wrote his dissertation "as required," and was barely successful in its defense, receiving "the lowest possible grade" needed to pass.[37] As a result, a read through his dissertation, which was eventually published in 1969 as *A Theology of Human Hope*,[38] is remarkably unlike the genres of Alves's future work. In a preface that he wrote for a later edition of that book—not published in English until a 2008 dissertation—he shares his grievances.

> I wrote uglily, without smiles or poetry, for there was no other alternative: a Brazilian student, underdeveloped, in a foreign institution, must indeed submit himself, if he wants to pass. . . . Today I would do everything in a different way. I would begin by informing my readers that theology is a play[,] . . . knowing that God is far ahead of our verbal ploys.

36. Ibid., 270.

37. Ibid., 274.

38. Alves's 1968 dissertation was originally submitted entitled "Toward a Theology of Liberation," three years prior to Gustavo Gutierrez's *A Theology of Liberation*. Alves's advisor and a publishing house's editor both agreed that the title should be changed, as "liberation" was " a name without theological respectability," and "hope" was much "more of the moment" (Linhares, "Nevertheless I Am Continually with You," 274).

> Theology is not a net that is woven in order to capture God in its meshes, for God is not a fish, but Wind that no one can hold . . .
>
> Theology is a net which we weave for ourselves, so that we might stretch out our body in it.[39]

Without another apparent alternative, Alves progressed in his scholarship, continuing to be dissatisfied with the "required" modality of academic theology. Indeed, he even began to become dissatisfied with liberation theology, noting in an interview that "it has little to say about the personal dimension of life. If a father or mother comes with their dead child, it's no consolation to say, 'In the future just society there will be no more deaths of this kind.' This brings no comfort!"[40] Personally disengaged from its overly political focus while simultaneously acknowledging that it is "absolutely essential," Alves had another vision for how it is that he could contribute: "The origin of my liberation theology is an erotic exuberance for life. We need to struggle to restore its erotic exuberance, to share this with the whole world."[41] In 1975 he decided that he would write only from that place of exuberance.

In that year his daughter Raquel was born and her birth became a marker after which he refused to comply with standards and expectations from the academy. In an interview, he once said, "I broke with the academic style because I decided that life is very short, very mysterious, and I didn't have the time to waste with academics. I would only say things in the most honest manner. If people like it, fine. If not, I can't help that. Today I couldn't write academically even if I wanted to!"[42] Thus, after years of struggling to find his voice when asked to speak in a register unfamiliar to his own, Alves finally settled into work which is recognizable as being theopoetically influenced. An intense period of work ensued, from which emerged a string of texts[43] that each thoroughly engaged questions of poetics, place, space, and flesh.[44]

39. Linhares, "Nevertheless I Am Continually with You," 237.

40. Puleo, "Rubem Alves." 193.

41. Ibid., 194.

42. Ibid., 188.

43. 1982's *Creio na Ressurreição do Corpo*; 1983's *Poesia, Profecia e Magia*; 1984's *O Que É Religião?*, and 1991's *O Poeta, O Guerreiro e O Profeta*.

44. While a number of Alves's texts have been translated into English, there is an increasing number of South American and Northern European scholars engaged in secondary scholarship about the importance of Alves whose work has not yet been translated into English. See, Boer and Cervantes-Ortiz in the bibliography.

As Alves departed from writing "uglily" and "without smiles or poetry," he didn't enter into a period of disengaged work concerned only with pleasing surface appearances, but rather moved into a style of writing where his method directly challenged the formal academy. Even though he aptly moves between Scripture, Hegel, and literature to great effect, the nature of his writing was far from academic in genre. Two passages will suffice to demonstrate, and as style, method, and content are bound up so tightly in Alves's later writing, to adequately allow for a sense of his work I include longer passages than one might often be inclined to provide. Note the conversational and lecture-like cadence to his prose. He is writing from the body.

~

This, I believe, is the secret of communion: when my body, transformed in words, is given to the other, to be eaten. And as she or he tastes it one says: It is good. . . . Back to Feuerbach: Man *ist* was man *isst*; we are what we eat. When the other eats eucharistically a piece of my body, we become "companions," in the original sense of the word: those who eat the same bread.

So I am no longer a professor. I have no lessons to give, no knowledge to communicate. I am a cook. I try to transform my body in words. Indeed, I try to say the words which make up the essence of my being. These statements should not cause any surprise, since they are nothing but a variation of the central motif of the Christian tradition, that the Word becomes Flesh. I speak only about myself.

Arrogance? How could someone not feel embarrassed to make such a statement—as if he or she were the center of the world?

I believe, rather, that such a statement implies a great deal of humility. I know nothing about God—I am not a theologian! I know nothing about the world—I am not a scientist. I know only this little space which is my body—and even my body I only see as a dim reflection in a dark mirror.

Confessions.

Not theology. Poetry.

The poet is the person who speaks words which are not to be understood; they are to be eaten. And his stove is his own body lit with the fire of imagination . . .[45]

45. Alves, "Theopoetics: Longing and Liberation," 159–60.

~

It is well known that Luther said that reason was a whore. Few, however, know, that this was his reply to Erasmus' statement that the body is a whore . . .

Erasmus was a citizen of the world of light. Luther, however, knew that amidst the glitter of reflections, Lucifer, the deceiver, is the one who bears the light (from the Latin *lux*, light, and *ferre*, to bear). Truth abides in the darkness of the body where a word is heard. Not the eyes, but the ears. Truth is "a Poem which became Flesh," the body of Christ, ubiquitous and hidden in the whole universe, even in the tiniest leaf of a tree.

It is not our doing. It is the doing of an "Unknown" . . .

In theological language: not justification by works but justification by grace. Grace is the forgotten word which speaks itself. . . . We are all feminine. We are the Virgin who is made pregnant by the Word which comes with the Wind.

A word is heard and the body trembles. But this trembling is only possible if body and word are the same thing. "Words are the stuff with which we are made," says Octavio Paz.

Our bodies dwell in oblivion, like the Sleeping Beauty. We no longer know how to play the tune which is written in our flesh. The reflections, ten thousand, we know. But the depth of the lake is beyond our reason. We learned that we are where we think: "I think, therefore I am." Now, the reversed theme: "Where I think, there I am not."

This is what poets have been saying all the time. No wonder that they have become marginal. They should not be invited to our academic dinner parties, because they speak as if they were drunk.[46]

~

What we read in but a few hundred words of Alves brushes against Eucharist, revelation, justification, Luther, Feuerbach, hermeneutics, and grace, not to mention a Brazilian poet, a Mexican author, and Sleeping Beauty. And this is normative, not exceptional at all, for Alves's later writing. His pacing and genre is such a departure from normal academic modes of discourse that even before Alves's great 1975 "break with the academic style" he received these comments in Thomas Altizer's book review in the *Journal of the American Academy of Religion*: "surely [Alves's

46. Alves, *The Poet, The Warrior, The Prophet*, 54–55.

dissertation] would not even have been considered for publication if it had not been written by a Third World theologian. . . . My one fear about the book is that it will yet further sanction that growing mass of homiletic literature which presents itself in a theological guise."[47] What Altizer seems to infer here is that "homiletic literature" cannot be theology, or, put another way, the form of theology is not something that can be accomplished in homiletics, which is more readily accessible and aesthetically pleasing than much academic writing.

Altizer's fears and assumptions aside, I believe that Alves's decision to take up a freer form of language was not mere whimsy or an attempt to dress up poetry in a "theological guise": it was the result of an intellectual stance regarding the nature of God and theology. His "break" with the academy meant that he had to give up on the idea that his theological language would ever be satisfactory or complete. He let go of a desire to prove, and was "no longer a professor," but "a cook," preparing words that captured a facet of the movement of spirit, crafting them in the stove heat of "his own body lit with the fire of imagination," and serving them to his readers that they might catch some taste of the experience of hope and God. By 1975 he no longer felt he was doing theology at all, but theopoetics instead.

> God is the Wind: it comes, it goes, it cannot be put in paper cages or word cages. . . . After it goes the only thing which is left is the memory of its touch on my skin. I can only speak about this: reverberations on my body, as it is touched by the Wind; sometimes a chill, sometimes a warm feeling, goose-pimples. . . . Not theology. Poetry. If you like—theo-poetics.[48]

A Thread Unites

At the core of their work, I believe that Wilder and Alves were both profoundly uneasy with the discontinuity between lived experience and academic text, and both desired to do something about it. For Wilder, firsthand exposure to the European fronts of World War I left an indelible mark on his awareness, and for Alves the chaos and upheaval of his native Brazil meant that the pabulum and tame did not speak to the depth of his

47. Altizer, "Review of *Tomorrow's Child*," 376.
48. Alves, "Theopoetics: Longing and Liberation," 161.

experience.[49] Both insisted on a vibrancy to theological language without which they felt that it was somehow falling short of the mark. Without either writer ever citing one another, there is an incredible resonance between them:

> It is at the level of the imagination that any full engagement with life takes place. It is not enough for the church to be on guard against the Philistine in the world. Philistinism invades Christianity from within wherever the creative and mythopoetic dimension of faith is forfeited. When this happens doctrine becomes a caricature of itself. Then that which once gave life begins to lull and finally to suffocate us.[50]

> I apologize for having written such a dull book. I did not want to, for I'm not that way. If I wrote this way it was because I was forced to do so, in the name of academic scholarship. It is thought that truth is something cold and even a funny way of writing was invented: always impersonal, as if the writer did not exist, thereby making the text look like it was written by everybody and by nobody. And it was this coldness that forbade beauty and humor from surfacing in scientific texts. Knowledge, you see, must be something serious. Without taste . . .[51]

Though both make use of the term "theopoetics," and that itself is rare enough so as to suggest some linkages, I propose that there is something that unites them more significantly than unusual similarities in diction. Framed as an effect, both Wilder and Alves offer that theopoetics is that which bridges the fractured, chaotic, and fleshy experience of life with the oftentimes removed and "ossified" attempt to create "scientific texts" out of theological articulation. Both want to capture the power and experience of the flesh without sacrificing intellectual rigor. Where they differ is in the emphasis of their methods and rationale. Wilder generally conceived of the move toward the theopoetic as one needed for *Christian* vitality and renewal, and routinely suggested the most significant missing element is that of imagination, or the "pre-rational way we deal with experience." Alternatively, Alves seemed to move toward the theopoetic out of a sense of necessity for his *own* sake, a feeling that he can no longer

49. Ashley Theuring argues that theopoetics has a particular utility in helping reconnect to God in the context of violence and trauma. See her work in *Expressing the Ineffable: Theopoetics of Abraham Joshua Heschel and Dorothee Sölle*.

50. Wilder, *Theopoetic*, 2.

51. Alves, "Foreword," 237.

speak of God in traditionally academic modes of discourse because they no longer sufficed to account for the experience of God, which he so dearly wants to reflect.

While Wilder's emphasis was a renewal and re-encouragement of the Christian imagination grounded in a lifetime of literary studies, Alves's is about the flesh, longing, desire, and the feeling and weight of exile.[52] Wilder's interests were propelled by a forward-driving desire to reinvigorate Christian discourse, while Alves's shift to the poetic was *pulled* from him by a sense of lack, a sense that there was yet something being called forth, a sense of beauty drawing him further into some furtive and fragrant garden like the sweet song of some exotic bird.[53]

Regardless of their varying trajectories, I believe that both Wilder and Alves were in resonance with Hopper and his assertion that "theology founded upon the mathematical models of propositional logic is founded upon a profound metaphysical error."[54] For all three it was necessary that theological articulation do more than talk *about* God: it had to somehow also capture the *experience* of the presence of God, the radically disorienting encounter with the Christ whose kingdom is not of this world. What is curious, however, is that though both Hopper and Wilder affirmed the need to encourage language that "evokes resonances and recognitions,"[55] abandons "hollow language," and requires "the unlearning of symbolic forms,"[56] neither made the shift in their own academic work. While both Hopper and Wilder were published and vocal champions of embodiment, imagination, and the creative, their academic work continued to rest in the traditional register of academic methodol-

52. Further reflection on the emphasis on longing and the flesh is taken up again substantially in chapter 3, when embodiment and knowing are considered. Alves's 2010 book *Transparencies of Eternity* is an excellent resource in this regard as well, as is *The Poet, The Prophet, The Warrior*.

53. Alves writes that the "foundation of [his] poetic and religious thinking" is "*saudade*," a Brazilian word that he explains as follows: "Translators with expertise in several languages say that there is no precise synonym for it in other languages. It is a feeling close to nostalgia. But it is not nostalgia. Nostalgia is pure sadness without an object. Nostalgia has no face. Whereas *saudade* is always *saudade* "of" a scenario, a face, a scene, a time. The Brazilian poet Chico Buarque wrote a song about *saudade*, in which he says that '*saudade* is a piece of me wrenched out of me, it's to straighten up the room of the son who just died.' It is the presence of an absence" (Alves, *Transparencies of Eternity*, 15).

54. Hopper, "The Literary Imagination and the Doing of Theology," 224.

55. Ibid., 218.

56. Ibid., 220.

ogy. Both Hopper and Wilder wrote poetry as well as academic prose, but the genre of their academic work remained relatively separate from their literary writing. This is not the case for Alves.

My intention is not to condemn or castigate either Hopper or Wilder. Their work has been profoundly influential on my own, and has paved the way for thinking about the importance and function of theopoetic language and perspectives. However, it is simply the case that this is primarily what they provide: language *about* theopoetics. Well-written, well-reasoned, and compelling, but ultimately not to be considered theopoetic itself. Their work was second-order discourse, while Alves attempted to engage theopoetics *theopoetically*. Wilder wrote powerfully as both an academic and a poet, taking care such that "each genre of his work stood on its own,"[57] while Alves flung himself headlong into an attempt to realize the kind of integrated theological and poetic language that Wilder and Hopper wrote about. I see Hopper's search for "resonances and recognitions" of God and Wilder's "plea for a renewed theopoetic" to be manifest in Alves and his declaration that "theology is a net which we weave for ourselves, so that we might stretch out our body in it." Indeed, it was in large part because of the vigor, artistry, and excitement I find in Alves's writing that I first felt drawn towards this work.

This is not to elevate one over the other, or to place Alves at the top of some academically theopoetic hierarchy, but to re-affirm with Paul that "each is given the manifestation of the Spirit for the common good"[58]: Hopper and Wilder were teachers and utterers of wisdom and knowledge, and while Alves was inclined to begin there as well, he eventually slipped into prophecy and the speaking of tongues. In some ways, *Way to Water* is intended to serve as a more clearly marked path between work like Alves's and texts that are more similar to a traditional academic genre. I believe that theopoetics possesses the means to assist more logic-oriented theologians and people of faith with a connection to a prophetic and poetic method and way into that which is eternal.

57. Beardslee, "Amos Niven Wilder," 5.

58. 1 Cor 12:7.

Limbo

In the end—if there is an end that is—we might not remember
this exchange. It may be simply washed away.

The words breathed between us evaporate
to particle & become—to swill, to sweep, to storm.

We go—once more, from the chest—into prayer
as we would a door, not really knowing if its entrance or exit,
departure or arrival.

How we might be the sentence God is breathless saying,
bodies balanced from divine tongue-tip,
a dancing king marionettes through his own forgiveness.

Or that God might be diving from the rim of our lips
into a manger or a cross or dribbled wine & wiped away.

& so it's outside in & inside out—a broke vocabulary puzzled
back to whole in portable shrine, in patterned pulse.

That name a marble in the mouth, swaddled in the air
as it begins to exit—bright bolt coughing in the vault,
an alphabet of rain, the bowls our fingers weave
to drink the water.

& this is you: standing at the door,
a curtain torn & soaking at your feet.

Our tangled roots, our messages,
our sapped and sinewed particles.

These invitations to which we've all said yes
before the envelope is opened.

PART TWO

Contemporary Contributions

3

Bodies and Tongues

Melanie Duguid-May and Scott Holland

> The essential is to know how to see . . .
> But this . . .
> This calls for deep study,
> Learning how to unlearn . . .
>
> I try to get rid of what I learned,
> I try to forget the way I was taught to remember,
> And to scrape off the paint they used to cover my senses.
> —ALBERTO CAEIRO[1]

THIS CHAPTER IS THE first half of an exploration of the related work of four contemporary authors who have engaged directly with theopoetics as a topic after the initial extensive foray by Hopper, Wilder, and Alves. These scholars will be of particular interest to those interested in theopoetics as they are the primary source of students who have become part of the blossoming American interest in, and publication on, the topic since 2000. While the next chapter takes up the work of process theologians Roland Faber and Catherine Keller, this chapter considers

---

1. Caeiro, "The Essential," 28.

the contributions of Melanie Duguid-May and Scott Holland, both with origins in one of the historic Peace Churches, the Church of the Brethren.[2]

Though the Church of the Brethren is not the primary focus of either of their theological careers, it can be considered as providing the platform upon which they both work. As opposed to schemas that tend toward the near-complete separation of the kingdom of God and the kingdom of the World, Anabaptists have traditionally affirmed that the ordering of the kingdom of God ought to have concrete, social, and this-wordly manifestations.[3] The theopoetic insistence on the importance of fleshly experience and the validity of the vision of marginalized perspectives seems to keep in resonance with this ordering. That being said, however, the methods by which Holland and Duguid-May arrive at support for the theopoetic are not directly via an appeal to Brethren theologies. For Holland, it is through a heady draught of American pragmatism, continental phenomenology, John Howard Yoder, and the work of Catholic theologian David Tracy. For Duguid-May, it is through a potent mix of feminist theory, Gordon Kaufman, and Michel Foucault.

Borrowing terminology from the work of Mikhail Bakhtin, theopoetics in the Duguid-May/Holland frame can be understood as "a dialogical enterprise." Theopoetics is that which acknowledges that all text is in continual dialogue with past and present texts and—perhaps Holland and Duguid-May might add—bodies as well. Language, "as a living, socio-ideological concrete thing . . . lies on the borderline between oneself and the other. . . . It becomes one's own only when the speaker populates it with his own intention, his own accent, when he appropriates the word."[4] Read this way, the viability of theopoetics is tied to its insistence on the particular, and a theological re-interpretation of the Imagist poet's maxim, "show, don't tell." Adrienne Rich's comments on poetry are applicable to theopoetics as well: "there is no universal Poetry anyway, only poetries and poetics, and the streaming, intertwining histories to which they belong."[5] In this way, theopoetics is an affirmation of intersectionality, an insistence upon the importance of each perspective and voice, and

2. It is outside the focus of this piece to consider the more profound potential reasons why it is that theopoetics is appealing to Anabaptist sensibilities, but it should be noted that Holland and Duguid-May are not alone in their interests. See also the work of Gundy, Guynn, Miller, and Poling in the bibliography.

3. See John Yoder, J. Denny Weaver, Donald Kraybill, et al.

4. Bakhtin, *The Dialogic Imagination*, 278.

5. Rich, *Poetry and Commitment*, 21.

a challenge to the social forces that—intentionally or not—cover over the senses with whitewash. The poetic epigraph that opens this chapter can serve as a guide-post to Duguid-May and Holland's work. They both take up theopoetics as a way to try to "forget the way [they were] taught to remember," and to try to "scrape off the paint . . . used to cover [their] senses." They want to recover a fuller measure of sacredness associated with the body and with the body's senses and experiences.

Though later chronologically, I see the work of Melanie Duguid-May as typologically falling somewhere between Wilder and Alves. She writes in a way that transgresses academic theological mores, and does so with a stated intent to re-affirm the body as a—if not *the*—supreme site of knowing and being human. That said, she never goes as far from standard theological style as does Alves, who all but abandoned prose, propositional argumentation, and the formal, systematic development of a thesis. Where Duguid-May overlaps with Alves is on the insistence that "the body knows." Though Holland also unites with a desire to ground knowing at least partially in the flesh, he is more like Alves in his eagerness to be a theological rabble-rouser for the sake of transgressing the status quo. Holland often says his academic transgressions are about challenging the "Constantinian assumptions of contemporary theology and culture,"[6] or, seen with a theopoetic sensibility, about scraping off the paint used to cover his senses. Holland's method then, while no less dedicated to fleshy, experiential knowing, is more purposefully provocative, less confessional than Duguid-May's, and significantly less poetic in genre than Alves's later texts. Regardless, Holland's work is compelling—focused on embodiment and the accessible nature of theopoetics[7]—and has become a vibrant part of the landscape of the conversation.

What we will see that unites these two thinkers is a commitment not only to affirming the validity of experiential knowledge, but also an assertion that the *exclusion* of fleshly knowledge is a tool of control exerted by systems of power, used to police discourse, control tone, and maintain the status quo. By championing the body and experience as an essential component in knowing and thinking, Duguid-May and Holland not only affirm our incarnational nature, they challenge those systems

6. Holland, "Editorial," 4.

7. *Entering Whitman's America: A Theopoetics of Public Life* is forthcoming from Holland and focuses on the intersection of populism and theopoetics in Whitman's poetic, social, and political thought.

and worldviews that attempt to operate as if the flesh can be ignored, or worse, *should* be ignored.

Melanie Duguid-May

Before delving into Duguid-May's work directly, it is worth a short detour through Gordon Kaufman, who served as her doctoral advisor at Harvard. Apropos of the conversation thus far, it is important to note that Kaufman also took issue with Bultmann's "de-mythologizing," but on separate grounds than did Wilder. Kaufman's method was to point out that even if one were to accept the Bultmannian method of removing the "crude and unbelievable mythological machinery" so that faith in God could once more blossom, unhindered by outmoded metaphors, and linguistic contrivances, there would still be another stone to turn over: "the problem is whether there is *any significant reality at all* 'above' or 'beyond' or 'below' the world we know in our experience, or whether life is to be understood simply in this-wordly, that is, secular terms."[8] Succinctly, Kaufman's position is that Bultmann's project does *not go far enough.*

For Kaufman, the most significant theological issue causing doubt with contemporary people was not "demons, angels, and other supernatural and superpersonal powers,"[9] but the very notion of the "exalted Christ" or the pure "Word of God," which Bultmann thought we would be left with if we could but remove the "naïve myths" of another era. Kaufman's move is to argue that by saying there will somehow be an "exalted Christ" left after clearing away the myth one simultaneously affirms—albeit perhaps unintentionally—that there is a "there" out there that is somehow entirely beyond that which humanity can perceive. Kaufman writes that this is a far larger stumbling block than the supposed existence of the demonic, and to truly address the issue adequately, "the meaning of the word 'God,' even in its reference to the 'transcendent,' must be developed *entirely* in terms of this-worldly experiences and conceptions[,] . . . that therefore the whole issue of a presupposed cosmological dualism . . . can be bypassed."[10] Though neither Duguid-May's methodology nor her project are identical to Kaufman's, she agrees with him that theology is an imaginative construct, and that it can be

8. Kaufman, *God the Problem*, 43.
9. Ibid.
10. Ibid., 45.

constructed such that it need not insist upon a dualism: that which is offered by the world we know is more than sufficient to know that God is.

Central to Duguid-May's work in the 1990s is a narrative regarding her transition from standard theological discourse to a more theopoetic one. Rather than methodological transformation catalyzed by the birth of a child, as was the case for Alves, Duguid-May found herself transformed by several experiences of cancer and the death of those close to her, as well as hope and new life beyond, and in, the moments of suffering. In large part because of her willingness to embrace her body's knowing, there is a clear development of the degree to which she is willing to step outside the boundaries of "acceptable" discourse between her 1989 *Bonds of Unity: Women, Theology, and the Worldwide Church*—a treatment of her Harvard dissertation—and 1995's *A Body Knows: A Theopoetics of Death and Resurrection*. Lifting up aspects of both of these works helps to clarify what Duguid-May's sense of the theopoetic is.

In *Bonds of Unity,* Duguid-May writes about the tension between wanting to belong to a community and a tradition and the ensuing struggles when one's individuality does not easily fit within the norms of that community. She is particularly concerned with the ways in which female voices and views are systemically left out of dominant systems, and the way in which this exclusion happens, especially in church communities. Her working method involves using numbers of interviews from women around the world, with whom she had worked as she served the World Council of Churches in Switzerland. As the text nears its close, Duguid-May transparently grapples with how to conclude a theological text that has methodologically been focused on dialogue and interrelation. She confesses to seeing the problem with having to make some final, definitive, and totalizing theological proclamation when her emphasis in the book has been about shared narrative and the particularity of individual stories.

> It is certainly incumbent upon the writer of a doctoral dissertation "to give her verdict," or "take sides" . . . but to do so at this point in this dissertation would be to fall prey to and thus perpetuate precisely that mode of thought from which I set, seeking a new way of life and thought. Throughout this text I have articulated my voice as it is woven together with other voices. I have not attempted an unadulterated account of either subject or object. . . . I have committed myself to this transgression in

hope of transformation, i.e. in hope of bonds of unity created in celebration not constraint of difference.[11]

Ultimately—and in a bold move that must have raised more than one set of Harvard eyebrows—she chose not to close with a proclamation, but with a decision to "participate with others, rather than to make predictions about a new creation."[12] She concluded her doctoral dissertation at Harvard without a conclusion! After scores of pages dedicated to the vision of women's liberation being tied to the survival of individual narratives, she felt that in integrity she could not then universalize the experience of the women whose stories she had been stewarding, pushing their faces into the background in favor of her "learned" conclusion. This marked emphasis on the particular stays with Duguid-May, and in *A Body Knows* it bears full fruit.

Each chapter in her later book is an account of one of Duguid-May's brushes against death—both her own and those of loved ones—and her experience of new life in the face of the crying of the flesh. Nothing in *A Body Knows* begins with theory or metaphysics and looks to experience for support. She anchors her exploration *first* in memories of her body and allows knowing to grow from there, affirming the essential physicality of Christianity. She writes that "to tell the truth about . . . life . . . is to participate in the realization of God's revelation," because "as Christians we confess that the truth is not propositional, but personal. Jesus Christ, we confess, *is* 'the way, and the truth, and the life.'"[13] Regardless of the supposed importance of the body in Christian belief and practice, she writes with an awareness of the way that society—especially the culture of the academy and the church—suppresses embodied knowing.

> Experiences of a lifetime have prepared me to write in this way. It nonetheless remains a challenge to relinquish the relentless requirements of razor-sharp ratiocination that characterized my formal theological training. I still ache as I struggle to stitch flesh and blood sensibilities into the apparent self-sufficiency of scholarship. I am still mending my own alienated choice to dissociate logic from life that I thought was the ticket to academic achievement.[14]

11. May, *Bonds of Unity*, 165.

12. Ibid., 170.

13. May, *A Body Knows*, 85.

14. Ibid., 14.

A Body Knows runs the narrative of her own experiences of bodily pain, recounting life-threatening illnesses and the new life she found on the other side of them. In the course of her story she lifts up her own sense of resurrection, claiming that her theology has become a doxology, affirming that, "what our bodies know is a life-giving source of our knowledge of God."[15] She is grateful for her life and speaks of that gratitude into the Mystery, glad to have received its gifts and not needing to understand them in entirety. In a way, Duguid-May is treading the same path as early Christians, speaking of God not out of a desire to contain and comprehend, but from a place of thanksgiving. Early prayers and psalms were not systematized theologies or ordered ontologies, but instances of language grasping at slivers of the Spirit, attempting to speak personal experience into the Mystery, hoping it would catch.

Duguid-May writes in opposition to perspectives like that of George Lindbeck who asserts that "language creates the possibility of religious experience,"[16] and that "religious experiences in the sense of feelings, sentiments, or emotions . . . result from new conceptual patterns instead of being their source."[17] While Duguid-May does not engage Lindbeck directly in the text, his value for this section is to see her project's trajectory more clearly by placing it beside one which is oriented in full inversion. Where Lindbeck argues that "Luther did not invent his doctrine of justification by faith because he had a tower experience, but rather the tower experience was made possible by his discovering the doctrine in the Bible,"[18] Duguid-May's conviction is nearly opposite to this. She sides with an insistence that understanding "ourselves as embodied selves expands the range of pastoral theological interests," providing "a methodological tool to critique the inadequate views of personhood and bodiliness with which much Christian theology operates," affirming that "*knowing*, as such, happens through our bodies as well as our minds."[19] Succinctly, Duguid-May is convinced that embodied knowing is not only faithful to the Christian tradition, but also engenders a more vibrant engagement within communities of faith.

15. Ibid., 23.

16. Holland, *How Do Stories Save Us?* 79.

17. Lindbeck, *The Nature of Doctrine*, 39.

18. Ibid.

19. Moore, *Introducing Feminist Perspectives*, 15.

> Too many of us are dead while we breathe: dead to feeling, to imagination, to truth telling. Too many of us live satisfied with a shallow seriousness—sanguine or sober—since we assume what we now know is all there will be. I write to awaken myself, and others, to an awareness of death as integral to life, to awaken us to the joy of resurrection, that is, to new life abundant.[20]

Whereas Wilder issued a plea for "rooted-ness, creaturehood, [and] embodied humanness,"[21] but did not much address the pain and suffering that comes with that creaturehood, Duguid-May insists that pain and bodies must be acknowledged as unavoidable aspects of humanity and the Incarnation, and as such, vehicles by which we can come to know God's movement. Following the significant role that Foucault played in *Bonds of Unity,* Duguid-May makes repeated use of his thought regarding the ways in which bodies become sites of social control.[22] She picks up on the Foucauldian theme of emotion, physicality, and socially constructed madness being categorized as "unreasonable," and thus a tool used by those in positions of authority to alienate and devalue the offerings and very *lives* of women and other marginalized voices.

Wanting to subvert this type of alienating activity, she sides with Kathleen Jones in suggesting that rather than associating authority with "a disciplinary, controlling, rule-ordered concept," in a Christian context it can be rightly reinterpreted as a "contextual, relational process of communication and connection."[23] Within this framework, a healthy unity is achieved not by enforcing some totalizing *Ordnung,* pressing all voices into place, but by allowing—and inviting—each voice to speak, trusting that by God a place has been made for all voices.

> Authority is bearing witness in one's body—in word and deed—to the Good News so people can see and come to seek promised life abundant. Authority cannot accomplish this by command of control. For bearing witness is revelatory, regulatory. Authority as bearing witness is revealed in persons who themselves in their lives incarnate the proclamation that Christ is risen, that God's new creation in Christ is already present.[24]

20. May, *A Body Knows,* 15.
21. Wilder, *Theopoetic,* 14.
22. May, *A Body Knows,* 32, 64, 71, et al.
23. Jones, "On Authority," 125.
24. May, *A Body Knows,* 75.

A Body Knows is important to the theopoetic conversation not so much because Duguid-May says something in particular that upsets the theological status quo, but *that* she says it in the particular way she does. She writes that she wants to "invite others to participate in an ongoing process of naming, clarifying, and loosing again: to honor *Poesis* as making and remaking without ceasing."[25] The book is not some strident polemic against theology *de rigueur,* but is instead a kind of lament, a doxology of suffering and joy that defies norms, not via virtuosic proof, but because it acknowledges uncertainty, pain, and death, emerging from stories of personal suffering and joy in her body. She writes that she was assured of resurrection, not because of doctrine, but through the *experience* of new, abundant life.

Scott Holland

Working from Catholic thinkers David Tracy and Andrew Greeley, Holland desires to develop a method of theological articulation that resonates between two positions: "the Protestant dialectical imagination [that] envisions life within a sacred text," and "the Catholic analogical imagination [that] imagines life in a sacramental universe."[26] Like Duguid-May's Kaufmanian move to identify theology as an imaginative construct, Holland affirms that theology is a type of writing, and like Duguid-May's insistence on the importance of the body, Holland's work affirms the *experience* of the believer is to be a key component of any contemporary articulation of faith. Also like Duguid-May, he voices the importance of the erotic and ludic dimensions of a life of faith, citing his appreciation of Diane Prosser MacDonald, Jeanette Winterson, and bell hooks, along with their respective notions of "Creative Transgression," "ecstasy and effrontery prior to epistemology," and an "erotic pedagogy wherein transgression itself exposes and undermines the politics of domination."[27] Holland reminds us that the body is not just the container of our rational mind, but the seat of emotion, desire, and imagination as well. For all their similarities though, if Duguid-May is typologically situated somewhere between Wilder and Alves, Holland is somewhere between Wilder and Duguid-May.

25. Ibid., 25.
26. Holland, *How Do Stories Save Us?* 5.
27. Ibid.

Rather than Duguid-May's move to read theopoetics as doxology, Holland offers that it is a type of "fictive writing" along the lines of Emerson's notion that fiction reveals truths that reality obscures, or perhaps even better, Lewis Carroll's request that "When describing, / A shape, or sound, or tint; / Don't state the matter plainly, / But put it in a hint; / And learn to look at all things, / With a sort of mental squint."[28] Theology and theopoetic writing isn't "made up" in the sense that it is a falsity or a fantasy,[29] but it *is* a creation of humanity striving to articulate the Divine, not infinite truth poured into the container of language. This willingness to think and write in a way that requires a "mental squint" is a positive thing for Holland, as its lack of mechanistic clarity engenders dialogue and promotes a radical acceptance of plurality regarding personal experience of the Divine. Furthermore, since "personal experience of the Divine," happens only by means of our bodies—how often this simple fact is forgotten!—Holland closely associates theopoetics with an affirmation of the importance and centrality of the flesh in Christian tradition.

> We are reminded at Easter that unlike the Greek philosopher Socrates, who faced his sentence of capital punishment with a calm, welcome acceptance as the cup of poison hemlock was placed in front of him, Jesus, the Jewish rabbi, resisted his death with the anguished plea, "Father, if it is possible remove this cup from me." For Socrates, the body was the mere prison of the soul. For Rabbi Jesus, the body and the book and the beloved world were imagined as united in God and thus believed to be blessed by God.[30]

Theopoetics is compelling for Holland because it is an embodied and populist approach to God-talk. While modern philosophy, theology, and to a large degree, even poetry, have become isolated in the rarefied atmosphere of academia, theopoetics remains the means through which common people may begin to voice their sense of the Divine. He does not believe that "theopoetics" as a term is readily employed by "the people," but argues that all experientially inspired articulation of God—via popular music, over kitchen tables, in novels, movies, etc.—is a form of theopoetic expression. As such, experiential commentary of God ought to be

28. Carroll, "Poeta Fit."

29. Working from within a Ricœurian frame, Holland is not concerned with "reproductive" imagination, but with the "productive" imaginary. See Taylor's "Ricœur's Philosophy of Imagination" for more on this distinction.

30. Holland, "The Anabaptist's Will."

acknowledged as a type of legitimate theological communication, opening up the category such that it is accessible to more than those trained in the academy.

Holland refers to Plato's exile of the poet from the ideal republic because of his distaste for the manner in which poetry can excite the masses in ways that are unpredictable. Holland rejoices in this unpredictabilty. He writes, "philosophers make the eternal Logos, Word, or Reason inhabit political structures and moral forms, but poets, dangerous poets, make the flesh become word."[31] This dangerous action, this flow of Word into flesh into liberating word, is exactly what Holland would like to see more of. He is concerned with the distance at which theology holds itself from the world, and envisions a language of God wherein "a theopoetics and a hermeneutics of gesture finally meet on the tongue of language and taste."[32] Theology ought not just be *in* the world: it ought to be sensing and rubbing against it as well.

Holland sees theopoetics as a means of returning to a sense of God among present perspectives of postmodernity, and yet claims that the call toward a theopoetic is discernible as far back as Samuel Taylor Coleridge, who understood poetry to be a providential gift that supports "those delicate sentiments of the heart . . . which may be called the feeding streams of religion."[33] For Holland, the theopoetic impulse acts as a "divine lure" of sorts, pulling at the heart's sentiments, irresistibly drawing people into physical action and not just thought.[34] On more than one occasion, as a pastor in a Church of the Brethren congregation, he has encouraged those gathered to "search out God in the streets like a spy," urging them to find and share reflections of the Divine wherever they might.[35]

An explicit champion of "theology written in the shadow of postmodernism," Holland is nonetheless a critic of the postmodern turn in theology. He finds that far too often postmodern theologies provide "a God without wonder, subject positions without souls, multiculturalism without analogies of being, bodies without passion, sex without real

31. Holland, *How Do Stories Save Us?* 132.

32. Ibid., 136.

33. Ibid., 137.

34. See Barry Whitney's article for further consideration of the "Divine Lure," and see chapter 8 in which Matt Guynn's work, "Theopoetics and Social Change," is considered.

35. Holland, *Personal Communication*.

bodies, aesthetics without art, and poetry without strong poets."[36] He resonates with Paul Tillich's assertion that "to be a theologian one has to be a non-theologian"[37]: to speak meaningfully about God in the world one must know God *and* the world. This grounded emphasis of theopoetics is reminiscent of an interview with national poet laureate Stanley Kunitz. In it, he evokes William Blake, claiming that his success as a poet is completely tied to the degree that he has been capable of evincing the "minute particulars" of a situation. The *specificity* of corporeal experience is vital.

Asked the secret to his long-lasting career and popularity as a poet, Kunitz responded that it was because he loved gardening more than poetry. He commented that "it is an advantage for the poet not always to be immersed in poetry, not to become incestuous with his own art. . . . [Too] much poetry is airy. It is spun only out of the need to write the poem and is not nailed into the foundations of the life itself."[38] In his garden, Kunitz came to literal grips with that life, fending off an "incestuous" obsession with poetry by immersing himself in the "minute particulars" of his flower beds. In turn, Holland's tended rows are the cheap seats of a Pirate's game, the scratchy comfort of a first-pressing Pete Seeger record, and the worn edges of a pub stool where he and his steel-working neighbors head at the end of the week. There he finds enough expression of the everyday to hedge against a type of airy theorizing and abstract theology that theopoetics seeks to avoid. Moreover, for Holland an avoidance of *any* claims to metaphysics is profoundly important.

In a substantial passage of *How Do Stories Save Us?*, Holland recounts the history of Immanuel Kant's origins as a poetic thinker, reminding us that at the relatively young age of forty-two he was invited to the University of Berlin to take up a full professorship in poetics.[39] Holland makes much of Kant's refusal of that offer, holding it in view as part of what he calls "Kant's longing for fixed points, for a metaphysics of morals over a poetics of obligation," a longing, he says, that can be understood to culminate in Kant's trilogy of *Critiques*. Even when Kant again takes up aesthetics in *The Critique of Judgement,* he writes "a rather

---

36. Holland, *How Do Stories Save Us?* 17.

37. Ibid., 19.

38. Luphor, "Language Surprised," 6.

39. Holland, *How Do Stories Save Us?* 115.

disembodied doctrine . . . wherein ethics proceeds aesthetics."[40] This is the same problem, argues Holland, which led to Plato excluding poets from the republic: Kant believed that "the transgressive body of the strong poet must submit to that which underwrites the categorical imperative, the philosopher's reason."[41] Emotion, sensation, and aesthetic experience must come under the thumb of rationality. Holland argues that this trajectory is, if not nearing its end, at least not as useful to people of faith as is a more theopoetic approach. That is, "we now live east of Eden and its pure and perfect foundations. The safely detached 'observation towers' where men [*sic*] once sat to colonize reason, homogenize language, unify ethics and thus domesticate the Divine have forever fallen."[42] We may not yet have complete maps for this east-of-Eden place, but staring longer at Eden's cartographies will not help.

In place of Kantian "observation towers," Holland advocates for models of theological thought that have a "mutually critical correlation between the texts of one's religious community and common human language and experience."[43] He rejects approaches like that of Lindbeck and Hauerwas, who he says too firmly shut out other worlds, words, and communities for the sake of an internally-coherent and hermetically sealed hermeneutic. It is indicative that Holland more closely aligns himself with the Catholic Tracy, who is more likely to "converse with thinkers like Lacan, Derrida, Benjamin, Kristeva, Levinas and others as part of the practice and pleasure of composing theology," than with fellow Anabaptist theologian Hauerwas, "who suggests we can be helped most by the explicit Christian witness of Barth, Yoder, and the Pope."[44] A brief exploration of Holland's opposition to the early Barthian tendency to distance God beyond all knowing will prove illustrative of Holland's desire for "mutually critical" theological thought.

> How can a theology which negates the cultural history of how we have come to think about ourselves and how we view the world ever hope to connect with our contemporary loves, longings, and losses? Can a word that strangely falls like a stone from heaven ever hope to be incarnational and truthful

40. Ibid., 116.
41. Ibid.
42. Ibid., 107.
43. Ibid., 89.
44. Holland, "Damn the Absolute!," 4.

to those living and loving in the fleshly texts of dreams and bones? How can there be genuine dialogue and compassion in communities of discourse that almost bless the category of the incommensurable?[45]

At the heart of Holland's work there is a striving to make a space between (1) totalizing proclamations of abstract "monotheory," (2) tepid, lowest-common-denominator approaches to universalism that do not honor difference, and (3) the cacophonous chorus of individuality that shattered meta-narratives. For Holland it is vital that God be found not only in the "beyond," but in the here-and-now. He is diametrically opposed to Barth's assertion that "when God enters, history for the while ceases to be, and there is nothing more to ask; for something wholly different and new begins—a history with its own distinct grounds, possibilities, and hypotheses."[46] While Holland locates God's call as coming "from the margins, from life's liminal spaces, from somewhere *other*, from somewhere *beyond*," he feels—in marked resonance with Duguid-May—that the other-ness of the temporal and physical *present* is more than sufficient. Indeed, to have the other able to be voiced *here* is critical for Holland. He sees "the voice of the other as a genuine possibility of disclosure inviting transformation."[47] He seeks to encourage transformation in concrete, observable ways, here.

If God were wholly apart from contemporary creation then the possibility of concrete transformation dependent on God would be inconceivable. That being said, Holland is aware that "the return to the body in critical theory risks falling into a new essentialism in which it is almost implied that there is a 'natural' state of embodiment outside of cultural-linguistic scripts and symbols," and reminds readers that "nature" and the flesh are not our only residences: "language and culture, art and religion are also our homes."[48] Holland's plea is not for a theopoetic for theo-poetics's sake, but because the embodiment of the method means that greater value will be given to those voices too often placed at—or forced to—the margins of public life; voices more at home in their bodies and their experiences than in the academy. Theological discourse *de rigueur* excludes—perhaps even unintentionally—those who have not acquired

45. Holland, *How Do Stories Save Us?* 20.
46. Barth, "The Strange New World," 32.
47. Holland, *How Do Stories Save Us?* 89.
48. Ibid., 37.

the correct tone and cadence of the field, even if what is being said bears power and truth.

> Even we constructive theologians who have become skilled in redeeming the pleasures of Babel in the task of public theology need to be reminded not to neglect the voices from the margins. The sexy ones are becoming easier for most of us to hear, but the suffering ones still speak . . .
>
> Good theology is a kind of transgression, a kind of excess, a kind of gift. It is not a smooth systematics, a dogmatics, or a metaphysics; as a theopoetics it is a kind of writing. It is a kind of writing that invites more writing. Its narratives lead to other narratives, its metaphors encourage new metaphors, its confessions invoke more confessions, and its conversations invite more conversations.[49]

Scraping Paint

Duguid-May and Holland represent a kind of hybridity between the theological/devotional exuberance of Alves and the academically pro-theopoetic position of Wilder. I believe that both Duguid-May and Holland would stand with Alves, who writes that "the body has a philosophy of its own," asserting that "there are words which are not to be thought. They are to be eaten[;] . . . the angel, in the book of Revelation, was a poet. He gave the little book to the seer and ordered him not to read . . . but to eat it."[50] Theology has much to gain when it comes to accept that it can grant more emphasis to our pains, joys, and pleasures.

Both maintain—Duguid-May more in method, Holland more in content—the vitality and validity of experience over primary adherence to metaphysics. Both deny essentialist claims that religious experience is either (1) fully private and embodied or (2) solely inscribed within "cultural-linguistic scripts and symbolism." Both agree that theologians write best at home in two worlds, aware of the particulars of individual experience and the historical narratives and words that shape traditions. Holland and Duguid-May write in a spirit of solidarity with Alberto Caeiro: "I try to get rid of what I learned, / I try to forget the way I was

49. Ibid.
50. Alves, "Theopoetics: Longing and Liberation," 166.

taught to remember, / And to scrape off the paint they used to cover my senses."[51]

In resonance with Hopper's Heideggerian claim that "we can learn thinking only if we radically unlearn what thinking has been traditionally,"[52] Duguid-May and Holland resist framing theopoetics as a form of God-modeling, or as a replacement for theology. Indeed, if it were such it would be vulnerable to the same challenges and critiques that both provide. Theopoetics is not about the retroactive creation of a user manual for faith, not even if that manual is multi-media and compelling. It is a way of "forgetting the way we have been taught to remember" theology, ways that for Duguid-May and Holland are too enmeshed with systems of exclusion and domination. Framed as an effect, Duguid-May and Holland offer theopoetics as that which re-opens the senses and affirms the role of the body in theological discourse, encouraging dialogue and reminding us that the tongue—that primary organ of discourse—is for language, yes, but also for taste, and for sex.

Far from a "tepid universalism," the theopoetic invitation is a challenge for others to begin to speak their truth and to test it with others, making space for marginalized voices to safely enter the discourse. Theopoetics discourages a gate-keeping mentality wherein people must learn to speak and think a certain way to have their voices heard. Conversely, it engenders dialogue from many voices and many perspectives. More writing, more narrative, more metaphor, more confession, and more conversation. More invitation into the kingdom of God realized such that a place is made *here* on *earth* for every voice and body.

51. Caeiro, "The Essential," 28.
52. Hopper, "The Literary Imagination and the Doing of Theology," 221.

Every Prayer a Blasphemy at Last

So easy to mistake the sky for heaven
& the ground for all we've got. But gravity does
her thankless job & we forget what keeps us pinned to earth.

We shuffle through days, forget small graces found
in a peeled orange, a nearly finished book, an audible hum.
We go right to the knees & call it communion—rehearsed
    reverberation,
reunions & address—as the way we think God wants it heard.

The heart a little atlas with many islands to explore;
the mind an anthology of losses shriveled in the arid evening air.
& both may bring us closer to the vapor in the hull.

In each of us, words cloud to vision: cirrus, stratus, cumulus—
wish to capture every shifting sweep to recollect the story.
Hands white-knuckled to the unknown like it's a parachute.

But we're braided constellations roaming out the earth, we're wound
about God's finger so we might not be forgotten,
& we're kissing gravity on her contented mouth, lucky
to survive the fall from such a height.

Amen Amen Amen we shrink and crumble to a dream,
& thankful for the distance plummeted between the scapes,
that words can only fly so far & are bound up in our lungs.

Poet and Streams

Roland Faber and Catherine Keller

Coming to grips with your embodiment is one of the most profound philosophical tasks you will ever face. Acknowledging that every aspect of human
being is grounded in specific forms of bodily engagement with an environment requires a far-reaching rethinking of who and what we are, in a way
that is largely at odds with many of our inherited Western philosophical and
religious traditions.

—MARK JOHNSON[1]

WHILE NEITHER MELANIE DUGUID-MAY nor Scott Holland are
eager to emphasize a metaphysics, putting forth a theo-poetic
in place of a theo-logic, process theologians[2] are firmly committed to

1. Johnson, *The Meaning of the Body*, 1.

2. While a detailed articulation of process theology is beyond the thrust of this
work, it is worth noting a few features of process theology that directly play into its
theopoetic trajectory. A standard claim of process theology is that God is fully involved
in, and affected by, temporal processes. While traditional Christian theology claims
that God is "non-temporal (eternal), unchanging (immutable), and unaffected by the
world (impassible)," process thinkers argue that "God is in some respects temporal,
mutable, and passible" (Viney). The consequences of this are that God is conceived of
as still active in the world, affected by human suffering, and always in the process of
becoming (as opposed to a perfected and finished being).

the production of a metaphysical model that attempts to correlate the language of the model with the actual, ultimate workings of reality. Where process metaphysics differs from "inherited Western" models is that rather than focusing on subject and object distinctions, there is an emphasis on process, becoming, and creation. While Hellenistic models of reality might posit that an ultimate Platonic concept of God exists in its fullness only in a higher realm of ideas, process thinkers are eager to talk about how it is that God is fully becoming in the world, how it is that God is constantly at work drawing forth creation, engaged in it directly. This aspect of process thought, focusing on the content of God's actual engagement with the material world is quite in line with the kind of writing and thinking done by Duguid-May and Holland, and yet the process method is divergent from that taken by the thinkers addressed thus far.

While those closer to Hopper or Alves's modalities tend toward theological reflection being crafted as a form of prayer or evocative doxology, process thinkers are "committed to metaphysical clarity and coherence."[3] The result is that reading how it is that process thought understands theopoetics is a markedly different experience from a more literarily weighted consideration, such as how Alves writes. Reading process theology can be a very demanding exercise of academic prowess and intellectual acumen, precisely—at first glance—the kind of gentrified working method challenged by the authors I've taken up thus far.[4] This is not to say that there is not merit to the process project, but to hold that the methodologies of process thinkers initially seem to be in explicit tension with those considered thus far.

Taking up process thought in the context of theopoetics is important in that it provides insight into a substantially different articulation and perspective of the topic. Moreover, whereas prior to 2005 almost the entirety of literature referencing theopoetics cited Hopper, Wilder, or Alves, in the intervening years, there has been a steady and increasing stream of work being produced that never cites any of those authors, focusing instead on thought originating with Whitehead and his process

---

3. Epperly, "Process Theology," 2.

4. As this chapter is in itself an engagement with the methodology of process thought, readers less interested in the language and internal reasoning of process thinkers and more eager to simply have the process perspective contextualized and the process effect of theopoetics articulated can turn to the final section of this chapter, "Decentering Spins."

philosophy.[5] That this is the case necessitates serious consideration, even if at first it seems that process thought and theopoetics make use of divergent methods and originate with alternate intents. In fact, that the process method seems so divergent provides for an interesting opportunity through contrast: while the methods and articulated goals are markedly different than the biblical and literary focuses of the early theopoetic authors, I believe that there are some underlying claims that unite even the most systematic of process thinkers with someone like Alves who has all but abandoned sustained argumentation. As such, and so as to consider a broad range of perspectives in the development of the three definition of theopoetics that come in chapter 6, this chapter takes up the explicitly theopoetically-focused work of process theologians Roland Faber and Catherine Keller, exploring the ways in which their intended purpose—if not their methods—resonates quite well with other, more literary and populist, theopoetic methodologies. The chapter closes once again with an articulation of a process theology perspective on the effects of the theopoetic.

Roland Faber

If Alves occupies the far pole regarding adherence to typical academic discourse, followed sequentially by Duguid-May, Holland, Wilder, and Hopper, then some significant distance later Faber stands off to the side: concerned with plurality, multiplicity, polyphilia, and theopoetics, but writing in a thoroughly academic genre. His doctoral training was as a systematic theologian at the University of Vienna through the Catholics-Theological Faculty, though it is interesting to note that prior to his career in theology Faber was a classical music composer of some significant repute, earning a number of national awards in Austria. Currently he occupies the John B. Cobb Chair of Process Studies at Claremont, the most significant process theology teaching position in the world, also serving as the executive director of the International Whitehead Research Project.

Faber's most substantial book to date in English, *God as Poet of the World*, is quite comprehensive regarding process theology, and in it his

5. It should be noted that while Stanley Hopper never formally considered himself a process thinker, he was a student of Whitehead while he was in Boston. Thus, while Melvin Kaiser writes that Hopper "made use of Whitehead to criticize Heidegger" he also adds that "Hopper does not seek some final refuge in Whitehead either" (Kaiser, "The Artistry of Theopoiesis," 11).

articulated perspective regarding theopoetics is thoroughly influenced by the thought of Alfred North Whitehead. Faber's writing is firmly ensconced in academic distance, rich with neologisms and dense language that makes no apparent attempt at being stylistically poetic, personal, or popularly accessible. What he does provide is a thorough explication of a system of thought that outlines theopoetics as a "theology of perichoresis (of the mutual coinherence of all things) in which the universe represents God's creative adventure and God [represents] the event of creative transformation of the world."[6] Earlier than that book, though, Faber had recounted the means by which he came to use the term "theopoetics." In a lecture given at the Claremont School of Theology in 2006 he addressed his understanding of the term explicitly.

> [When asked "What is process theology?"] what came to my mind was not a definition, but rather a tentative network of associations that gathered around three suggestions as to a probable description of the field of process theology.
>
> Being conscious of this inability to pin this field down further, I added an opening space, which I filled with possible answers to this question that I asked experts around the world. As you can imagine, none of the answers agreed. These "voices," indeed, revealed process theology not to be a clear-cut method or subject, but rather to describe a certain region. One moves into an "undefined land" in which one experiences differently, begins to think differently, and is encouraged not just to adapt to, but to create new theological language.
>
> Today, I think that not only can we not control this field or region in fact, but that it is of the essence of process theology to be an uncontrollable undertaking in the infinite adventure of God-talk, and consciously so, in modes that I came to name "theopoetics."[7]

Faber's interest in the theopoetic is tantamount to his interest in the "uncontrollable undertaking in the infinite adventure of God-talk" made manifest in the "undefined land," of theological experience and articulation. Theopoetics as outlined in Faber's book is open and pluralistic. One is reminded of Whitman's assertion, "I contain multitudes," and indeed, Faber uses the word *polyphilia* (love of multiplicity) often, arguing that a theopoetic perspective will always "hold open a 'moving whole' that

6. Faber, *God as Poet of the World*, 15.
7. Faber, "Process Theology as Theopoetics."

never, at any point, resists revision and progression of thought."[8] At best, this approach suggests, any articulated vision of God, no matter how complex, will only be but an aspect of a Divinity that is eternally in the process of becoming other than that which it already is at any given moment or point.

Faber writes that the "theopoetics of process theology is not a method for reductionism, but a field of re-interpretation, de-construction and re-construction, of shocking the surface of seamlessness."[9] For him, the theopoetic impulse is one that always "seeks to roughen up unified appearances by differentiating the various deep-lying, multiple voices hidden under various powerful contenders of an alleged 'orthodoxy' of content, method, and direction of thought."[10] Here I think he is envisioning something akin to a process translation of Leonard Cohen's "There is a crack in . . . everything. . . . That's how the light gets in."[11] Faber's theopoetics is that urge to point out how things are not as simple as others might want them to seem. Desiring, then, to "let the light in," Faber forwards a theopoetic perspective on theology that entails the rejection of any system that claims a complete and closed system of thought regarding the Divine. In place of a self-enclosed system of thought, process theology becomes "a wealth of different endeavors, adventures, and practices—different manifestations of this new God-language, different poetries of this becoming and relational God, often not compatible with one another, but all of which are folds of a poetry of salvation that Whitehead, at a certain point in *Process and Reality*, called the vision of the 'poet of the world.'"[12] Here it is worth taking some space to explicitly address Faber's and Whitehead's use of "poet," as it is at the core of the rationale by which process thinkers employ the term theopoetics.

As the progenitor of process philosophy, the work of Alfred North Whitehead is regularly made use of by process theologians, who often then employ the work of Charles Hartshorne, generally accepted as the originator of an explicit process *theology*. This is not the case for Faber, whose work can be seen as an effort to return to a pre-Hartshornian type of process thought. As such, Faber cites often, and directly, from Whitehead

8. Faber, *God as Poet of the World*, 318.

9. Faber, "Process Theology as Theopoetics."

10. Faber, *God as Poet of the World*, 318.

11. Cohen, "Anthem."

12. Faber, "Process Theology as Theopoetics."

himself, resulting in some constructions that, while fascinating in content, can be laborious in style for those uninitiated in process-speak:

> [Traditional Christian arguments have claimed] that the Christian God is a timeless and changeless God of no empathy who then was considered "creator" of a world of which "he" already knew its history a priori. Whitehead, instead, tried to recover the biblical God of empathy and solidarity who is responsive rather than controlling; saving what is lost, rather than creating what "he" knows will be lost. . . . While the all-creative "creator" seems to be indicating unilateral omnipotence and, hence, seems to operate within the elusive paradigm of all-controlling power, the all-patient "poet" now symbolizes all-receptive, all-relational, all-sympathetic, and all-healing reconciliation.[13]

For Whitehead—and therefore Faber—the phrase "Poet of the World" is not primarily intended to refer to a writer of poems, but to the Greek term for "creator." This follows Aristotle's classifications of knowledge, a reference "neither to *theoria* (knowing by meditation) nor *praxis* (knowing by doing), but *poietics* (knowing by creating)."[14] God as Poet is infinitely engaged in continuing to create the world, constantly existing in sympathy with all that occurs here, and drawing forth the world into possible reconciliation. The Poet of the World is not the producer of a poem that is complete: the "poetry" of God and the world has no end or beginning.

Here process thought seems to be in tension with both John's Gospel—"In the *beginning* was the Word, and the Word was with God, and the Word was God"—and Revelation—"I am the Alpha and the Omega"—where God is framed as present to, and at least *co*-causal with, a marked beginning and end. Nonetheless, the process position is that these firm stops as described in Christian Scriptures are not in keeping with the true character of the Divine, which is ceaselessly multi-valent and always in the process of becoming something more. As Faber writes, "theology becomes poetry precisely when we take the 'absolutes' out of the metaphors of God-language! Divine poetry is infinite, the patient and fragile embodiment of the infinite wealth of unfolding and refolding beginnings and endings. The 'poet' is the God of an ever-becoming world

13. Faber, "Process Theology as Theopoetics."
14. Ibid.

in which there is nothing but becoming."[15] This vision, though it might be in tension with traditional interpretations of the gospel, provides a framework for powerful social action and ministry.

I believe that at the root of the process insistence on taking "absolutes out of the metaphors of God-language" there is a concern with the repercussions of abused metaphors. As Faber offers, "if we understand abstractions not as instruments of mental simplification of the folds of becoming, but emphasize them instead of the multiple becomings, we begin to misuse them as instruments of power with which we think we can control. . . . It is here that the imperialistic seductions begin to corrupt our perception."[16] When we overly flatten language and discourse and attempt to make things black and white, we begin to theologically err. Nothing is ever lost or beneath reflection for the process thinker: there is never a point at which a full clearness can be settled upon by which certain people and things are known to be cast out of God's work. This metaphysical claim is paralleled by an equivalent concern for an open-ness in social and ecclesial settings as well. It is therefore worth noting that for all of the insistence on the importance of philosophical and theological metaphysics, process theologians also have a very significant practice of being directly involved in concrete works of service: they actively resist not only rigid and fixed theological abstraction, but also the social ramifications of others who use rigid thought as instruments of oppressive or imperialistic power.

From John Cobb's work in economic justice and sustainable farming to Monica Coleman's healing work with the survivors of abuse, many of the major contributors to the process conversation have significant engagement with direct service as well. Note too, the resonance between Faber's fear that Christians can "misuse [metaphors] as instruments of power with which we think we can control" and Duguid-May's suggestion that rather than associating authority with "a disciplinary, controlling, rule-ordered concept," in a Christian context it can be rightly reinterpreted as a "contextual, relational process of communication and connection."[17] Where Duguid-May arrives at these claims primarily via feminist perspectives and Continental philosophy, process thinkers arrive via Whitehead and Hartshorne. That these resonances exist be-

15. Ibid.
16. Ibid.
17. May, *A Body Knows*, 75.

tween process theology and the literary tradition of Wilder's theopoetics without sharing a single citation is interesting indeed, suggesting that there is something more in common than a mere word. Further evidence of similarity in purpose—if not in method—is found when Faber posits two explicit implications of his formation of theopoetics:

1. The "poet" never closes the case of becoming. In God's view, everything is always in becoming. . . . In a theopoetic view of the world, we might like to look into the becoming of matters, not their being, even if they are past; we might become sympathetic fellows of the pilgrimage of the other, even if it is unsettling, or disturbing at times. Theopoetically, we may like to always seek the many folds, and cracks. . . . This "poetry" is always in love with manifoldness.

2. The only "security," the Divine poetry grants us, is God's love for our diversity, including the poetic diversity of our pilgrimage with God. The uniqueness of our experiences may be what God wants us to explore, seek, find, communicate, adventurously pursue. God is "in the making" by insisting on our poetry, by saving our ways with the "poet," in all unimaginable manifoldness, into the immediacy of the Great Poem.[18]

Theopoetics construed this way does not demand the strictures of dualism, the "firm ground" Descartes sought to find, or Kant's detached towers of observation. Like Holland's attempt to create a space between a totalizing proclamation of abstract "monotheory" and the tepid, lowest-common-denominator approach of a universalism that does not honor difference, Faber's theopoetics is in line with Plato's notion of *khôra*, "the empty space that in Whitehead's *Adventures of Ideas* reappears as 'Receptacle,' as empty space of 'mutual immanence' and the 'medium of intercommunication' of the manifoldness of becoming."[19] Put another way, theopoetics holds open *khôra*, a generative space in which possibility—as opposed to certainty—is primary. This articulation, one in which neither immanence nor transcendence is emphasized, seems to accomplish precisely what Holland states as his goal when he seeks to find a theology that resonates with both "the Protestant dialectical imagination [which] envisions life within a sacred text," and "the Catholic analogical

18. Ibid.
19. Ibid.

imagination [which] imagines life in a sacramental universe."[20] That is to say, while the process perspective that Faber articulates does present theopoetics in a metaphysical mode, his proposed implications of theopoetic work are comparable to other conclusions drawn through vastly different means.

For all the metaphysics that produced them, the heart of Faber's claims that "the poet never closes the case of becoming," and that "the only security the Divine poetry grants us is God's love for our diversity," can easily reflect Continental postmodern trajectories as well. For example, Jean-François Lyotard's *petits récits* are nothing if not an attestation of multiplicity and variation,[21] a promise that "the case of becoming" always remains diverse and will never close or become mono-vocal. Similarly, Kaufman's insistence that theology is an imaginative construct means that while we humans yet remain imaginative and striving to more fully know God, theology will be endlessly spun out in new directions and variations, being fitted to communities and contexts as needed. That this is the case is not a refutation of Faber at all, but an affirmation of his method and its place within the theopoetic conversation, even if its voice is heavily accented by Whitehead and metaphysics. Perhaps *because* its heavy accent marks it as foreign and the "only security the Divine poetry grants us is God's love for our diversity."

Catherine Keller

To complete the methodological sketch of the continuum of those directly engaged with theopoetics, Catherine Keller would be placed somewhere in the midst of Wilder and Holland, willing to speak from the first person, aware of the provisionality of theology, and present to the materiality of being in the world, yet propositional in her genre. Among all current scholars she is the clearest in articulating her understanding of theopoetics in relation to that which has come before, situating herself and other process thinkers as somewhere other than the arc in which can be found Hopper, Wilder, Alves, Holland, and Duguid-May.[22] In the

20. Holland, *How Do Stories Save Us?* 5.

21. Lyotard, *The Postmodern Condition*, 60.

22. Keller writes that by the time she arrived at Drew in 1986, where the Consultations on Hermeneutics had taken place, and both David Miller and Stanley Hopper had been faculty, "there lingered no echoes of the term," such that she writes "I thought

2013, Faber-edited volume on theopoetics, Keller offers her analysis of the theopoetic traditions, claiming that there are three distinct streams: Eastern church theosis, Hopperian post-Death-of-God scholarship, and the process emphasis on God's multiplicity and infinite-becoming. Since she is the most explicit process thinker to frame her own position in relation to the Hopper/Alves stream, it is worth considering how she categorizes each typology.

Her first articulated stream follows *theopoiesis* back to the term *theosis*, which is normally translated as "deification" or "divinization" within the Eastern church. She references the fact that Clement of Alexandria defined theopoiesis as an "assimilation to God as far as possible," that Irenaeus developed the concept with his claim that "God the Logos became what we are, in order that we may become what He Himself is," and points to the Athanasian christological formula as a concise example of a call to theopoiesis: "God became Man so that Man could become God." In short, Keller characterizes this first stream as providing "a certain internal resistance to the theology of dualistic transcendence," in that it allows for human interaction with, and transformation through, the Divine, rather than having God inhabit a solely transcendent plane.[23] She sees a significant resonance between this traditionally Hellenistic account and process theology, noting that as with the concept of theosis, "process theology has not been shy in claiming a high-Logos Christology—and with it, the 'God manifest below.'"[24] Furthermore, following John Cobb's notion of "creative transformation," she also affirms "the possibility of human transformation in a cosmologically scaled narrative," such as is articulated in much of Orthodox theology.[25] What Keller is interested in seems to be the degree to which theologians can find ways to articulate the interrelationality between the Divine and creation, including humanity. Thus, to the extent that theopoetics allows for this possibility, she is willing to consider its utility.

Yet even with these similarities, Keller believes that process thought has "hardly explored theopoiesis . . . because it is embedded in the classical substance metaphysics . . . and in its perfectionism it draws the

---

I had coined it" (Keller, "Pluri-Verse," 184). Yet, by as early as 1988 she used theopoetics in direct reference to Amos Wilder (Keller, "Goddess," 63), suggesting that if not at Drew, there were at least echoes of it elsewhere from which she could acquire the term.

23. Keller, "Theopoetics and the Pluri-verse," 182.

24. Ibid., 183.

25. Ibid.

individual soul toward a changeless immateriality."[26] This is exactly the kind of thinking that the metaphysics of process thought hopes to replace, positing that God is infinitely becoming, decidedly *not* eternally immutable: the God of process theology is not the substance of a perfect fixed being as much as Becoming itself. That being said, Keller *does* see some possibility for fruitful "conviviality" with theopoeisis in an acknowledgement that there are significant parallels between "the Whiteheadian dissemination of the incarnation to every creaturely becoming," and "the classical panentheism that characterizes precisely the Eastern Christian tradition," a type of panentheism that "already conditions the immanence of divine transcendence upon God's presence—as the logos—in all creatures."[27] As yet she has not more fully fleshed out the implications of these parallels, but she does well to point them out as they potentially widen the theopoetics conversation into the circles of Eastern Orthodox theology as well.

Keller's second articulated stream of theopoetics is that in the vein of Hopper, and rather than re-capitulate that trajectory, which is addressed in the first chapter, I'll include here only her commentary *upon* that perspective. In general, she characterizes this arc as "a mid-twentieth-century strategy to dislodge any fixed logos,"[28] and makes significant use of David Miller's work to explore her own understanding. Following Miller, she makes a clear distinction between theopoetics and "theopoetry." For Keller, theopoetics in the Hopper stream is essentially "after the death of God," and she includes in this lineage "the work of Thomas Altizer and Mark C. Taylor," arguing that it "involves a poetics and not a poetry, i.e., a reflection on poiesis, a formal thinking about the nature of the making of meaning, which subverts the -ology, the nature of the logic, of theology."[29] This is in contrast to the markedly less radical category of "theopoetry," which resonates less with work after the death of God and more with "the assertion that all theological language is really already metaphor."[30] Theopoetry is just a reinscription of "extant religious faith or theological knowledge"[31] into new terms. Citing Miller, she writes, "in theopoetry, as

26. Ibid.
27. Ibid., 192.
28. Ibid., 181.
29. Miller, "Theopoetry or Theopoetics?" 8.
30. Ibid.
31. Ibid.

opposed to theopoetics, theology does not end with the death of God, because there is no death of God."[32] For Keller, the work of Wilder borders too closely to new words for old ideas, and she prefers to distance herself from that stream.

Whereas theopoetics engenders an acceptance of "difference, fragmentation, and multiplicity,"[33] theopoetry works primarily by the creation of novel comparisons on traditional themes: a new coat of paint without first scraping the walls down. Thus, it is only to the extent that theopoetics is a subversion of traditional thought, which affirms "the logic of identity, essence, substance, noncontradiction, exclusion," that she believes "process theologians may say amen."[34] Put succinctly, while Keller utterly rejects a desire to encourage theopoetry, she does unite with the project of theopoetics as articulated by Miller and Hopper insofar as it is conceived of as an opposition to a "dependency upon the unquestionable referents," "Heidegger's ontotheology," and "Derrida's Transcendental Signifier."[35] She believes that process theology shares this very same critique of dependency. In spite of this, she is yet wary of process thought too closely self-identifying with theopoetics, even of the Hopperian stream. Beneath the surface resonances, she believes there is a significant amount of disconnect between the methods employed by Hopper and Whitehead.

For all of its critiques of empire, permanent meaning, and objectifiable referents, process theology is nonetheless "doggedly pushing on toward a better theology[,] . . . knowingly constructing that becomingly non-coercive, ecofeminist, and relationally sensitive God, God the Poet."[36] For Keller, this acknowledgement means that it is either the case that (1) the theopoetic rejection of metaphysics remains complete and process theology cannot participate in the theopoetic conversation or (2) the theopoetic project must accept that a clear metaphysics is an acceptable option given the particularities of process thought. To further the possibilities of this later option she proposes that the third stream is a transformation of Miller's claim that "theopoetics begins where theology ends."

32. Keller, "Theopoetics and the Pluri-verse," 185.
33. Ibid.
34. Ibid.
35. Ibid., 186.
36. Ibid., 187.

> Theopoetics begins not where theology ends, but where it be-
> comes. That is, where theology negates itself becomingly. For
> in the event of its self-negation theopoetics repeats the tradi-
> tion of negative theology, with a difference: now it understands
> the affirmation that is made possible by the negation not as the
> changeless truth of the hyperousiologial neo-Platonic One, but
> as the construction of a language that is already always unsay-
> ing itself. It relativizes its own utterances not as an act of self-
> abnegation but as the affirmation of its own unknown future
> and the beauty of its innermost history of becoming.[37]

In her re-framing of theopoetics as a negative theology that invites
the "construction of a language that is already always unsaying itself,"
Keller seeks to allow for continuing proclamation: speak with vigor and
yet be open to change. In her own words "we had best stay autocritically
tuned to our own theopoiesis in order not to trip ourselves with impa-
tient literalisms."[38] Though she is "doggedly pushing on toward a better
theology," she is aware that even new theologies can become hollow and
tools of institutional preservation rather than hope and new life. Wanting to acknowledge this tension she writes that, "we do not want to
find ourselves decorating even a loveable and poetic God's coffin with
theopoetry."[39] She is aware that the most ardent of Radical Theologians
and those seeking to work in the explicit wake of the death of God will
likely see her project as but another piece of theopoetry: safe, familiar,
and not radical at all. To that potential challenge Keller is clear in her
response: "for the sake of intellectual honesty and dialogue . . . we might
want to leave ourselves open to the charge that we worship an undead
God. We might want to turn a cheek to it."[40] Why turn a cheek? Because
she maintains that it is an absolute necessity that process theology be able
to argue against oppressive theologies, and she is willing to accept the
charge of idol worship in turn for being able to articulate challenge to
oppression. This necessity is an enormous component of Keller's articulation of how it is she believes theopoetics *is* used—or ought to be used—in
the context of process theologies.

37. Ibid.
38. Ibid.
39. Ibid.
40. Ibid.

For Keller, the strength of process theology is that it is a strong, intelligent, rational means of challenging systems of oppressive thought.[41] She warns that if "theopoetics weakens the capacity of process theologians to make confident arguments in debates, in teaching, preaching, and pastoral care, then I don't think we should indulge in it. If, by either its discursive playfulness or philosophical mysticism, it does dilute the force of the process counter-orthodoxy, then we should stop now . . ."[42] Thus, desiring a continued capacity to debate, Keller primarily values the generative capacity of theopoetic perspectives and articulations, affirming their possible role in adding movement and energy to the rigid "game of guarantees." Though she is firm on producing a metaphysics that attempts to explain the ultimate nature of things and/or processes, she is supportive of the way theopoetics opens doors to other discourse.

> The theopoetic impulse works to uncork the energies of icon, story, and metaphor that every systematic form of theology cannot but dampen—and this energy is needed now if progressive forms of theology are to persist in the face, the Janus-face, of fundamentalism and secularism, which will always outdo us at the game of guarantees. On the other hand, the linguistic indirection of theopoetics, its kinship both to negative theology and to post-structuralism, is fostering sustainable negotiations with a matrix of secular discourses.[43]

Indeed, Keller herself often writes in ways that show evidence of "uncorked energies" and excitement. Her books have an ear to the earth, never forgetting the importance of the body and of mystery. Her book *The Face of the Deep: A Theology of Becoming* is an evocative and seminal text on creativity, science, and creation. Her focus is often on the materiality of the world and the ways in which the tangible things of our lives play important roles in our theology. She is a deft writer, a brilliant thinker, and for all of her drive to produce a technically sophisticated, systematic, all-encompassing structure of theological thought, often quite a beautiful wordsmith as well.

---

41. I agree with her that theopoetics needs to be able to address the tangible realities of the world and speak to them directly, but I am not so certain that the style of speech required is point and counterpoint.

42. Keller, "Theopoetics and the Pluri-verse," 180.

43. Ibid., 181.

> I am sitting in a brook as I write. . . . I don't know how many books have been written in brooks. But in this environmental congruence, I am settled (almost too happily to write) on a hospitable boulder, softened by aeons of stream running down from the northern face of the Catskills.
>
> It is almost too easy to meditate on the universe as God's body, here. Yet it does not occur to me that this rock is God, this water is God. These neighborly pines rooted stubbornly amid the layers of rock bed; this waterskimmer floating with such elegant insouciance on the water—ah, no, it is a couple, a coupling, a water-waltz, limbs forming delicate pontoons that rest, speed, and fish upon the surface. They do not announce to me, "We are God." When my (human) friend Mary glances over at me from a neighboring boulder, I do not think, "She is God." It is always a different sort of thought—and a thought it is, a way of seeing in thought, an in-sight, never a knowledge. If God is the right word for it, God is somehow somewhere in this all, every ripple and all, every bite, flight, scramble, or stillness of it.[44]

Beyond her predilection for fleshly prose, the above passage also highlights an important aspect of Keller's work in general: her championing of the work of Sallie McFague, particularly her development of a panentheistic theology of God in the world. A theology of this sort is predicated on an assumption, as Keller puts it, that "if God is immaterial, God doesn't matter."[45] Consequently, McFague's, and therefore Keller's, assertions revolve around the eco-theological idea that creation is a body of God and that our relationship to the Divine must be similarly "enfleshed."

Just as the poet must bring new eyes to the particulars and details of life so as to more fully capture them in verse, Keller suggests that theologians bring a renewed perspective on creation to more fully capture how God moves in the world. She is quick to note that our society has a tendency to perceive a duality between self and body that finds itself paralleled in the common separation of God and world. With Faber she affirms the theopoetic gesture of removing "absolutes" from the metaphors of God-language, hoping not to transcend and synthesize this theological separation, but to interpret it such that the truths of both interpretations interweave with one another, transforming both. She writes

44. Keller, "The Flesh of God," 96.
45. Ibid., 91.

that "the challenge is to think of the difference of 'God' and 'world' with a radicality that actually deepens their interdependence. Or put differently, we will want to complicate the boundaries by which these two terms are opposed, while releasing mystery into the first term and creativity into every level of the second."[46] Following McFague's lead, Keller desires a panentheistic model not to build a God of the gaps, but as a guide that helps Christians to see the world differently, and because of the new sight, become inspired to engage it for the better.

Keller acknowledges that tensions between the dominance of Greek epistemological constructions in modern academia and the process understanding of the ever-becoming nature of God can lead to a temptation to abandon the task of theology entirely: there simply is no way to get the whole of God in words just right. She resists this temptation though, and drawing from Nicola Cusa's *docta ignorantia*, recapitulates a tenet familiar to Duguid-May's theopoetic perspective via Kaufman: the task before us is not to resort to skepticism or disbelief, but to "keep always in mind how humanly constructed are the models whereby we know anything at all."[47] As people—theologians and otherwise—deepen their relationships with Spirit and develop their understandings of the Divine, there is every reason for articulations of God to continue to develop as well.

Any sense of God then is profoundly relational. Truly seeing creation does not happen without a seer. As such, the more that people become aware and attuned to the possibility of theophany, of the relationship between creation and Creator, of the sacred in the profane, the more likely they will be to see it, consequently having their own perspectives and habits transformed. Keller's emphasis on relationality is a touchstone of poetic thought as well: the genius of the poet is not the production of the wholly novel, but of the realization that even in the strange there is the known, and deep in even the familiar, there is the mark of mystery which is worthy of our attention and respect. Indeed, "the metaphor of theopoetics itself will wash out quickly if it is not occasionally renewed by the poetry that circulates as the art of all languages."[48] As always, Keller is pushing towards a connection between the Divine and the created, between a renewal of theological language influenced not only by other words but also by material and actions. And there is perhaps no action

46. Ibid., 94.
47. Ibid., 103.
48. Keller, "Theopoetics and the Pluri-verse," 193.

more significant than God's infinite-becoming and the ways in which that becoming is revealed to us in the body of the world.

Decentering Spins

Though far from identical, the process perspective on the nature and function of theopoetics is resonant with writers from what Keller identifies as the "post Death of God" stream. Wilder, Holland, and Duguid-May emphasize that theopoetics is an attempt "to overcome a long addiction to the discursive, the rationalistic, and the prosaic,"[49] a type of "writing that invites more writing,"[50] and a "struggle to stitch flesh and blood sensibilities into the apparent self-sufficiency of scholarship."[51] Not entirely identical with any of these lenses, process theology seems to understand theopoetics as more polemic. Framed as an effect, process thought offers that theopoetics is that which destabilizes and decenters, seeking out the "various powerful contenders of an alleged 'orthodoxy' of content, method, and direction of thought," and revealing "the various deep-lying, multiple voices hidden underneath."[52] It does so by affirming the multiplicitous and creative nature of God and reality, a type of creativity in the world that draws out creative action from us while reminding us that those words we find to articulate God's nature and action are a "construction of a language that is already always unsaying itself."[53]

Process theologians firmly maintain that to engage with the theopoetic "is not to relinquish all truth claims or ontological references, but to acknowledge that we spin such language in the darkness of an infinitely complex universe, and out of the contexts of our endlessly distorting socializations."[54] Moreover, *that* we continue to "spin such language" is part of our nature and the nature of God, who calls us forth into action, the result of which is a continuous stream of striving—of becoming—without end. Indeed, perhaps there is a process paraphrase of St. Maximos the Confessor's definition of theopoeisis as "total participation in Jesus Christ": theopoetics is a full acceptance of, and action based upon,

---

49. Wilder, *Theopoetic*, 3.

50. Holland, *How Do Stories Save Us?* 37.

51. May, *A Body Knows*, 14.

52. Faber, *God as Poet of the World*, 318.

53. Keller, "Theopoetics and the Pluri-verse," 187.

54. Keller, "Goddess, Ear, and Metaphor," 65.

God's invitation into a many-folded type of creative transformation, a full saying of "yes" to God's multiplicity, and a full willingness to let die the notion of "the hyperousiologial neo-Platonic One."

That being said, this conclusion seems too tidy, too much mono-lith, too much of a punctuation mark and not enough of an invitation to *khôra*. . . . It *is* the case that process theologians believe the effect of theopoetics is a challenge to oppressive orthodoxy by means of interject-ing creativity and multiplicity, *and* that is a gross reduction of the fullness of their perspectives. Perhaps I should try to conclude again . . .

In the spirit of Roland Faber, who was wary of attempting to pin down a definition of process thought too firmly and thus "added an open-ing space, which [he] filled with possible answers," I will add an open space of another sort. Having gone through all the technicalities of God as becoming, non-Substance metaphysics, and trying to "stay autocriti-cally tuned to our own theopoiesis," perhaps the apt conclusion to this chapter is not more fixity and proposition . . .

> God may be the poet of the world but the world itself does not speak. We therefore look to poets and preachers, artists and intellectuals, scientists and gardeners, powerful uneducated persons, the young, and mothers of families to help us name ourselves and render God's name in history.[55]

Perhaps my conclusion here ought instead be an invitation to draw close to an *enacted* affirmation of the tension and unity between God and world, an instance of language spun out not to prove, but to show. A rendering of God's name made with words crafted so that they fall apart in your mouth, leaving you with a trace of the reason why we turn again and again to ideas when what we want is God enfleshed off of the paper. God alive. God in life.

55. Holland, "Foreword," 11.

Bone Cartography

No. It cannot be a named reliance—the map
has its own folds and tatters—a silence
which we must respect, but not always reach.

The way an infant ladders the ribs searching the terrain
of a breast, hunger blinking in her breath or the blade-scratch
down the hill of cheeks & hair washed through the drain.

Always what we give away brings us back together.
This compass, this magnatic abandon to the grace
of weathered pattern: pantapon hues, moon-rise,

dusk-matter, snow. What matter trembles in the sky
is just as inexact. & we—yes, we—annunciate the angles
of our prayers by moving just enough to bump into our walls.

We keep naming the body by what it isn't or what
it was or what it can't become. The turning in
& turning toward eastward slow stab, tendoned topograph.

O, to get it right just once would be so nice—this asphalt,
this fission, this jupiter light tangled in the stars & it's our better
angel sketching out a way to remember close to what we are.

PART THREE

Affinities and Conclusions

Fire and Rubble

Peter Rollins and John Caputo

> Our theological language is always in need of being broken apart and
> reformed, our common lexicon stretched and reshaped. Language under the
> pressure of divine weight always crumbles. Theological writing must come to
> grips with the reality that it is always lo(o)sing its grip,
> always arriving on the scene too late.
>
> —J. BLAKE HUGGINS[1]

IN THE FIRST SECTION of this book I explored the work of Hopper, Wilder, and Alves, the three early authors most often cited when theopoetics comes up academically. Section two worked with four contemporary theologians who have also woven theopoetics into their work. In this third section I will complete the theoretical exploration of theopoetics by drawing on the work of philosophers whose projects are resonant with the theologians already considered. This chapter takes up the writing of Peter Rollins and John Caputo, and the next examines Richard Kearney and Karmen MacKendrick before finally offering a triad of definitions for theopoetics, which, when taken together, account for each of the authors considered. While none of the philosophers in this section have spent

---

1. Huggins, "Writing on the Boundary Line," 128.

much time writing explicitly on the topic of theopoetics, each has used the term in one form or another, and more importantly, the work that they regularly produce bears a strong resemblance to theopoetic thought even without the term itself appearing with any consistency. Why is that resemblance present? Primarily because both Continental philosophy and theopoetic thought offer critiques of "hollow language," "ossified doctrine," and "empty doxologies and litanies."[2] Both want to draw attention to the way that language shapes our understanding of reality.

Following in the footsteps of Nietzsche, Freud, and Marx—dubbed by Paul Ricœur as "the masters of suspicion"—contemporary Continental philosophers of religion are eager to critique the ways in which the church and its theological and metaphysical constructs foster a kind of personal stagnation in, and control over, people of faith. While analytic philosophy long stayed away from reflecting on religion, as the field began to drift from the necessity of logical positivism, faith once again began to be an acceptable area of investigation. In the analytic tradition, however, philosophy of religion still very much employs a Hellenistic, propositional methodology and metaphysics, not particularly concerned with the role of flesh and hermeneutics in the way that meaning and knowledge are constructed. Conversely, the Continental tradition has been enormously influenced by the work of Martin Heidegger, Michel Foucault, and Jacques Derrida, each of whom can be seen as eager to explicate how it is that experience, culture, and knowledge interact to create meaning.

To the extent that analytic philosophy remains bound up in metaphysics, Continental philosophers continue to ask skeptically with Tertullian, "What indeed has Athens to do with Jerusalem?" Conversely, to the extent that fleshly experience is given value and human-pronounced theological epistemology is not considered fixed and final, Continental philosophers suggest that Jerusalem might want to consider having something to do with Paris and Marburg. In the past two decades it has become increasingly common for Continental philosophers of religion to blur the line between what exactly it is that constitutes a "philosophy of religion" and a "theology of religion."[3] This chapter takes up the work

2. Wilder, *Theopoetic*, 2.

3. This philosophical "turn toward the theological" is neither complete nor accepted in all quarters. See, for example, Dominique Janicaud's essay in *The Theological Turn in French Phenomenology*, which is very critical of the "theological takeover" of Continental thought.

of two related thinkers who have all but erased that line, and in so doing, have invited the church to directly consider how it is that deconstruction might be a useful tool for theological reflection.

I will begin with the Irish philosopher Peter Rollins and follow with John Caputo, a thinker that Rollins has often, and explicitly, named as a seminal influence. In each writer there is an emphasis on the utility of the poetic as a tool—perhaps *the* tool—for theological utterances in the face of profound unknowing and doubt. They both employ elements of Derrida's deconstructive method to destabilize the institution of the church, but both are hopeful for the future even if the institution as it stands may be in need of radical transfiguration or dissolution. The chapter closes, greatly assisted by the work of the Canadian theologian Jeffery Hocking, with a pointed comparison between theopoetics and deconstruction, ultimately concluding that the theopoetic method accomplishes many of the same beneficial critical gestures, but allows for a profession of faith and a generative re-engagement with the church, which deconstruction is not well-suited to handle. As such, the chapter closes with an articulation of a theopoetic effect that is two-pronged: Rollins and Caputo are useful in seeing how it is that theopoetics can be seen as a type of quasi-deconstruction and Hocking provides insight into what theopoetics does over and above the deconstructive gesture.

Peter Rollins

Perhaps most widely known in circles related to the more socially progressive spectrum of the American emergent church conversation, Peter Rollins is an engaging and increasingly read author. Born in Belfast, Ireland, and coming of age during The Troubles, Rollins became part of an American-inspired Pentecostal church in his early adulthood. By his late twenties, however, he had left the church and devoted himself to philosophy. From Queen's University in Belfast he took his Bachelors, Masters, and Doctoral degrees, in scholastic philosophy, political theory and social criticism, and post-structural theory respectively. By the time he completed his work in post-structuralism he had begun to specialize in phenomenology, particularly phenomena pertaining to religious experience and faith. Before moving to the United States he was a founding member of Ikon, a Christian-inspired, "subversive, public performance art collective."[4] He now lectures regularly at post-evangelical and emergent conferences, posts and engages frequently with social media.[5]

In his earlier work Rollins gave a lecture he called "From Theo-logos to Theo-poetics: Re-imagining the Language of Faith,"[6] but in his most recent two texts this relatively calm phrase and his use of theopoetics has been replaced with an emphasis on something he calls "pyrotheology." A much more aggressive and energetic phrase, Rollins cites that it is a take-off of Spanish anarchist Buenaventura Durruti's quip that "the only church that illuminates is a burning church."

> Pyrotheology . . . is not a systematic, constructive, or narrative theology. It is not concerned with building upon, supporting or altering the current understanding of Christianity. . . . Rather it represents a fundamental questioning of these ideals and signals an approach to faith that claims the central event of Christianity is nothing less than a type of white-hot fire that burns up all we believe about ourselves, our gods and our universe . . .
>
> In pyrotheology the truth of faith is not seen to be located in one interpretation or the other. Nor is this truth thought of as a type of container within which all such conflicts are ultimately reconciled. But rather the truth of faith is seen to be expressed in the antagonism which generates the conflict and causes us to readjust our thinking in light of new contexts. The truth then is not that which remains after the fire which burns away the old ideas, but rather the fire itself.[7]

Functionally, this "pyrotheology" is an amalgam of deconstruction, theopoetics, and its precursor, the Radical Theologies of the Death of God. As a manifestation of deconstruction it follows Jacques Derrida's method of overturning binary oppositions such that "the truth of faith is not seen to be located in one interpretation or the other,"[8] but rather, in the fire which "burns away the old ideas," and "overturns the Church as it presently stands."[9] This position seems very similar to Derrida's claims that deconstruction exists to create new ideas and concepts by marking

---

4. Hunt, "Inhabiting a Space," 4–7.

5. PeterRollins.net.

6. Rollins, "MatterCon."

7. Rollins, "What is Pyrotheology?"

8. Derrida, "Interview with Julia Kristeva," 21.

9. Rollins, *Insurrection*, xiv.

their difference(s) and their "eternal interplay."[10] Indeed, that the "truth of faith is seen to be expressed in the antagonism which generates the conflict," can be seen as the rough theological manifestation of Derrida's *différance*, the "systematic play of differences, of the traces of differences, of the spacing by means of which elements are related to each other. . . . It is also the becoming-space of the spoken chain . . . a becoming-space which makes possible both writing and every correspondence between speech and writing."[11] That Rollins emphasizes antagonism over a Derridian empty space which invites is indicative of Rollins's method in general: "pyrotheism burns up all we believe."

Focusing on the "fire" of pyrotheology, that which causes us to constantly readjust, Rollins's refusal of binaries also parallels Wilder's claim that biblical interpretation must be done in view of the fact that the Scriptures "were meant neither literally nor symbolically." Pyrotheology also resembles—if not replicates—Altizer's insistence that Radical Theology exists as "a challenge to everything that we can know or name as God."[12] That being said, Rollins is directly relevant in a way that none of these other thinkers have been: one need only look at his continuous speaking schedule and the amount of time he spends in churches, seminaries, and at church conferences to see that he is fulfilling some desire or need.

As a former charismatic Christian who has now embraced postmodern, post-structuralist philosophy of religion, Rollins is perfectly situated to appeal to the increasing number of American evangelicals who feel disenfranchised and disconnected from the church. He speaks to the condition of those raised in Christian families throughout the 1970s and 1980s who no longer feel that the model of church in which they were brought up suits them, but are not quite willing to leave the church in spite of it. It is perhaps fitting, then, that Rollins has become closely associated with Jay Bakker, who himself had to struggle with a loss and rediscovery of faith as the son of televangelists Jim and Tammy Faye Bakker. Working from within the church, Rollins explicitly lifts up the appropriateness of doubt and questioning, a long-held taboo for many Christian communities, and as such, a stance many find refreshing. In fact, more than mark it as appropriate, Rollins actually prioritizes doubt, subtitling his book *Insurrection*, "To Believe Is Human To Doubt, Divine."

10. Derrida, "Interview with Julia Kristeva," 21.

11. Ibid.

12. Altizer, *The Call to Radical Theology*, 4.

Taking aim at the ways in which doubt and uncertainty have tried to be suppressed, Rollins notes that pastors often serve as the avatars of belief for their congregations, standing in their stead and believing so that those in the pews don't have to. This serves as a maladaptation, says Rollins, allowing for a buffer that "protect[s] us from a direct confrontation with the world and with ourselves."[13] When Christian leaders discourage doubt and questioning, asserting that they have it figured out, the status quo remains unchallenged and there is a form of stagnation and covert suppression at work. It numbs and pacifies church-goers, but ultimately it is not actually church that is being engaged in, merely a kind of church-like play acting for comfort.

It is precisely this maladaptation Rollins wishes to confront when he writes that the ultimate goal of his pyrotheology is to "rupture" and "re-configure Christianity,"[14] so that the result is somehow both entirely new and yet still authentic to its previous incarnations.[15] Part of this re-configuring would entail "leaders who openly experience doubt, unknowing, and a deep mystery,"[16] effectively removing the "buffer" between the congregation and the world and allowing for a re-engagement with the terror of the world, the fear and unknowing, the experience of Christ crucified and God dead. This is a key—and existentialist—move for Rollins, as he claims that the proper function of the church is not to offer supposed means to avoid suffering, anxiety, and pain, but instead to acknowledge these struggles and process them in community.[17]

Under Rollins's framework, congregational life is about building collectives "to fan the flames" and draw "those who attend into the event of absolute loss reflected in the Crucifixion so that they might experience Resurrection . . . ."[18] In function, Rollins refers to this fanning work as "transformance art," and uses Kierkegaard's definition of a poet as a model for leadership.

> What is a poet? An unhappy man who hides deep anguish in his heart, but whose lips are so formed that when the sigh and cry pass through them, it sounds like lovely music. . . . And people

13. Rollins, *Insurrection*, 110.
14. Ibid., xiii.
15. Ibid., xiv.
16. Ibid., 65.
17. Ibid., 179.
18. Rollins, "What is Pyrotheology?"

flock around the poet and say: "Sing again soon"—that is, "May new sufferings torment your soul but your lips be fashioned as before, for the cry would only frighten us, but the music, that is blissful."[19]

Rollins's pastoral speaker of the truth of faith isn't a philosopher king or priest. It is the poet. In fact, insofar as we colloquially use "truth" to mean a fixed and complete fact, or use "knowledge" as a justified, true belief, Rollins wonders whether it is applicable at all to talk about these terms in the context of theology and ministry. Instead, he wants us to approach the idea of "religious truth," not as a way of firmly defining the world, but as a means of affecting transformation on reality. In doing this, he suggests that, "instead of truth being an epistemological description, it [can be] rediscovered as a soteriological event[,] . . . an understanding of truth as that which transforms us into more Christ-like individuals."[20] This is an interesting facet of Rollins: he believes that people can be transformed into "more Christ-like individuals," even though he seems to suggest that it is not possible to develop any personal relationship with the Divine, writing that "loving God in any direct way is closed off."[21] The best we can do, Rollins seems to suggest, is participate in some blissful articulation and reception of love and sorrow by which we *indirectly* connect with God, the name of the source of that bliss, love, and sadness.

Rather than construe Christ as some cosmic panacea that alleviates all present sorrow, Rollins—true to the phenomonological method—engages with the truth of the experience of Christian life: bad things still happen and we still feel bad about them. Christ may be the light that shines in the darkness, which darkness cannot overcome, but in the sense that pain and suffering have been banished, that victory is simply not a part of the everyday experience of most Christians. Here, for all his claims to be a philosopher, Rollins brushes right up against one of the thorniest of theological questions: how it is that a God of utter goodness and infinite power can allow bad things to happen and needs go unmet?

> What if we cannot grasp the manner in which Christ is the solution to the problem of our darkness and dissatisfaction precisely because he isn't the solution? . . . To put this another way, what if Christ does not fill the empty cup we bring to him but rather

19. Rollins, *Insurrection*, 73.
20. Rollins, "Christian A/Theism."
21. Rollins, *Insurrection*, 123.

smashes it to pieces, bringing freedom, not from our darkness
and dissatisfaction, but freedom from our felt need to escape
them? . . .

In the figure of Christ we are confronted with an atomic
event that does not destroy the world, but rather obliterates the
way in which we exist within the world. . . . This means that the
darkness and dissatisfaction that make their presence felt in our
lives are not finally answered by certainty and satisfaction but
rather stripped of their weight and robbed of their sting.[22]

Kierkegaard's poet models an acceptance of sorrow and a transformation of that sorrow into song that Rollins sees as quintessentially
Christian. A crucial distinction that Rollins makes though is that there
are at least two types of responses possible to the Poet's "anguished cry
that sounds like lovely music." The first results in an image of the Christ as
"breaker of our addiction to certainty," and the Poet/Pastor as the source
of a song "we may be gently drawn into . . . undergoing the same emotional release that would have taken place if we had [wept ourselves]."[23]
This perspective is one that resonates with Hopper's vision for language
that "evokes" and "echoes" experience rather than attempts to explain—
and thereby flatten—it. It is a response to the Poet which utterly depends
on the listener: the Poet cannot simply draw the listener in, cannot make
herself be heard as blissful, if the listener has no experience of his own.
Indeed, it is as Joseph Joubert claimed, "you will find poetry nowhere
unless you bring some of it with you." Rollins's model of Christian leadership has the pastor serving as a type of wounded poet, and the gathered
audience as those who relate to the wound. Care must be taken though,
for the audience must hear and relate to the Poet's pain or something has
gone awry.

The second type of response to the poetic cry follows from the next
line in Kierkegaard's text: "And the critics come forward and say, 'that's
the way, that's how the rules of aesthetics say it should be done.' Of course,
a critic resembles a poet to a hair, except he has no anguish in his heart,
no music on his lips." Far from being disconnected from the Poet, the
critic "resembles a poet to a hair," and yet "never enters into the experience that the musician invites us to participate in."[24] In the first type of response, when the Poet sings her heart's anguish and joy, we can be pulled

22. Rollins, *The Idolatry of God*, 4.
23. Rollins, *Insurrection*, 74.
24. Ibid.

in and transformed by the song. In the second, we can remain in distant observation towers refusing to be moved. In a parallel manner, even if contemporary liturgy, theology, and preaching resembles the message of Christ "to a hair," without music on the lips and anguish in the heart, it falls short of actually engaging with Christ's ministry and presence. Rollins's Christian leadership is dependent not upon critically perfect articulations, but upon words truly rooted in experience, which is sometimes full of doubt and uncertainty. This makes Rollins something like a parable-telling evangelist for deconstruction and doubt. He endlessly spins out words intended to cause questioning, and yet is not satisfied when the questioning begins, eventually moving to question questioning as well. In Rollins's own words, "that which we cannot speak of is the one thing about whom, and to whom, we must never stop speaking."[25] Ours is the task to endlessly sing, making our lives into questioning song.

John Caputo

Jacques Derrida once famously declared that "I quite rightly pass for an atheist," raising suspicious philosophical eyebrows and forcing people to grapple with the implications. If he "passed" as one, did that mean he wasn't one? Why not just say he was? Why the doublespeak? Enter John Caputo.

Respected American Continental philosopher of religion, former faculty in both religion and philosophy departments, Caputo is one of the foremost leading scholars on Derrida's "turn to religion," as well as the theological turn in Continental philosophy more generally. More than a scholar of Derrida, Caputo's 1997 *On the Prayers and Tears of Jacques Derrida* is the field's seminal text on the exploration of Derrida, religion, and the postmodern turn to consider faith. Once a confessing Christian and Catholic initiate, Caputo has considered Derrida's sideways declaration of atheism explicitly.

> When asked why [Derrida] does not say "I am" an atheist, he said it was because he did not know if he were, that there are many voices within him that give one another no rest, and he lacks the absolute authority of an authorial "I" to still this inner conflict. So the best he can do is to rightly pass for this or that, and he is very sorry that he cannot do better. That, it seems to

25. Rollins, *How (Not) to Speak of God*, xii.

me, is an exquisite formula not only for what might be called Derrida's atheism, but also for faith. Rightly passing for this or that, a Christian, say, really is the best we can do. It reminds me of the formula put forward by Kierkegaard's "Johannes Clima-cus" who deferred saying that he "is" a Christian but is doing the best he can to "become" one.[26]

Rather than a superficial kind of performative *via negativa* in which the believer professes God's ineffability and unknowable nature and yet ultimately is firm in his belief of that God, following Derrida, Caputo proclaims a more rigorous unknowing. His profession is that it is not merely that God is ineffable, but that the best that can be done is merely hope that there is a God behind all that ineffability. For Caputo, this intense hope in the face of unknowing circumvents the possibility of a firm ontotheology or theological metaphysics, and he sees this as a good thing, as humanity is then drawn forward with a promise of an event which is to come but has not yet arrived.

> By allowing [God's] name to fluctuate in all its undecidability and provocativeness, by releasing it from its servitude to being in order to free it as a promise, we free it from its service as the name of a *res* [thing], even the most real of all real beings, but we do not deny thereby that it has any reference to reality at all. Rather, we enlist it in the service of a certain "hyper-reality," of a reality promised beyond that what is presently taken to be real, the hyper-reality of the beyond . . . .[27]

Caputo's work on Derrida and faith can be seen as an attempt to rescue Derrida's deconstruction from the label of "joyous nihilism," and reveal that it is better filed under "infinite hope." To do this Caputo problema-tizes readings of Derrida that too narrowly focus on deconstruction's critique rather than on that hope. Conversely, an emphasis on the hope in deconstruction yields a very different approach.

I work from an understanding that the basic premise of deconstruc-tion is that "all systems (which include linguistic, artistic, social, scientific, or technological) impose structural limits on the power to appreciate ma-terial reality."[28] These limits consequently lessen our capacity to engage with the world around us: it is hard to connect with that which we do

26. Caputo, "Jacques Derrida," 8.
27. Caputo, *The Weakness of God*, 11.
28. Pronger, *Body Fascism*, 12.

not perceive. This lessened capacity in turn "undermines our political power to formulate alternative constructions of reality."[29] Emphasizing its critical function, "the point of deconstruction is to expose the insensitivity to the power of limitation that lurks within a system and to show that this insensitivity prevents our having ethical relationships."[30] Caputo argues that while many understand that deconstruction functions to destabilize traditional texts and patterns of discourse, most miss that the destabilizing action in Derrida's work is "not a reckless relativism or an acidic skepticism," but rather "an affirmation, a love of what in later years he would call the 'undeconstructible.'"[31] Caputo sees this as a movement toward greater connectedness and sensitivity to the other and alternate interpretations of reality. The hope is that we can more fully come to see the various others that our lives are dependent upon.

By acknowledging the category "undeconstructable," Caputo believes that Derrida opened the way for a kind of messianic hope, a faith that though our current systems are all limited, there may yet be more. This is not to say that what is to come will then itself not be deconstructable, but that there is always more than that which currently is. The undeconstructible, then, is "the subject matter of pure and unconditional affirmation—'*viens, oui, oui*' (come, yes, yes)—something unimaginable and inconceivable by the current standards of imagining and conceiving[,] . . . the stuff of a desire beyond desire, of a desire to affirm that goes beyond a desire to possess, the desire of something for which we can live without reserve."[32] For example, Caputo notes that Derrida's hope was not deconstructing Justice and "leveling laws in order to produce a lawless society, but of deconstructing laws in order to produce a more just society."[33] The full content of Justice's call, which our laws attempt to embody and enclose, will always be beyond that which humanity creates. This is precisely why Derrida says that Justice is undeconstructable: it is that which calls to us, not in a fully-apprehended logic and metaphysic, but in traces and whispers. In a poetics. The call of the undeconstructable comes "packing only vocative power—not power pure and simple, but the powerless power of a provocation or a summons, a soliciting, seduc-

29. Ibid.
30. Ibid.
31. Caputo, "Jacques Derrida," 7.
32. Ibid.
33. Caputo, *The Weakness of God*, 27.

tive power—but it does not have an army to lend it support, and nothing stops us from turning a deaf ear to it."[34] For Caputo, this is the good news[35] of deconstruction: whatever it is that we think God is, and however it is we construe the church to function, there is something more which has yet to be seen, and the action by which all those future somethings will come about is not demanded from us, but asked of us. Constantly and pleadingly calling us forth.

> To deconstruct the law is to hold the constructedness of the law plainly and constantly in view so as to subject the law to relentless analysis, revision, and repeal, to rewriting and judicial review, in the light of the unconditional demand of Justice. . . . The deconstruction of the law is made possible by the structural and necessary gap between the name of the law, which is constructed, and the event of Justice, which is undeconstructable, between the law, which is conditioned, and the event of Justice, which is an unconditional demand.[36]

Caputo's championing of deconstruction as a theological tool for the church has implications that parallel those of Gordon Kaufman's claim that doctrine and theology are "imaginative constructs." It is not that theology and church should be abandoned as activities, but that the cultivation of a hermeneutic of humility is more than warranted, a hermeneutic that, while not perhaps demanding a theopoetic articulation, is certainly resonant with one. If Christians are to continue to produce words about God, to work doggedly toward better theology, to help shape hearts and minds such that justice is more prevalent, and if we are to do so knowing that our work is provisional, contextual, and fallible, then it doesn't seem to serve our purpose or modality to proclaim with a fixed finality.

Caputo suggests that both Augustine and Derrida ask "what do I love when I love my God?" and that both possess Augustine's "restless heart." But while Augustine is able to sublimate that question and settle his heart with an abstract notion of God, Derrida finds that question "stir[s] up still more restless inquiry," because for him "the constancy of

34. Ibid., 13.

35. Caputo writes that "the good news deconstruction bears to the church is to provide the hermeneutics of the kingdom of God" (*What Would Jesus Deconstruct?* 137).

36. Caputo, *The Weakness of God*, 27–28.

God ... does not have one settled and definite name."[37] Caputo's God is not an Aristotelian Unmoved Mover, but the possibility of motion that has not yet shown itself but for excited rumor of its arrival.

> Deconstruction is satisfied with nothing because it is waiting for the Messiah, which Derrida translated as the ... figure of the "to come" (*à venir*), the very figure of the future (*l'avenir*), of hope and expectation. Deconstruction's meditation on the contingency of our beliefs and practices ... is made in the name of a promise that is astir in them, for example, of a democracy "to come" for which every existing democracy is a but a faint predecessor state.[38]

Following this perspective suggests that by crafting theology too firmly and representing it as an eternal truth we set ourselves up to make it all the more likely that we will succumb to the temptation to begin to worship the form and the words of our teachers instead of listening for the continuing guidance and call of the Word made flesh. For Caputo, theopoetics is "a deployment of multiple discursive resources meant to give words to the event, but without miscasting it as a gift coming down from the sky (supernaturalism) and without laying claim to the high ground of the Concept (metaphysics) which dominates it from above, without asserting that one knows the secret, the code, the rule that governs events."[39] Caputo's theopoetics is about contingency and the possibility of hope, not assurances and fulfilled promises. This is precisely the benefit of Caputo's work.

Indeed, Rollins's articulation that "an understanding of truth as that which transforms us into more Christ-like individuals," can be seen as a direct development of the kind of thinking Caputo puts forth when he writes that "to be in the truth means to be transformed by a call, to have been turned around, to have been given a new heart. The Kingdom's truth, the truth of these biblical narratives, is a truth that we are called upon to make come true, to realize, not the truth of a record or a journal kept by eyewitnesses of magical events transpiring in the world."[40] Language itself can lure us into transformation, guide us to enact the things that allows stories to continue to be told. Though numerous crit-

37. Caputo, *Philosophy and Theology*, 64–65.
38. Caputo, "Jacques Derrida," 8.
39. Caputo, *The Insistence of God*, 95.
40. Caputo, *The Weakness of God*, 16.

ics of postmodernism might read Caputo's position here and charge him as advocating a radical relativism, Caputo argues that it is not so much that "anything" goes, but that the way it usually goes gets turned upside down. The powerful do not inherit the kingdom and forceful arguments and proofs do not carry the day. While the world demands logic, the kingdom calls for song and prayer and supplication, for a transformation at the foot of the cross where God is not merely laid low and made meek, but *killed*.

For Caputo, Jesus functions as "the centerpiece of a poetics of the kingdom of God found in the New Testament, of a kind of theo-poetics . . . in which the task of converting that poetics into reality falls squarely on our shoulders."[41] The call of Christ is the insinuation of a promise of something to come, of a promise of things hoped for, but not yet seen. It does not coercively demand or castigate, but draws forth faithful people into "the symbolic space one obtains in the kingdom," and into "the dynamics of a desire beyond reason and beyond what is reasonably possible, a desire to know what we cannot know, or to love what we dare not love, . . . a desire not extinguished by the impossible, but fired by it."[42] The emphasis of Jesus on the cross is not victory given *to* us, but the poetic asking for action *from* us. This is not a justification by works, but a response to an anguished cry, a poetic obligation. In a theopoetics, says Caputo, "the name of God is something to *do*, . . . the weakness of God must be addressed by the strength of a response, which is its chiasmic partner."[43] Jesus as the great Poet of the World, a fully-fleshed man who carries deep anguish in his heart, but whose lips are so formed that when they sigh and a cry passes through them, it echoes through the ages and asks us to reach out and help where we might: *Eloi, Eloi, lema sabachthani? My God, my God, why have you forsaken me?*

Sin Boldly

While acknowledging all the resonances between theopoetics and the philosophical projects of Caputo and Rollins, it is important to be clear that deconstruction and theopoetics are not the same thing. Rooted in the same concerns perhaps, but certainly not equivalent. As marked as

41. Caputo, *What Would Jesus Deconstruct?*, 134.

42. Caputo, *The Weakness of God*, 104.

43. Caputo, *The Insistence of God*, 116.

their similarities are, it is instructive to explicitly contrast the ideas so as to clarify both by means of differentiation. In his brilliant essay "Risking Idolatry? Theopoetics and the Promise of Embodiment," Jeffery Hocking does precisely this, exploring the nature and function of theopoetics and deconstruction as compared to one another.

Hocking begins with a categorization of deconstruction as a "method for preventing self-enclosure, ever-vigilantly guarding against the ossification of language."[44] To the extent that this helps Christians guard against the creation of idols, he believes that it has a utility in the church; however, he is concerned that it is precisely this "guard" against idolatry that can cause a "paralyzing preoccupation"[45] from which nothing can be spoken. Cleverly, he then goes on to say that while this paralysis is often critiqued by "accusing deconstruction of making an idol out of its own aversion to idolatry," he believes a more fruitful tact is to be found with Martin Luther and an emphasis on embodying God in the world, on becoming the flesh of the body of Christ that is the church.

> I am here recommending that we open ourselves up to the risk of idolatry for the sake of creating newness and embodying the presence of God in the world. Luther's oft-repeated invocation to "sin boldly" . . . is able to serve as a guide at this point. Luther does not recommend sinning boldly for sin's own sake, but because the world is not yet a place where justice resides. . . . What I hear Luther saying when he says to "sin boldly" is to let one's sins be in pursuit of justice—to not let attempts at purity to get in the way of embodying the presence of God in the world.[46]

Not stopping with Luther though, Hocking also points to John's Gospel as evidence that we are called into the world: "the one who believes in me will also do the works that I do and, in fact, will do greater works than these . . . ."[47] That is, asks Hocking, "what if in God's absence (i.e., after Jesus ascends to the Father, but before God becomes all in all [1 Cor 15:28]), we are called to risk idolatry?" If that is the case, then "in its hyper-vigilance against conceptual idols, deconstruction closes down the authentic calling of the church."[48] Hocking seeks a means to

44. Hocking, "Risking Idolatry?" 3.
45. Ibid.
46. Ibid., 5.
47. John 14:2
48. Ibid., 8.

include deconstruction in the conversation, but wants to pair its constant entropic drive with something generative. Hocking does not think there is a discrete period of deconstruction, followed by re-construction, and then, finally, a better, remodeled faith. Deconstruction is ever present in all human construction. And so too, argues Hocking, is the call to risk idolatry for the sake of possible life.

Framed as an effect, Hocking suggests that theopoetics is that which causes a cyclical motion that both (1) critiques and deconstructs any system that attempts to self-enclose or claim eternality, *and* (2) in the constant wake of that deconstruction, puts forth a new thing, a new try, a new response to God. A theopoetic articulation is one that we know—before we even begin—will be insufficient, but that we put forth nonetheless out of a care and concern drawn out from us by an anguished call from the cross.

> It may well be that deconstruction has already served its therapeutic purpose in certain church bodies; it has done its work of breaking apart the containers through which theology has attempted to control the transcendent. Perhaps it has tilled the compacted, barren earth and made way for the seeds of theopoetics. However, the call to live as the embodiment of Christ in the world may take precedence over continual visits to the therapists couch for the exorcism of new conceptual idols . . . .
>
> While deconstruction is busy dismantling, standing ready with a hammer in hand to perform its style of therapy on any new construction, theopoetics is quietly building something new on another site, on different ground. Certainly this new construction risks becoming an idol, but if it does, [theopoetics] simply moves on to another site, in hopes that people of faith will leave the building that has become self-enclosed and participate in the construction of a new space on promising new ground . . . .[49]

If I might indulge in some Derridian language play, I'd suggest that there is an intersection, an overlap, and an event here: where deconstruction creates the *khôra*, the open space between, and beyond, binaries, the empty center that "gives place" and becomes the "receptacle—as it were, the nurse—of any birth,"[50] theopoetics invites the *kora*, harp of the African griot, the music that accompanies songs of remembering, longing,

49. Ibid., 17.
50. Derrida, "Circumfession," 123.

loss, and hope. Deconstruction may well help to break apart damaging constructs of a coercive and idolatrous god, but it is theopoetics that wades into the rubble, not to build anew, but to sing of what might have been and what might yet be, encouraging others to imagine beginning again, nearby, and listening.

Loving Thy Neighbor

Baking bread, I've run out of flour. So now I must go door-to-door
& ask for what I need. I've bled up my gall to stand on your little stoop.
Funny, there was no door on which to knock, & worst of all
I couldn't even make a fist—forgotten how—& I couldn't find a way
into your house. All this audacity I have made moot by the things
I couldn't see, the stuff in me that leavens then recedes: courage,
    cowardice,
craving, or clarity. That when I ask, I rarely want to know the answer.
So, are you comforted by such a creatured thing? Asking, that is.
Are you happy with the little mind I have?—whipping up metaphors
to symbol out a truth, to circumstance & qualify the process or the
    means?
Sure, I've heard the rumors—people saying that you're dead—
but that seems harder to believe than some other things I've heard.
& if it's true it isn't news—we killed you long before
& now we've just begun to see you're gone.
Perhaps you're simply smaller than you were before—age I'd guess.
Emaciate from growing old, slighter each day with the calendar page
you tear back from the year. Once so monolithic
but now just some grouch retiree . . . .

My god, please come to the door.
My god, my god—do you need a drink? Do you need a thing to eat?
Forget the ingredients I'm asking for—are you okay in there?

         . . . You're the tchotchke
we've corralled into a hutch, curio to possibility. What you were
is what's harder to imagine: wings & robes turned pillboxed medicines
& an empty cup of orange juice; clouds & tongues of fire turned tepid
    water
ringed grimy in a tub. I've been around the block enough to know
the tragedy of lonely widows, pregnant teens. I've seen the evidence
we've leveled & it's not too pretty. Hell, I'm part of it myself.
But friend, can you get up one more time & let me know
you're there? I'll bake you bread if it means I'll see your face.
Your body traded for my offering—to a neighbor who has moved
or is asleep, or fallen down & needs help getting up, or isn't inhaling.
Or maybe you're just rising & waiting for a visitor, maybe you're
    breathing
deeper than you ever were before. & I'm here now
to catch your breath, & brush your teeth, & sit & hold your hand.

6

Everyday Seduction

Richard Kearney, Karmen MacKendrick,
and Three Definitions

> In the Aztec design God crowds into the little pea that is rolling out of
> the picture.... In the white man design ... God is everywhere, but hard to see.
> The Aztecs frown at this.
>
> —WILLIAM STAFFORD[1]

THIS CHAPTER IS THE culmination of the historical and theoretical
consideration of theopoetics. Chapters 7 and 8 are a sketch of some
of the ways in which a theopoetic perspective might be employed within
concrete Christian practices, and the closing epilogue is a type of denoue-
ment, a reflection of the project in more poetic prose. Whereas much of
what has preceded this chapter has been writing primarily *about* the authors considered and a cataloging of the effects of theopoetics from their
perspectives, here I will turn to writing *with* two authors whose work
functions as a theopoetic Rosetta Stone of sorts, revealing what it is that
theopoetics has been up to all this time. While neither author makes any
regular published use of the word theopoetics or focuses on it any more

---

1. Stafford, "Ultimate Problems," 61

than in passing, they nevertheless provide key insight into the grammar and lilt of the language of theopoetics.

While there have been a number of articulations of theopoetics given[2] that express its historical context (Miller), theological method (Hopper, Keller, Faber), and linguistic character (Holland and Guynn), there has not been a sustained accounting of theopoetics with an emphasis solely on the function and effect of theopoetics itself.[3] By means of co-opting insights from Richard Kearney's concept of "anatheism" and Karmen MacKendrick's interpretation of theology as a form of seduction, this chapter serves put forth a functional definition of what theopoetics does, capturing a sense of each of the effects encountered thus far.[4] Having canvassed the vast majority of extant literature on the topic, I intend for this chapter to draw together a number of the recurring themes that have surfaced throughout the text thus far.

Upon closing, I will have brought together arguments for more embodied thinking, an emphasis on the pre-rational, a method by which we might avoid objectifying God, and a claim that a poetic sensibility in theological discourse allows for the pursuit of theology as a spiritual activity in and of itself, weaving them all together via a loom built from the work of Kearney and MacKendrick. My intention is that this chapter will provide a definitive theological response to the question "Why should we nurture the development of poetic sensibilities in theological discourse?" I will answer it by means of an articulation of what it is that I think is accomplished by the use of theopoetics.

Seeds of the Ordinary

One recurring theme throughout the theopoetic literature is that experience—or the articulation of experience—is a valid site of new

2. An appendix of "definitions" of theopoetics is included at the end of this book.

3. This is not strictly true, as Alves's work can easily be seen to focus on the intersection of word and flesh. However, given that Alves engages this topic in his idiosyncratic style, it hasn't been widely communicated in scholarly circles. As has been made clear previously, I have no desire to "rescue" Alves from his choice to eschew academia—indeed, his choices interrogate my own work by the mere virtue of their existence—and yet it still seems worth considering some of the topics he addresses in a more formalized, sustained way.

4. I actually provide three definitions: varying perspectives on the same scene, so as to discourage the flattening effect that explication can sometimes have.

understanding. This has been held to be true even if it conflicts with some extant authority.[5] The claim is not that *every* articulation about God is equally valid, which would be nigh on impossible given the diversity of perspectives that abound. Instead, the call is to create space for new articulations to be weighed and considered, rather than immediately being dashed upon the rigid rocks of proclaimed orthodoxy. Theopoetics encourages me to ask with Augustine "What do I love when I love my God?" and inspires me to respond both that I don't know *and* that I will not stop trying to love regardless. This is a mark of the theopoetic: an acceptance of a cognitive uncertainty regarding the Divine, an unwillingness to attempt to unduly banish that uncertainty, and an emphasis on action and creative articulation in spite of it all. A theopoetic perspective entails a willingness to entertain the uncertain and employ a hermeneutic of hospitality whose implications are far-reaching. In an attempt to explore this stance we will be assisted by another Irish philosopher living in the United States, Richard Kearney.

As was noted in the second chapter, Heidegger's contributions to hermeneutics and phenomenology were essential components of early conceptualizations of theopoetics. Nearly fifty years after the Third Consultation on Hermeneutics at Drew University, Kearney offers another phenomenological account of contemporary religious experience. I believe that it elucidates part of what it is that theopoetics accomplishes. In his essay, "Epiphanies of the Everyday," he calls for the establishment of a fourth phenomenological reduction, which he terms "micro-eschatological."[6] Kearney's response to the post-Nietzschean question, "What comes after God?" is a return to a renewed God. This return,

---

5. For more on the gatekeeping role of theology and some possible ways in which theopoetics may explicitly challenge the defensive maintenance of the status quo, see my chapter, "Toward A Theopoetic Response to Monorthodoxy."

6. So as to avoid what would be the necessarily lengthy diversion were I to get into the technical aspects and phenomenological details of Kearney's point, this footnote will have to suffice: his proposal accepts and follows Edmund Husserl's transcendental reduction, Heidegger's ontological reduction, and Jean-Luc Marion's donological reduction of givenness, but then goes further (Kearney, "Epiphanies," 5). In effect, Kearney's proposed new methodology: (a) accepts Husserl's epistemological techniques for filtering out habitual patterns of thinking so as to more readily approach a transcendent consciousness and the essences of meaning, (b) accepts Heidegger's means of raising of awareness of ontology with *Dasein*, (c) acknowledges Marion's articulation of the givenness of "saturated phenomena," and (d) suggests that while these reductive methodologies are in place, one may return to a concrete experience of the world that yields a "renewing and creative perspective."

though, is not a book-of-Revelation-styled second coming in which en-
emies are swept aside and true Christians are left sated and pure; rather,
it is much more akin to John's record of Mary Magdalene and Jesus after
the resurrection: God close enough to touch but unrecognizable through
her tears, until she hears her name being called.

Instead of imposing a presumed theology or metaphysical structure
regarding God's ultimate and complete return at the end times, or *eschaton*, Kearney explores where and how it is that God—and traces of the
eschaton itself—is in the everyday.[7] In his words, the process of returning
to experience is akin to "that indispensable loop on the hill path that
enables us to climb higher before doubling back to the valley below. The
step forward as the step back. And vice versa."[8] In embarking on the journey to create a phenomenological methodology that can contemporarily
grapple with God, Kearney has set out not to "define the proper style
for God-talk, so much as perform it by example."[9] His writing is both
a model in its content and its form, and he draws examples from film,
television, and contemporary events just as readily as he does from theology and philosophy. For Kearney, thinking faithfully entails a necessary
re-engagement with the small things of life, which then, in turn, are seen
as more profoundly signifying of the divine. As he writes, "in our rush to
the altars of Omnipotence we often neglect theophanies of the simple and
familiar."[10] These "simple theophanies" are tied into his sense of "eschaton," hence his nomenclature of the reduction as "micro-eschatological."

The *eschaton* is that time/place/experience in which God's *kairos*
time eclipses humanity's *chronos* time and we "touch the sacred enfolded
in the seeds of ordinary things."[11] For Kearney, the encounter with God
in the seeds of the ordinary requires the laying down of certainty. Just as
Mary Magdalene's experience of the Resurrection was held at bay because
of her certainty that Jesus had already been carried off, Kearney offers

7. It should be acknowledged that this framing is not at all that dissimilar from
Jesuit spirituality and Ignatius's maxim to "find God in all things." See, for example,
Richard Peace's, *Noticing God*. While Kearney does not make immediate connections
between his project and an Ignatian worldview, it is worth noting that Kearney was
raised Catholic and that these ideas would not be foreign to him.

8. Kearney, "Epiphanies of the Everyday," 19.

9. Keller, "Richard Kearney's Endless Morning," 890.

10. Kearney, "Epiphanies of the Everyday," 3.

11. Ibid.

that we may be dampening our experience of God by making strident insistence upon God's nature, location, movement, and plans for return.

In his most recent work, Kearney has abandoned the term "micro-eschatology" in favor of the book's title *Anatheism*, a neologism from *ana-* meaning "coming back to," that clearly owes much of its function to his previous work as foundationally set in "Epiphanies." In his introduction to *Anatheism*, Kearney offers an explanation of the term as "a call for a new acoustic attuned to the presence of the sacred in flesh and blood. It is *amor mundi*, love of the life-world as embodiment of infinity in the finite, of transcendence in immanence, or eschatology in the now."[12] This is undeniably resonant with Duguid-May's insistence upon the Kaufmanian position on the sufficiency of the material world to signify the presence of God, but it also bears more than a passing resemblance to Caputo's Derridian framing of the "call of the undeconstructable," which comes "packing only vocative power . . . the powerless power of a provocation or a summons, a soliciting, seductive power."[13]

> [Anatheism] is about repetition and return. Not in the sense of a reversion to an anterior state of perfection . . . nor, indeed, in the sense of a return to some prelapsarian state of pure belief. . . . The "ana" signals a movement of return to what I call a primordial wager, to an inaugural instant of reckoning at the root of belief. It marks a reopening of that space where we are free to choose between faith or nonfaith. . . . Anatheism, in short, is an invitation to revisit what might be termed a primary scene of religion: the encounter with a radical Stranger who we choose, or don't choose, to call God.[14]

This "primary scene of religion," the choice to see God or not, is of utmost importance for Kearney. He understands it as a decision for, or against, radical hospitality. Do we invite in what might be God or not? Indeed, Kearney sees hospitality as a Judeo-Christian imperative not only in terms of social ethics, but also in the development of our interpretive lenses and our constructive theologies. His call is one of invitation to walk in a place of hospitality and welcoming, even when the welcomed guest may prove hostile. Making the choice for faith may indeed be frightening and unpredictable, but hospitality may well call us to that. This is perhaps

12. Ibid., 166.

13. Caputo, *The Weakness of God*, 13.

14. Kearney, *Anatheism*, 7.

best exemplified in Kearney's reading of the Genesis 18 encounter between Abraham and the "three strangers," who foretell that Sarah will
bear a son. There Kearney sees the commentary that religion "is capable
of the best and of the worst. . . . Abraham's heartless banishment of Hagar
and Ishmael is totally at odds with his hospitable reaction to the arrival of
the aliens from nowhere. Capable of the most cruel acts, Abraham is also
capable of receiving potentially threatening nomads into his home with
open arms."[15] Abraham, the great father of the Judeo-Christian lineage,
contains multitudes. Making the choice for faith does not mean that all
will become singularly clear.

What I want to suggest by means of Kearney is that a vital part of
any project of theopoetic interpretation is to remember that no duration
of hosting will ever co-exist with the knowledge its ending provides: how
our interaction with the other will influence us is not known until it happens, and sometimes not even then. So too with the other of the everyday,
with the other of the text, and with the personal other whose articulation
of God and God's movement "fails" to meet the claims of our existing
orthodoxy. This is not to say that we invite the guest in hoping to be ac-
costed or destroyed, but that the call is to acknowledge that whenever we
host the Stranger in any form—personal, textual, or otherwise—we are
entering into a situation of profound uncertainty and possibility. Kearney
believes—at least for hermeneutics and theology—that we are both called
to invite the other in *and* to do so without any insistence or promises
made regarding our safety.

Kearney offers that this temporarily suspended moment of
(un)knowing in the act of hosting is more than amicable to the Judeo-
Christian worldview, as it is well-modeled by the theophany on Mount
Horeb. The Divine, he writes, "is a God who puns and tautologizes, flares
up and withdraws, promising always to return, to become again, to come
to be what he is not yet for us. This God is the coming God who may-be.
. . . This Exodic God obviates the extremes of atheistic and theistic dogmatism in the name of a still small voice that whispers and cries in the
wilderness: 'perhaps.'"[16] In that whisper we are brought to an ecotone, an
edge space that marks a continual re-entrance into the liminal area on the
threshold of faith.

15. Ibid.
16. Kearney, "The God Who May Be," 85.

Anatheism is the moment in a film wherein the audience knows they have just witnessed something that is pivotal to the picture and will figure into later narrative, but at the moment of their witnessing, they are clear only as to its import, not its intent. It is in those moments, Kearney suggests, that people of faith decide again if they will do the work needed to stay the course and hear that "perhaps" again. What he proposes is an articulation of God akin to the form of Eve Kosofky Sedgewick's "besides," a way of philosophically and theologically coming into the presence of a topic without demanding that it hide something beneath or beyond it, or that it necessitates anything other than what it is. Set up as a "besides," Kearney sees anatheism not as some kind of Hegelian synthesis of—and above—theism and atheism, but as a kind of thinking that is perpendicular to both.

> "Besides" is an interesting preposition . . . because there's nothing very dualistic about it[;] . . . a number of elements may lie alongside one another, though not an infinity of them. . . . Beside permits a spacious agnosticism about several of the linear logics that enforce dualistic noncontradiction or the law of the excluded middle, cause versus effect, subject versus object. Its interest does not, however, depend on a fantasy of metonymically egalitarian or even pacific relations, as any child knows who shared a bed with siblings. Beside comprises a wide range of desiring, identifying, representing, repelling, paralleling, differentiating, rivaling, leaning, twisting, mimicking, withdrawing, attracting, aggressing, warping, and other relations.[17]

Kearney isn't looking to confirm or deny prime tenets of either position, but to encourage dialogue and hospitality among, between, and beside them both. For Christians this means that if we are to accept that God is a God of creation and newness then we might also want to accept that our answers to Augustine must remain provisional, lest in our answering we forswear a fuller future understanding of God's nature or action. We know experientially that we love God, but we don't know—at least not in any final, self-enclosing way—the fullness of what exactly it is that "God" means. As such, we would be well-served by learning "to speak of God without allowing the name of God to function as a rhetorical trump card that alleviates thought of all paradox or aporia."[18] By inviting in *poeisis* we invite in that which is not fully formed, that which

17. Sedgewick, *Touching Feeling*, 8.
18. Huggins, "Writing on the Boundary Line," 5.

could emerge as friend, foe, or—perhaps more frightening than a foe—an instance of sublime otherness so profound it does not become the object to our subjective will, but *reconfigures* that will, transforming our very sense of subjectivity and relationality, momentarily fusing the horizon(s) of our own sense of self with that which is decidedly *not* us. This invitation affirms a mutuality present in the theopoetic position: it calls for a continual interplay between a speaker of a "new world-experience"[19] and a receptive ear willing to harbor the vision of a world which is not yet fully known. The speaker risks transgression against (a possible) God, risks idolatry in the hope of more vision and union, and the host risks the same by virtue of the invitation for the speaker to continue, to carry on.

By means of this framing I propose that we are already always engaged in the anatheistic wager. The givenness of the world is such that in every moment we can invite in the strange text of the world and hear it speak, or we can attempt to immediately name it and know it into fixity. As a Christian, I see this as exactly the same fulcrum upon which the power of sacramentality turns. If a sacrament is "an outward and visible sign of an inward and spiritual grace given," then the world can be seen to be full of possible signs and words that we might invite to speak to us of God's grace. Perhaps anatheism is simply an articulation of the human condition: we live in a world of signs such that we might at any turn stumble across/into the living God. Yet without a cultivated sense of listening and reception we may well miss the invitation to an audience. Theopoetics is an invitational stance that accepts the anatheistic wager by ceding the necessity of proof, willing to accept that the world as it is already bears sufficient seeds of Divine possibility. Whether the seeds will take root—or even sprout at all—we can not yet know.

Seducing God

Following Kearney's anatheism, the theopoetic gesture is an invitational one, a prioritizing of hospitality above fixity and hermeneutic safety. What has yet to be addressed though, is why the invitation is to be accepted at all. What is there to budge us up off our comfortable couch of certainty and answer the knock on the door from only God knows who? Why enter the fecund-but-foggy theopoetic jungle when the cut-and-dry

19. Wilder, *Theopoetic*, 1.

library of clear theological doctrine is open and well-lit around the clock? Two answers occur to me.

First, and perhaps more readily discernible, because formalized and institutionally centered doctrinal certainty tends to support status quo systems of social power, and thus, to the extent that current systems and structures appear to be in collusion with unjust forces, attempts at challenging the mode of discourse might allow for the encouragement of voices that might not otherwise be given space. As a Christian, particularly as a member of the Religious Society of Friends with Anabaptist tendencies, I find that my interpretation of Jesus's ministry and message consistently points me toward acknowledging and lifting up voices that do not occupy seats of worldly power. This is a type of pragmatic answer most resonant with Alves, Duguid-May, Holland, and Kearney, for whom the power of the theopoetic is in its ability to create hospitable spaces for dialogue, to affirm the wisdom of the body, and argue that voices need not be "academic" to articulate wisdom of God and God's movement. It is, however, a different reason for letting theopoetics in that is the focus of the remainder of this section.

Without a poetic sensibility and perspective within theological discourse, without occasionally coming up besides mystery and fog, I believe that we are somehow living less than we might, refusing to receive and fully honor our bodies and our fleshly finitude. When we craft theology so that it attempts to be self-enclosing and make claims with a certainty and finality, claiming to be based in knowledge instead of hopes and understandings grounded in *faith*, we are trying to think thoughts that we cannot think, and make claims about outcomes we cannot know or control.[20] Without the poetic we risk becoming too full of theological hubris, too sure we can force words and thoughts to do as we wish, and not accepting enough of that which is: we are limited, failing creatures with a limited language; those who cannot ever hope to have a grasp on the fullness and nature of God. Theopoetics accepts this and is a way to understand why—given the fact that we know our words will never be sufficient—we might want to continue to make them regardless. Theopoetics is an acceptance of God's invitation, or as the poet Rilke would have it, God's *imperative* to Divine embodiment: "You, sent out beyond your recall, / go to the limits of your longing. / Embody me."[21] Gone to the

20. cf. Isa 55.

21. Rilke, *Book of Monastic Life*, I 59.

limits of our longing, wanting to put into language that which is beyond all language, theopoetics is a way to respond "Yes" to the words that I dimly hear: a way to sing praises to the Lord and offer up laments without trying to force a response from God.

Theopoetics invites, it does not demand. In giving voice to our hopes and fears in a way we know to be inherently limited and lacking, we embrace that we too are limited and lacking and that we will do the best we can with what we have. The reason to entertain the guest of the poetic in theological discourse is because without it we fall short of fully honoring our embodied and finite nature, our limitedness besides God's infinity. Our human being is finite, and is therefore incapable of fully enclosing—or disclosing—the infinite. To attempt to deny this or to try and force it to happen does not result in a perfect, infinity-capturing theological articulation, but in a God-flattening depiction.

I believe that we do indeed "dwell poetically on the earth,"[22] and we are yet clay-footed creatures whose lives are beautifully unsorted portfolios of onionskin, palimpsest, and meaning. I also believe that God is simultaneously the catalyst of those words that we carry, and the most eager audience of our songs and scraps of poem. It is precisely *because* of our inability to fully grasp God that there is cause to continually renew our cries of praise and lament. The limits of my longing include a desire to name a God that we know we cannot fully name, and a desire to articulate how it is that God moves in the world when there is no certain way to know that movement. And yet, even without certainty, we can put words to our experience and hope, being open to hear the hopes and experiences of others. This listening, an attention to intention and receiving the articulation and sense of the other, is a cornerstone of Karmen MacKendrick's work in the history of philosophy and theology.

> Remaining secure in knowledge of what the world signifies, we will have no idea, and no way to discern, what strangeness might arise before any of our senses. But when we listen to another person, we listen to the call, not only of her words, but also of the world to which those words call us and in which those words respond: the world in which they have their sense, the praise into which they join. We try to hear the sense of her faith—not the list of beliefs, but the desires and delights, revoiced in praises and laments, which give sense to her world—but the only way to try to hear this is to suspend the presumptions that underpin

22. Heidegger, *The Piety of Thinking*, 213.

our usual understandings. . . . Fidelity reads signs in light of
desire: the world is sacramental not simply insofar as it "is," but
as it is read; in the voice of praise we not only hear, but echo, in
paying attention. We listen not only for another's web of meaning, but also for the astonishment of other desires.[23]

What MacKendrick offers is a tantalizing re-conception of theology
as a form of seduction, as an extended love poem and an act of mutual,
public courting between theologians and God. In allowing ourselves to
be open to how the world calls out to God and by being willing to host
whatever "strangeness that might arise before any of our senses," we prepare ourselves more fully to be caught up in God's invitation. Viewed
this way, as the natural, open-ended, human response to God's desire,
theopoetics asserts that the "imperfection" of human language about
God is not something against which we must struggle, but something
in which we can rejoice! That is, "the incomplete, finite nature of words
may be something other than a flaw: it may correspond exactly to what
words do and even ought to do, which is not merely show us answers, but
also to keep drawing us into questions."[24] I am reminded of the difference
between a wedding and a marriage, of the moment of public witness that
is the wedding itself, and the years of love-building and life-making that
it marks the beginning of. Is the wedding itself a perfect symbol of what
is to come? No. *And* . . . it is how we mark that something more is on
the horizon. We affirm the couple, form community around them, and
remind them that there is a great—and joyous/trying—work to be done.
What MacKendrick asserts is that our articulations are symbols of what is
to come and they mark the advent of eternally-arriving horizons of hope
and struggle.

In her call for a deep listening, MacKendrick asks us to prepare for
the strange and unexpected, asks us to accept that that which we have
known may not be all that there is. She asks us to "listen" to the world,
to receive it not just as it "is," but also in the way that others see it, how
they read it, how it calls out to them. Implicit in this conception is an understanding and acceptance of multiplicity, and an awareness that what
ought be sought is not some single, smooth, systematic articulation of
reality and God, but a rough, textured, polyphony of cries, songs, and
praises. This should be familiar to the Christian as when the Holy Spirit

23. MacKendrick, "The Hospitality of Listening," 105.
24. MacKendrick, *Divine Enticement*, 28.

descended in Pentecost, and its flame came to rest upon each of the heads gathered with Peter, there was not a sudden shift to one, Godly, language, but rather the ability for each to understand each though many tongues were spoken.[25]

Those gathered were not given a new language for the sake of talking about God, they were given the gift of hearing that all could speak in their own way. Because MacKendrick sees the world as full of a multiplicity of signs that affirm God's possible presence, she realizes that she must then accept that it is the whole world that points to God, not only the things we like or call "good."

> The efforts to disentangle beauty and destitution, enticement and fear, joy and sorrow are also efforts to tidy the sacramental promise back into a contract fulfilled and finalized and kept: to read simple signs that inform us of a clearly defined divine entity, ideally one in which power is neatly divorced from vulnerability, one we can praise without lament. Much, probably most, of Christianity does just this, but it thus takes the sacramental firmly out of the world thus rendering the promise unsigned, the word invisible. If we want to remain in the world that is, if we really want any sense of the sacramental, we are recalled to attention . . .
>
> The world and the other, destitution and beauty, call; they do not impose with the ineluctably of logic or physics. They call to desire to attend, to faith to say the strange too: the strangeness of discerning divinely. If we accept the responsibility of response to the call, it is not simple joy that follows; it is rather the far more complicated joys entangled in the passing of time, joys that fight against our own immense capacity for inattention and self-absorption.[26]

It strikes me that what MacKendrick is doing is a kind of unintentional re-framing and resolution of Feuerbach's critique of Christianity, using a novel blend of Continental philosophy and Catholicism. In *The Essence of Christianity*, Feuerbach takes issue with claims that it is possible to know that there is a God just because revelation says as much. He then cleverly points out that if it were so clear then the theologian would "make himself a negation,"[27] no longer necessary because anyone

25. Acts 2:1–11.
26. MacKendrick, "The Hospitality of Listening," 104–6.
27. Feuerbach, *The Essence of Christianity*, 206.

could see clearly that God existed. This doesn't happen—says Feuerbach's imagined theologian—because God's full nature can never be revealed as itself: it can only come to us via human reading and reason, or it would be too infinite and astounding to be understood. As such, we need to keep mining Scripture to further understand God. Feuerbach points out that this formulation of revelation sets up an internal incoherence.

If God cannot reveal the entirety of the Godhead to humanity directly, but has to arrive via revelation and reason (which itself cannot even disclose the fullness of God), then what is termed interpretation of "revelation" is really just a self-enclosed cycle: humanity is merely revealing humanity to itself. That is, the "secret of theology is . . . anthropology."[28] This kind of reasoning allows Feuerbach to conclude that religion is "nothing else than the consciousness of the infinity of the consciousness,"[29] or "human nature reflected, mirrored in itself,"[30] and that "God" is just the projection of a collective assemblage of human hopes and ideals. Put another way, "God springs out of a feeling of a want," and therefore God is merely a "conscious or an unconscious need."[31] On several points MacKendrick and Feuerbach agree, but they differ wildly in their use of those points and the conclusion they reach using them.

MacKendrick whole-heartedly agrees that revelation isn't usefully conceived of as "proof" of God's existence either: no more so than love letters to the beloved prove that there is a beloved. "But," I can imagine MacKendrick saying, "it does pretty convincingly show that love, desire, and longing exist." This longing and desire is the focus for her, a "conscious need" worth examining, not because of what is needed, but because there is a need at all.

Citing the influence of Deleuze and Guatari,[32] MacKendrick offers that "the subject, who is lacking, is drawn by that desire/desirable object outside herself, but the *desire* is that drawing power, not the lack within the one drawn."[33] Whereas Feuerbach claims that "God springs out of a feeling of a want," I again imagine MacKendrick saying, "No. That is *theology* you are thinking of. God is that which *allows* for the wanting."

28. Ibid., 207.

29. Ibid., 3.

30. Ibid., 63.

31. Ibid., 57.

32. "Desire does not lack anything; it does not lack its object. . . . Desire and its object are one and the same thing" (Deleuze, *Anti-Oedipus*, 28).

33. MacKendrick, *Word Made Skin*, 20.

> The infinitely iterable "why" of theologian and child is grounded in a dual amazement: at the sheer fact of somethingness, on the one hand, and at the nothingness that dis-encloses[;] . . . that the world is astonishing, wonder generating. It astonishes when we attend, and what is wondrous about it is what draws our attention. Absence is mysterious, enticing, but so too is what there is; it is in this interplay that the world opens up to a query that never intends to get to the bottom on it, for which more is always possible.[34]

There is some marked measure of both familiarity and transcendence in the Divine, a compelling call that seems to move me into action, not because of a promise or command, but because of an almost-heard whisper, or the insinuation of a curve or line housed in the twilight, which we would not have seen were it not for our listening and attention. Indeed, MacKendrick is very clear on this point: the Divine does not ever give itself over to us fully. That, she says, would be to confuse the seductive with the pornographic, to claim that "the elusive, veiled, and glimpsed" is the same as the "fully presented, obscenely detailed image with nothing to offer that is not already given."[35] Her emphasis is not on satiation or satisfaction, but on desire. On seduction.

Via MacKendrick, theopoetics can be seen as a way to mark and embody our desire to draw closer to God. Just as the satiation of desire in the beloved does not end the desire for the beloved, but draws us even closer, so too can our spiraling and failing words momentarily bring us both a measure of joy and—when reflected upon—a desire for more. That being said, the satiation in its moment is the entirety of the desire and focus. It is impossible to enter fully into the abandonment and self-less-ness of material and sexual satisfaction while conceiving of the act as a means for some other ends. It is not the case that one ever cries aloud in ecstasy, "Oh this moment is sublime because I will later be drawn closer to this beloved!" Theopoetics unites with MacKendrick in this tension between being fully present to a mystical moment and the desire to have that moment mean something more. In every instance though, she resists the move to attempt to fully disclose—and perhaps enclose—the Divine, an act which she says "aims at a complete unveiling and equally complete satisfaction, leaving nothing to desire."[36] Too often theology "tells the

34. MacKendrick, *Divine Enticement*, 53.
35. Ibid., 28.
36. Ibid., 29.

whole story, closing the narrative," when instead it could be crafted so as to "draw forth desire with an eye to continuing so to draw, not with some other goal or *telos* in mind."[37] MacKendrick invites us to endlessly seek after an utterly illusive and wholly desirable God.

While theological discourse is too varied to fully comply with the totalizing categorization of "self-enclosing," the methodological orientation of academic theology—whether systematic, constructive, practical, or contextual—is often toward a better understanding of God and God's movement in the world. Alternatively, the emphasis of theopoetics is not a fixed "goal" as such, but the cultivation of a disposition of hospitality toward God, of a spiritual sensibility that invites the possibility of the infinite into the stuff of everyday life. Indeed, although von Balthasar does not appear anywhere in *Divine Enticement*, MacKendrick perfectly parallels his claims that "every worldly being is epiphanic," able to reveal both "the Being of the created world, the beautiful light in which all things show themselves to us as fascinating, mysterious, and worthy of exploration," and also "God the Creator, the glorious light in which all things show themselves as inherently good, mysterious, and worthy of redemptive love."[38] Thus, what I want to suggest is that even MacKendrick's "theology as seduction" position, which at first might seem radical, is—just as Kearney says of anatheism—"simply a new name for something very old and . . . constantly recurring in both the history of humanity and each life . . . ."[39] The cultivation of an endless love for an endless Spirit that calls us all forth into that which is to come is not a new idea, but it too may benefit from a renewed articulation.

What MacKendrick has done is to re-open the conversation regarding the validity of natural or general revelation, but in such a way that the "reading" of experience is done on even terms with the reading of Scripture. Whether it is the Bible or the immaculate row of a summer flower bed, she asks us to give over to possibility, give up fixity, and yet nevertheless continue to sing, cry, and make propositions. She asks this because she is in agreement with Kearney: "without the abandonment of accredited certainties we remain inattentive to the advent of the Strange; we ignore those moments of sacred enfleshment when the future erupts through the continuum of time."[40] Theopoetics is a method of encour-

37. Ibid.

38. Mongrain, "Von Balthasar's Way," 63.

39. Kearney, *Anatheism*, 17.

40. Ibid., 7.

aging exactly those moments when the strange reveals itself as familiar, when the gardener is seen as Jesus, and there is some momentary realization, eruption, and momentary in-breaking of the kingdom of God.

Whereas theology without poetics might be construed as "fully presented, obscenely detailed images with nothing to offer that is not already given," ever since Hopper, theopoetics has been envisioned as shared expressions of spiritual experience that "evoke resonances and recognitions."[41] Via analogy, if theopoetics at its best encourages an ever-deepening desire for, and relationship with, God, then scientistic theology at its worse can tend toward making the Word a site of sexual objectification. And yet, once again, this seems too clear of a dichotomy, too clear of a division. Who wants to enter into a relationship which is only ever endless desire without consummation? MacKendrick also sees this problem with the analogy, and answers directly, citing Catherine Keller:

> Theological truth . . . cannot be captured in propositions, no matter how correct. But neither does it happen without propositions. . . . Theology, not the truth it seeks, comprises a shifting set of propositions, frayed and porous at the edges. . . . To propose is not to impose, but to invite. A proposition may be more like an erotic appeal than a compelling argument: we get propositioned![42]

What MacKendrick suggests via Keller is a methodological parallel to Kearney's anatheism and Wilder's theopoetics. As anatheism is neither atheism, theism, nor some synthesis of the two; and as Wilder asserted that Scripture was to be taken "neither literally nor symbolically," but theopoetically; so too does MacKendrick conceive of theology as seductive. It is neither rigid nor without form, but a kind of writing "at the very edge of writing's possibility,"[43] a kind of writing that "pulls itself apart even as one pulls it all together."[44] MacKendrick's articulation of seductive theology is also the articulation of theopoetics: a response to the intersection of the apophatic and mystical drive toward a reverent silence in which we accept that nothing produced from our humanity will ever fully capture the divine, and the cataphatic and cognitive desire

41. Hopper, "The Literary Imagination and the Doing of Theology," 218.

42. MacKendrick, *Divine Enticement*, 41.

43. MacKendrick, *Fragmentation and Memory*, 2.

44. Ibid., 6.

to cry, sing, scream, and explain the various joys, glories, and terrors of the world.

MacKendrick is perhaps simply reminding us of something already captured in the wisdom of the Hebrew language, as recorded in Genesis. Knowing God can be less about being able to control and name the experience and more like the kind of knowing when Adam knew (ידע *yâda*) Eve, and she conceived. Perhaps instead of conceptualizing theological discourse as an attempt to grasp and hold God, we might conceive of it as touching God, as tracing the hollow of the Divine's collar bone not to clasp and claim, but to feel where we end and it begins. Theology as seduction reminds us that when we give in to our desire for fixity and objectification we may be closing off the possibility of a deeper desire. We allow ourselves to lose God behind some prop cardboard cut-out of God, mistaking the menu for the meal, and forgetting that music is the stuff of sound and motion, not marks of ink on paper.

I titled this section "(A) Seducing God" in an attempt to capture MacKendrick's both/and gesture. It is both the case that (1) God is a seducing God (if the Divine is a reality, and yet we only apprehend the barest of God's traces . . . then what a tease God is!) *and* that (2) we often try to seduce God, working to make God come closer to us or trying to find out what God needs to let us move closer ourselves. There is a kind of resonant libration in MacKendrick's position, an intellectual oscillation between cataphasis and apophasis, word and silence, immanence and transcendence. We desire to both simultaneously be drawn toward God and to take pleasure in the desire before contact, allowing it to last infinitely. As MacKendrick puts it, "the enticement of the infinite is precisely an enticement without end . . . ."[45] This tension, this eternally vibrant undulation is masterfully depicted in MacKendrick and is a vital mark of the theopoetic as well.

An Enticing Wager

While much of Christian theology has functioned to mine both testaments for various ethical exhortations, seeking to uncover or interpret directives by which the Christian might most properly live her life, theopoetics invites us deeply into the register of the aesthetic. This is not to

45. MacKendrick, *Divine Enticement*, 30.

say that theopoetics does not engage ethical concerns,[46] but rather that its method does not lend itself to issuing a diktat. When Scriptures are approached with a theopoetic perspective they are "released from the fate of being either a rather muddled and frequently inaccurate history or pedantic and often puzzling prescription."[47] Moreover, rather than simply being a freeing hermeneutic for the reading of Scripture, theopoetics can be the lens for not just sacred texts, but also for "theophanies of the simple and familiar."[48] Theopoetics is an invitation to give more time and attention to reading the world and word.

The power of the poetic for theology is not in the exercise of certain aesthetic skills but in the intention to draw people into an engagement besides reason. One does not come to be a poet through mere mastery and appreciation of technique. That person becomes Kierkegaard's critic. A poet is she who has developed those skills and yet has never let them fully dominate her, turning again and again to the world and the limits of her longing, allowing her cries and songs to be put into words: poetry as distilled life. To the extent that an individual has been taught that poetry is a certain kind of form with certain rules that uses certain literary devices to produce certain meaning through metaphor and simile, theopoetics is nothing more than a rather staid genre-study. On the other hand, when the notion of poetry is not slavishly tied to technique, but rather is taught as "imaginary gardens with real toads in them,"[49] there is something being cultivated that is of use to the theologian. The theologian with a poetic sensibility must not write with a blind eye to her longings and the world which calls out to be noticed, calls out and whispers, reminding us of God.

The theopoetic theologian does not search revelation or theology as if they are manuals to success from which doctrine and ethics can be wrung out and extracted. This may be important to human thriving and flourishing, but it is the work of ethicists, law-makers, and managers, not those entrusted with "drawing forth desire with an eye to continuing so

46. A number of writers have explicitly addressed the connection between theopoetics and ethics. See especially Wilder's *Theopoetic*, 23–27; Guynn's "Theopoetics and Social Change"; and Gouizuta's "U.S. Hispanic Popular Catholicism as Theopoetics." Each of these are taken up in chapter 8's section, "Spiritual Formation and Service."

47. MacKendrick, *Divine Enticement*, 203.

48. Kearney, "Epiphanies of the Everyday," 139.

49. Moore, *Complete Poems*, 267.

to draw."[50] Theopoetics does not supplant theology as another, replacement discipline, but functions as an insistent reminder that if we are truly trying to develop an invitational stance to God we must be willing to entertain the strange and uncertain, hoping that at times, that which reveals itself will in turn invite *us* in with suggestions of more to come.

> Scripture seduces in its promise of the secret of signs: it promises truth itself, and it tells of the materialization of that truth. It tells in words we know through our senses the story of word and flesh, speaking and world. And because bodies and words alike arouse and sustain our desires, so too, so much more, does the body of a text about the body that somehow is the book, the text that tells us how meaningful the sensuousness of our world is . . . .[51]

If theology is only to be considered as "nothing but abstract propositions about God's truth presented to the intellect for its purely cognitive assent,"[52] then I am both uninterested in theology as a discipline and believe that theology is not of much use to the church. If, however, it can be acknowledged that theology "has always been, at its height, a spiritual activity,"[53] then what counts as theological cannot be solely intellectual or cognitive: we were created as finite, embodied beings and our theology should reflect that. Theology is not merely an exercise of the mind, but an expression of faith that serves best when it strikes us as true beyond more than the intellect, when it discloses its truth bodily, does more justice to the symbolic and prerational, and ceaselessly evokes "the sensuousness of our world."

Theopoetics seduces us, leading us away from what is certain while it entices us with what might be,[54] awakening and arousing an awareness for the minute particulars which might not quite fit within our current schema for the world. Eventually, though, as we shift our attention from the theopoetic text, or the anatheistic moment, we will be brought back again to where we were before we began, required to confront the reality that there *are* experiences that simply refuse to comply with our

---

50. MacKendrick, *Divine Enticement*, 29.

51. Ibid., 203.

52. Mongrain, "Von Balthasar's Way," 57.

53. Von Balthasar, *Epilogue*, 121.

54. The etymologies of "seduce" and "entice" are very interesting in this regard: (Latin: *se-* "aside, away" + *ducere* "to lead") as well as (Old French: *enticier* "to stir up [fire]").

vision and hope for the world. Whether through their abject horror and atrocity, through their category-shattering beauty and awe, or the sudden profundity of the mundane, there are experiences that lead us away from what we thought was sure and we must reassess. Then, arriving again at the site of our convictions, which look different now in the light of our enticement, we come to that "primordial wager," the "reopening of that space where we are free to choose between faith or nonfaith." This is theology cast as a spiritual activity, a plunge into a space of recalibration and a request that we make the wager *as* a wager, understanding that it is exactly *because* we enter into belief unsure that it becomes faith.

Taking Inventory

Throughout *Way to Water* an attempt has been made to note how each of the authors considered has contributed to an understanding of the effect of theopoetics. Methodologically this followed Marshall McLuhan's enjoinder that, when investigating a form of media, one should begin by cataloging its effects, working backwards to arrive upon its nature only after seeing what it does. Before moving on to consider how Kearney and MacKendrick assist in the articulation of the nature and function of theopoetics, let us consider the effects which have already been noted.

> Chapter 1: Leads us into a new language where theologies are not rigid, logical assertions, but ecstatic expressions that plunge us into an experience of mystery and a primal being; a theology that is "not theo-*logic* but theo-*poiesis*."
>
> Chapter 2: Bridges the fractured, chaotic, and fleshy experience of life with the oftentimes removed and "ossified" attempt to create "scientific texts" out of theological articulation.
>
> Chapter 3: Re-opens the senses and affirms the role of the body in theological discourse, encouraging dialogue and reminding us that the tongue—that primary organ of discourse—is for language, yes, but also for taste, and for sex.
>
> Chapter 4: Destabilizes and decenters, seeking out the "various powerful contenders of an alleged 'orthodoxy' of content, method, and direction of thought," and revealing "the various deep-lying, multiple voices hidden underneath."

Chapter 5: Causes a cyclical motion that critiques and deconstructs any system that attempts to self-enclose or claim eternality, *and*—in the wake of that constant deconstruction—puts
forth a new thing, a new try, a new response to what might be
God.

Having considered the literature of the majority of the major theopoetics thinkers in the academy, this chapter explored Kearney and
MacKendrick, whose work provided key theological understandings for
"enticement" and "wager," ideas that seem in resonance with previously
noted theopoetic effects. With all this in place I can now consider a definition that attempts to succinctly and evocatively capture a sense of each
of the effects cataloged. To this end, I propose Definition 1: *theopoetics is
the roughing up of our ideas of God through an enticing wager on God, the
results of which are at least dialogue and at best an encounter with the Divine.* If MacKendrick is correct in her framing of theology as seduction,
this definition should feel somewhat underwhelming: we have arrived at
a completed culmination, and so the enticing promise of that fulfillment
has come to a close. This destination seems less that what we'd imagined
it to be.

Yet, I do not claim that everything addressed thus far easily collapses
into that phrase—indeed, what an ironic gesture that would be! What I
am suggesting is that, as a shorthand, that phrase is a useful pointer toward the important markers of the theopoetic. Theopoetics "roughs up"
those patterns of thought and naming that lead us into objectivizing our
experience of the divine and lessening the potential for the acceptance
of future experience. It does this by means of a wager that if we hang up
as many of our preconceptions as possible and invite in the stranger we
may be greeted with news that Sarah will bear a son, that the impossible
will spill over into the real. We accept this wager and make the invitation
because we are courting God, because though what we usually experience is but a mere trace of the Divine, it is nonetheless enough to compel
us forward into desire. Even if the wager is "lost," and nothing responds
to our invitation, we'll at least have the story of the time we thought we
heard a knock. Then, in sharing that story we may find that others have
their own stories of knocks in the night, and perhaps it is the case that the
wager wasn't lost like we thought it was . . . .

I think about theopoetics like a gyroscope, whose massive moving
center is the means by which the object as whole can be kept upright.

Our tendency, where God is concerned, is to overemphasize a particular quality of divinity at the exclusion of other aspects in what I understand as a misguided attempt to name and claim God. The result in every circumstance is an off-balanced worldview: too rigid or too permissive, too individualistic or too exclusive. Instead, I am proposing that theopoetics is always in motion, stable *because* it is in motion. When we say "yes," we invite in the other of the text and the world with a hermeneutic of humility, wanting to speak out against injustice and for righteousness, but also accepting that God might well be calling us to move toward better words and ways of seeing. So perhaps, in writing words that are already unsaying themselves I'll offer instead—or additionally—Definition 2: *theopoetics is believing in a manner akin to the way the evening primrose flowers: bold and fleeting in the dusk, new blossoms bursting forth only as tomorrow nears, always dancing with the setting of the sun.*

To the extent that theopoetics can provide a way in the wilderness that leads to Living Water, it is because there was a path beyond the desert all along, a narrow ridge that remained hidden when we thought we were looking for steel cables and spires to save us. Theopoetics may indeed be a bridge between the aesthetically experiential and the systematically theological, but if so, it is certainly not a bridge in the sense of a constructed and lumbering artifact built mid-desert and destructive to the fragile systems of life already present there. The bridge of theopoetics is as much an interior discovery of a path as it is the creation of a theological method that provides a possible way out of the desert of criticism. What I want is a way toward water. I do not need an artifice of contrivance and engineering if it does not give me that.

When we cry, "I believe, help my unbelief!" perhaps the inflection should be such that we are lamenting our belief, saddened by how shallow it is, how much it limits our experience. Perhaps we might want to entertain that it is not, "I really do (and want to) believe, help rid me of unbelief!" but rather, "I believe and that believing stops me from seeing the fullness of what is in front of me. Help *encourage* my unbelief so that it breaks that which keeps me from seeing what is truly here!" or perhaps even, "I persist in employing a strong metaphysics that objectivizes thinking and speaking such that I can only see what has already been said, help me move away from abstraction toward experience, from theologic to theo-poetic." Perhaps. And perhaps a better way would be one that is itself endlessly spinning, as in Definition 3:

*[Theopoetics is] an acceptance of cognitive uncertainty regarding the Di-
vine, an unwillingness to attempt to unduly banish that uncertainty, and an
emphasis on action and creative articulation regardless. It also suggests that
when the dust has settled after things have been said and done in the name
of God, the reflection and interpretation to be done ought to be grounded
in dialogue and enacted with a hermeneutic of hospitality and humility, an
acceptance of cognitive uncertainty regarding the Divine, an unwillingness
to attempt to unduly banish that uncertainty . . .*

As a Christian thinker, what is most compelling about theopoetics
for me is its insistence upon the incarnational, not just in content, but
in method. Theopoetics accepts the limitedness of humanity and affirms
that there is a possible power in our words without having to pretend
otherwise. It is a language of mutuality, dually calling us all forth toward
God as poets and readers of this world. It is the language of theology
spoken in the accent of someone whose first tongue is not academic but
sensual, whose dialect betrays an origin of flesh, and whose tone suggests
that at any moment we might be caught up in some grand dance.

Why should we encourage the development of poetic sensibilities
in theological discourse? Because we were all—even theologians and
pastors—made to dance, not merely think of dancing. Because when we
close our eyes there is a gripping *duende* to the music of this world, which
makes us want to cry and make love. Why theopoetics? Because I believe
we owe it to ourselves and to the hope of our God to live and write and
pray as if the world was a gift and each other a reminder of that which
gives.

Hallelujah I'm A Bum

I was told the way to water: go down to the river to pray.
& so it's what I did—followed the highway till a bridge emerged.
It wasn't easy, but I took the hill careful & stumbled. I took the hill
not knowing what to look for—not knowing if our paths would cross.

I should have seen it coming: graffito, dilapidated couches, cans
of beer & metal scrap. Not so much surprised as let down—
a stop for mendicants or rebel teens: nothing really mystical,
no elegance or majesty—just a silent mucked-on river moving slow.

So I started counting out the junk—the litter & the rocks—
thinking salvation might arrive. But goddamn—it took so long
I grew a beard & had an itch to wander. But you already know that
don't you, friend? Already know the time

we waste seduced by possibility of change—wishing for a vision
instead of simply taking in the scene. Yes, I got tired. Yes, I sat down
in the ashes & dust of the given day with no one around
to see me cry. Human, I know, but so is counting I suppose.

& I wondered what it must be like when snow settles
on the river here, the canopy of bare trees there—I imagined
all the seasons that I'd missed before I came, the little ways
we measure out the life: skimmed waterbugs, cattail cloak,

leaves blundering their color to recede—anything, really,
to semaphore an evidence that things stay as they're made.
There's joy in knowing everything evolves—that even you
must sing a different song to each stone buried under sand,

to every animal teeming in the water. & the garbage
that we make even has it's place upon the shore—
orange filters crunched against the curb, bottle caps,
& broken glass: every little thing accounted for & placed.

I was so relieved with revelation I reclined the sooty couch
& picked my fingernails, & read the writing on the wall. Above me
droned the intermittent cars, rolling their engagements to the future,
cargo hurried over bridge & bath, taxied to an unnamed destination.

& I wondered who might let me hitch & where I might be going next.

PART FOUR

Possible Application

7

Theopoetics through the Sermon and Pastoral Care

There is a risk that theopoetics will remain just a conversation corner in the academy: Yes, the writing may evoke more writing, but these rivers of words deserve to also flow into the sanctuary and toward the streets.

—MATTHEW GUYNN[1]

WHAT I HAVE TRIED to establish thus far in the book is the historical use and theoretical basis by which I believe that theopoetics provides a fruitful tool for theological discourse. I have done that by cataloging the various effects of theopoetics and then defining theopoetics by means of drawing together those effects under three possible definitions. An affirmation of theopoetics as I have framed it implies a belief that encouraging the poetic within theological discourse allows for the continuing interpretation of God, God's word, and God's action, without necessitating any idolatrously fixed and supposedly final, certain, proclamation of God's nature. Furthermore, I believe that theopoetics more fully honors both the finite nature of humanity's embodiment, and the vast diversity of experience within the individuals that make up the body of Christ. Having articulated these things, I move in this fourth section to provide a brief sketch of some of the possible, practical implications

1. Guynn, "Theopoetics and Social Change," 107.

of a theopoetic perspective in five areas of day-to-day church life: the sermon, pastoral care, communal worship, spiritual formation, and acts of service.

I believe that encouraging a greater poetic, embodied, and herme-neutically hospitable sensibility in theological discourse can contribute to practices that help contemporary people of faith move beyond the "desert of criticism" and reconnect with a sense of the Divine. Moreover, I understand theopoetics as a means of making this move without hav-ing to regress to either of two equally undesirable extremes. On the one hand, poetics helps us to overcome a naïve and uncritical understanding of Scripture and tradition, and on the other, it helps us avoid thinking we have found Kant's "safely detached observation towers of reason," or what Richard Neuhaus calls the "toxic cultural air of disenchantment and suspicion."[2]

While perhaps the picture painted by Neuhaus's "toxic cultural air" is slightly melodramatic, I have observed various versions of his wonderless "disenchanted world" within many circles of Christianity, particularly in those communities where the drive for a particular social issue—whether it be for *or* against same-sex marriage, abortion, etc.—has idolatrously overtaken an emphasis on an encounter with God. Theopoetics has the potential to serve most powerfully in these places, in churches and in hearts that have all but forgotten the "theophanies of the everyday" in pursuit of a grander—and outcomes-based—goal. I am not advocat-ing some kind of purely contemplative quietism, but I do think that in contemporary society's headlong rush into the great valuations of util-ity, reason, and effectiveness, we sometimes lose our connection to the visceral and aesthetic character of the Christian tradition. Thus, I hope to provide some preliminary examples of ways in which church practices might be reconsidered so as to incorporate a more theopoetic perspec-tive, reinforcing and reconnecting parts of the path that leads away from towers and toxic air toward the possibility of the Living Water which—I wager—sustains us all.

I am particularly driven to seek out this reinforcement and recon-nection because of the work of Rebecca Chopp and how she identifies the poetic as a possible source of liberation. In her essay "Theology and the Poetics of Testimony" Chopp describes the ways in which social, psycho-logical, and epistemological silences around trauma might be broken with

2. Neuhas, *Death on a Friday Afternoon*, 25.

a notion of "testimony." In short, she notes that clear, discursive accounts of traumatic events are insufficient to communicate the—sometimes personhood shattering—effects of trauma. In its methodological adherence to a clear subject and object, rationalistic prose inherently suppresses the expression of experiences wherein one's very sense of self is violated, ruptured, or damaged. As a corrective she suggests that another form or style of discourse might need to be employed. Chopp feels that if we are to properly acknowledge the presence of trauma and its effects we must take more seriously the role that language plays in mediating—which includes affirming or denying—experience.

> [Poetics] is an invention, for it must create language, forms, images to speak in what in some way has been ruled unspeakable or at least not valid or credible to modern reason. Compared to rhetoric, poetics does not seek so much to argue as to prefigure, to reimagine and refashion the world. Poetics is a discourse that reshapes, fashions in new ways, enlarges and calls into question the ordering of discourse.[3]

Chopp thinks that by employing poetic discourse we may be able to say something with our silences and creations: poetry emphasizes the generative power of language to create new understandings by breaking language from its moorings as ordinary and immediately correlational. In the wake of this fracture, the world to which the old language referred is reconfigured as well, and new ways of seeing, doing, and being can emerge. Chopp advocates for the use of the poetic and the literary precisely because it shakes us up and offers us—through our fusion with its horizons—a strange world. Or the "normal" world, but seen with new eyes. A world where the voices of those living with the wounds of trauma are affirmed instead of denied and marginalized.

> I believe that poetics is essential to the work of theology. The poetics of theological discourse is about the conversion of the imaginary, which works not only by stirring "up the sedimented universe of conventional ideas," but also by shaking "up the order of persuasion," thus generating convictions as much as settling or ruling over controversies. . . . [T]heology must refigure and reimagine the social imaginary.[4]

3. Chopp, "Theology and the Poetics of Testimony," 6.
4. Ibid., 9–10.

Chopp argues that the poetic can allow voices that were *always* present to finally be heard over the din of dominant discourse. Indeed, elsewhere Chopp even suggests that one of the reasons that "poetic testimony" works as a form of powerful truth-telling is precisely *because* it does not use the normal register of argument and power. Employing non-propositional, aesthetic, and poetic dimensions of communication may help to bypass dominant cultural systems that might otherwise dismiss and/or filter out the content were it in another medium.[5] The practices discussed in this chapter and the next are ones that I think may well engender precisely this kind of liberative communication.

That being said, these two chapters are by no means intended to serve as a comprehensive manual for theopoetic Christian leadership. Rather, they are to be read as a conversation starter, the seeds of which have barely been planted, the fruits still far off. Regardless of its present bareness though, I believe that the soil is rich, and I am eager to at least hint at the pragmatic ways in which theopoetic perspectives may take root in the lives of those who comprise the church. This section is a land survey of sorts, an exploration of the places in church life where there may be fertile ground in which to plant the poetic. I began this book wanting to offer the possibility that theopoetics is a viable method for encountering what Paul Ricœur referred to as a "second naïveté," and these next two chapters begin to sketch what practices informed by theopoetic methods might concretely look like.

The Sermon

To consider what a theopoetic approach to the sermon might be, I want to first turn to Jesus and his anguish in Matt 27:46 and Mark 15:34. His cry of *Eli, Eli, lama sabachthani*, his pain of loss, is issued forth in Aramaic, the language of home, and of the everyday. Jesus's lamenting pain on the cross seems to point to a distance between God the Father and God the Son, a space that has been described by Jürgen Moltmann as a sense of the immanent "darkness of God, the inescapability of the process of the world and the absurdity of existence."[6] And it is precisely to this absurdity that Christ screams in affliction. When he feels most distant from God, he cannot help but cry out as he would have cried as a child, in

5. Chopp, "Reimagining Public Discourse."
6. Moltmann, *The Crucified God*, 217.

the language of home and of his people. Given how far we contemporary people can feel from God, what we need in our moments of sorrow is not the theologizing of great systems and structures, but the voice and language of the nearby and the regular with which to name our pain. I think that Jesus gave us permission to speak of our lament as we have need to, not worrying about how we give voice, simply gasping what comes out. Our task is to allow ourselves to feel the grief that this fallen world gives us, to find the words to cry it aloud and embrace the revelatory power of accepted anguish, hoping that in acceptance we may also find amazement and joy. Indeed, it may be that at times one's task as a Christian is only to acknowledge anguish so as to "bring together the internalization of pain with external transformation,"[7] a task we must put to ourselves and all those we serve. Luckily, we also have joy, love, and mischief, and the capacity to voice the experience of these as well.

When we force ourselves and those we serve into speaking a certain way to express themselves "properly" as Christians, we box in the capacity we have for voicing our pain, our joy, and the way we understand God's nature and action in the world. Does traditionally acquired Christian language give us new insight into our relationship with the Divine? Surely. *And* there is no reason why we need limit ourselves to expressing human experience solely via the formal language that has come before. In our quest to make sure it is being expressed correctly, we sometimes become more concerned with correctness than expression. We are children of God and have each been given a vital voice with which to proclaim, and praise, and lament. The bumps and flights of our lives in the Spirit are meant to be named and sometimes we will have to use words common to us, not just the words our churches have given us to use.

As a Christian, I want to put Kearney's anatheism into practice, sometimes letting the words and worlds of the church fathers and my tradition fall away so that I can invite God in again for the first time. I want to find the means to express how my life is shaped by the possibility of the in-breaking of Spirit, and I want to hear how it is that others experience the Divine, allowing them to speak of it as they will, using whichever voice suits them, and not just the voice of formal theology. The power of the gospel is not just in text on the page, but in that text as it is given breath in the lives and actions of the people who comprise the body of the church and whose work serves the kingdom of God. Practically speaking,

7. Brueggemann, *The Prophetic Imagination*, 91.

this has significant implications for the intended role of the sermon in a worship service, and there are at least two areas in which theopoetics suggests an approach that may be different than what might otherwise be employed. First, in how it is that we understand the role of the preacher, and second, in how we approach Scripture in preparing to preach.

Function of the Preacher

Given the theopoetic aversion to a proclamation of eternal fixity, the role of the preacher becomes less about proclaiming God's word to the congregation and more of an invitation into God's word with the congregation. In M. Craig Barnes's *Pastor as Minor Poet*, he develops a useful model of ministry to explain this position. He identifies the "major poets" recorded in Scripture as the prophets, whose lives had been given over fully to articulating their visions of God's revelation. In contrast, Barnes categorizes the pastor as a "minor poet," who provides poetry that fits in between, and is resonant with, the major poets of the Christian tradition. He suggests that "poet" be added to the figures of pastoral identity formation including healer, teacher, priest, etc. He does not intend that it become the only, or best, category, but that it get lifted up as equally viable.

For Barnes, poets are those who have "been blessed with a vision that allows them to explore and express."[8] They are those who "see the despair as well as the beauty and miracles . . . ."[9] Here there are echoes of Kierkegaard's poet who "hides deep anguish in his heart, but whose lips are so formed that when the sigh and cry pass through them, it sounds like lovely music."[10] However, where Kierkegaard's poet was grounded in the conversion of deep anguish into beauty, Barnes's pastor as minor poet hides the ordinary in her heart and her lips are so formed that when she preaches it reveals the extraordinary. In Barnes's words, "the parish minister's soul becomes a crucible in which sacred visions are ground together with the common—and at times profane—experiences of human life."[11]

8. Barnes, *The Pastor as Minor Poet*, 17.
9. Ibid.
10. Rollins, *Insurrection*, 73.
11. Ibid., 22.

A theopoetic approach to the sermon would be one that models the same oscillating movement as discussed in chapter 6: simultaneously drawing the congregation into the text and asking them to bring their experience forward, pointing out the possible signs and marks of God in the everyday. It would affirm God's infinity without denying the traces of the Divine in our flesh and the dust of the world. Melanie Duguid-May captures this sense of the sermon vividly.

> Preaching is not simply the proclamation of the Word that has already come into the world—Word becomes flesh—for the Word is the Word of the living God who still reveals God's self in the world and in our lives. Too much theology is written and too many sermons are delivered as if God were dead, as if God were not revealing God's self afresh each and every day. Preaching is . . . not the proclamation of a dead and deadening letter. It is an announcement of the Good News that is news addressed to us today.[12]

This poetic, embodied approach suggests that the preacher functioning as minor poet is called neither to provide a totalizing description of what is, nor to produce an ultimate prescription of what should be, but rather to lift up possible signs of God and God's movement in the mystery of what is happening in the present.[13] The preacher is less a didactic teacher of God's word, dispensing wisdom as culled from the text, and more of a tour guide to the strange new world of the Bible, standing side-by-side with the congregation looking out over the text. Whereas others might make the case for the preacher as apologist, the poetic move is to claim that, the "pastor is less interested in making an argument for the presence of Jesus Christ than in simply showing him to the congregation," and that "even when preaching out of the New Testament epistles, a poetic preacher doesn't stop at presenting the apostolic arguments, but digs deeper to find the ways in which these truth claims are revealed as the Christ at work in our lives."[14] Set up as a "minor poetry," the sermon is far less about argumentation and explication and far more about evoking a sense of God and an invitation into deeper relationship. I think that what Barnes says of poetry is equally applicable to the sermon.

12. May, *A Body Knows*, 86.

13. Barnes, *The Pastor as Minor Poet*, 26.

14. Ibid., 126.

> [Poetry] doesn't argue, buttress against doubt, or defend. It ex-
> plores. Then it unveils what it finds in voices such as awe, irony,
> or even anger and lament rather than instruction or debate.
> Poets are seldom accused of being convincing, but the best ones
> can transform the way we see life.[15]

To be clear, this is not the dominant perspective contemporarily employed by preachers, and even if used sparingly, it must be acknowledged
that a shift toward the theopoetic would require transition on behalf of
both the preacher and the congregation.[16] For the preacher to take up a
more theopoetic stance is not to begin to craft the sermon in verse, but to
craft it with an ear toward the metaphoric, an eye toward the world, and
a sense of exploration, invitation, and possibility. A theopoetic approach
accepts that the congregation will hear it as they will and cedes that no
matter how well-crafted the sermon itself is, the meaning of God that it
conveys will be insufficient. Instead, the preacher moves to a place of mutual exploration with the body, placing herself hermeneutically besides
the congregation rather than in front of it. This might mean something
as radical as the apophatic practice of open and "unprogrammed" worship within of the Religious Society of Friends, which accepts that God
might work through anyone present with vocal ministry; something less
unusual, such as allowing for a period of open prayer or conversation
with the congregation; or perhaps, in the very least, a realization that "the
sermon belongs not to the preacher, to the congregation, or even to God,
but to the holy relationship between all three,"[17] and the partnering between all three in hopes of more fully realizing the kingdom of God. Part
of the means by which the above-mentioned shift in the preacher might
take place has to do with the way in which the preacher understands
her relationship to the Bible and how she encourages the congregation to
consider that text.

15. Ibid.

16. It is important to note that there is likely to be some social turbulence if a more
theopoetic perspective is explored when a preacher has previously understood the
role of the sermon to be primarily discursive and didactic. The dynamics of such a
transition, and the steps necessary to promote a healthy shift, deserve further exploration, but while I do believe that there is much to be gained in exploring a theopoetic approach, I do not want to suggest that I think it is an immediately easy task to
accomplish.

17. Barnes, *The Pastor as Minor Poet*, 116.

Reading Scripture

While a full articulation of a "theopoetic hermeneutics" would have its own merit, I will gesture in only broad strokes, articulating what I understand the contours of such an approach to be. It is unlikely to be sufficient enough to satisfy a specialist in biblical hermeneutics, but it is my hope that it is of use in an applied sense for those who are grappling with what it might mean to develop a more theopoetic approach to the reading of Scripture.[18] In the anatheistic moments wherein we experience a micro-eschaton, experience the other in the daily, and have to re-make our articulations of God, we find exactly the kinds of encounters we can encourage people of faith to have in the reading of Scripture.

Something akin to Gadamer's "fusion of horizons" takes place in the moment of surrender to the possibility that in the meeting of God in the other our own sense of God, other, and self will shift.[19] I want to encourage people to give up thinking that "understanding Scripture" is something that can be done and completed as a finished act. Rather than seeing Augustine's "*crede, ut intelligas*" as a model of "faith seeking understanding," where people of faith are on some safari hunt for meaning with reason as their gun, it becomes an immersive experience in which reason is used to situate oneself "within a process of tradition, in which past and present are constantly fused."[20] Fused not so that our contemporary thought is burned out to some pre-modern naïveté, but so as to allow for a renewed sense of the source to which the tradition might be pointing. We read not to master the material but so that it "can really be made to speak to us,"[21] cascading over and breaking through our certainties. Barnes articulates the perspective succinctly.

> [Pastors] train their souls for their high calling by constantly moving beyond the rationalistic means of handling Scripture and congregations. They don't ignore these necessary exegetical and analytical tools, which provide a critical introduction to the text of the Bible and the organization that they serve, but as

18. Sandra Schneiders's essay "Biblical Spirituality" does exactly this, addressing how it is that theopoetics can be a useful hermeneutic lens.

19. An excellent explanation of Gadamer's fusion of horizons in the context of religious and theological reflection can be found in Kemal Ataman's *Understanding Other Religions: Al-Biruni's and Gadamer's 'Fusion of Horizons.'*

20. Gadamer, *Truth and Method*, 258.

21. Ibid., 358.

poets they know that when all that work is done, they still have miles to go before they sleep. . .[22]

It is important to have access to exegetical tools *and* they are not sufficient. There is a balance to be made between our knowledge, learning, and self-development on the one hand, and trust, exploration, and inspiration, on the other. That is, when "sailing toward the kingdom of God promised by the Gospels, we find ourselves in the mode of explorers with a theoretical understanding of a round earth and yet an abiding fear of dragons at the map's edge."[23] Our ships "cannot simply aim for an unmapped shoreline," but must—when the New World cannot yet be seen—"be aimed, as carefully and calculatedly as possible, at the horizon."[24] Scripture and our analytical tools are those maps and calculations that help us aim at the horizon where the new world begins. To get there we must go beyond the maps and into the deep.

This approach to Scripture is situated in such a way so that at least two extreme trajectories intercept here: those who tend toward an interpretation of the Bible as mere cultural artifact, fully claiming a detached mentality of distanced hermeneutical suspicion, and those who tend toward an interpretation of the Bible as a contextless, eternal vehicle for complete and pure transmission of Divine mandate. To both of these positions the theopoetic tracings of the non-quite-yet-fully-disclosed-God open up some room for exploration and hospitality without requiring either to abandon their post. A hermeneutic zone of hospitality is created during a theopoetic reading of text, an attempted suspension of both disbelief and belief, and the ability to talk to others hospitably while the theopoetic perspective is enacted. While I do not think Paul Ricœur had precisely these ideas in mind when he proposed it, the two passages which form the epigraph to the first chapter point to this:

> It is in the age when our language has become more precise, more univocal, [and] more technical . . . that we want to recharge our language, that we want to start again from the fullness of language. . . . Beyond the desert of criticism we wish to be called again. . . [25]

22. Barnes, *The Pastor as Minor Poet*, 109.

23. Laurent, "Incarnational Creativity," 190.

24. Ibid.

25. Ricœur, *The Symbolism of Evil*, 349.

> In every way, something has been lost, irremediably lost:
> immediacy of belief. But if we can no longer live the great sym-
> bolisms of the sacred in accordance with the original belief in
> them, we can, we modern people, aim at a second naïveté in and
> through criticism.[26]

Reading theopoetics through Ricœur,[27] the idea is not to come to
Scripture—or experience—expecting our demands to be met, but to enter into it with acknowledged hopes for the encounter, praying that some
insight be found, yet always aware that even our notions of insight might
be reoriented: our smooth expectations "roughed up" a bit. To paraphrase
a line from Nicholas of Cusa that Richard Kearney uses, "Scripture
disturbs, uproots, and reiterates the call of Yahweh to Abraham to 'leave
his house'; it shakes every edifice."[28] Both the jaded progressive Christian
who questions the authority of Scripture and the biblical literalist could
come to the table without having to give up their current position, as long
as both allow that something radical *may* happen in the encounter of the
other in the text—and at the table—that opens up some micro fissure into
the eschaton, from which hope flows.

Faith that the text will consistently give over its power to us is not a
faith at all, but an insistence that the human power of reason and interpretation is sufficient to extract God's will directly from language, as if the
entirety of God's humble majesty might be captured in text. I think that
theopoetic and anatheistic projects honor 2 Timothy's assertion that "all
Scripture is inspired by God,"[29] while remaining in dialogue with André
Gide's request that we cultivate "a disposition to receive" (*une disposition
à l'accueil*).[30] The call is to cultivate a receptive disposition, developing

---

26. Ricœur, *The Symbolism of Evil*, 351.

27. A fuller reading of Paul Ricœur and the implications of his work as pertains to
theopoetics has yet to be explored in publication. One is needed. I do, though, highly
commend Patrick Vandermeersch's "The Failure of Second Naïveté." In it he notes
that Ricœur believed that "the restoration of the full meaning of language and of the
power of the symbol [could] only be achieved by taking an active position of ongoing
interpretation" (Vandermeersch, "The Failure," 257). Unfortunately, though Ricœur
intended to discuss the method of such an interpretation, that is, "a description or
evocation of the way the will can be liberated from its own slavery," that planned book
was never completed (ibid., 253). I believe that the theopoetic project is one means by
which just such an interpretation might be articulated.

28. Kearney, *The Wake of Imagination*, 75.

29. 2 Tim 3:16.

30. Kearney, *Anatheism*, 14.

ourselves to better interpret Divine inspiration without trying to clutch tightly to that interpretation, holding it over others by some means of reason or "proof." The call is to accept the free floating moment of the invited, fertile, anatheistic wager, allowing it to inspire and disturb our reading of those things we hold most dear. This is just what I believe Ricœur suggests when he says that the Second Naïveté "starts from the symbols and endeavors to promote the meaning, to form it, by a creative interpretation."[31] Reading this way is tilling, sowing, and waiting work: an uncertain, hospitable encounter with the other of the text that results in experimentation with new language and new ways of living. With new language that leads to new ways of living, an affirmation that "semantic innovation can . . . point toward social transformation."[32]

Are there things to be suspicious of? Are there false teachings? Certainly. There is much to be gained in a critical evaluation of what presents itself, but for a person of faith there is a hope for something beyond naïve certainty *and* beyond cultural irony and doubt. A theopoetic approach to reading lets us come to the text critically and yet be startled—as we might at a suddenly getting a joke we've heard in a foreign language but never understood—by traces of the presence of God. I suggest that this willingness to be surprised, to cede that it is exactly its sacredness that *precludes* utter mastery of holy text, is a theopoetic way forward.

Pastoral Care

Another avenue in which theopoetics may well serve the day-to-day needs of the church is in the area of pastoral care. A very short detour through a major concept in the field of pastoral theology will help to make clear why it is that the poetic has great potential for the pastoral encounter.[33]

In a 1950 address to the Council for Clinical Training of Theological Students, Anton Boisen, father of the Clinical Pastoral Education (CPE) model, said that it was vital that those receiving care be considered as "living human documents." At stake was his desire to make certain that

31. Ricœur, *The Symbolism of Evil*, 355.

32. Kearney, *Poetics of Imagining*, 149.

33. I am indebted to the work of Andrew Tripp in his piece "Pastoral Theopoetics," where he gives a much more nuanced accounting of the relationship between pastoral care, theopoetics, and Heidegger's poetics.

the pastor not lose touch with concrete human experience in an attempt to employ Scripture and theology. For more than fifty years this phrase, "living human document," has had enormous traction in the field of pastoral care, and it was because of its influence that contemporary practical theologian Bonnie Miller-McLemore felt the need to address an underlying component of human experience that the phrase fails to address.

Believing that "living human document" does not capture the fullness of human intersubjectivity, Miller-McLemore encourages us to move toward "living documents within the web,"[34] thus affirming the interconnectedness between an individual's sense of self and the world in which the individual comes to understand herself. Following Boisen and Miller-McLemore, I then want to reassert and reinterpret the claims I made above regarding a theopoetic method for reading text. If the pastoral care encounter can be seen as a form of interaction with a "document" of any sort, then rather than tending to strictly adhere to a psychologically oriented, rationalistic, secular therapeutic model, the caregiver would proceed, praying that some insight be discovered, yet always aware that even his notions of insight might be reoriented: smooth expectations "roughed up" a bit. Indeed, pastoral theologian Donald Capps suggests that insights from poetry can be directly employed so that pastors can "feel free to go beyond the legitimately circumscribed domain of secular counseling" without resorting to "mere advice or religious platitudes."[35] Capps suggests that the synergy between pastoral caregivers and poets is significant and under-examined.

> The tendency of poets to be exploratory, questioning, and tentative, though not spineless or without conviction and a passion for truth, has a natural fit with the kinds of human experiences that have been of greatest concern to pastoral care, and with the ways that pastors, in confronting these situations, have found themselves responding to them. Again and again, pastors confess that they have been unable to communicate a theological "answer" to a parishioner in distress, not because the pastor did not know what such an answer would be, but because the answer would violate the experience itself, usually by imposing greater certainty or clarity onto the experience than the parishioner and pastor felt was warranted at the time.[36]

34. Miller-McLemore, "Revisiting the Living Human Web," 3.

35. Capps, *The Poet's Gift*, 39.

36. Ibid.

Capps's position is largely based on his realization that while much attention has been given to narrative and counseling, it is increasingly the case that "pastors no longer have the long-term, in-depth relationships" once common in pastoral encounters, and thus, while "significant personal encounters continue to occur . . . they are less routine, more haphazard, accidental, and episodic, much like the episodes that Jesus relates in his parables."[37] This socio-cultural reality leads Capps to think that poetic reflections may be more useful than narrative ones as "among contemporary literary genres, the modern poem is the most direct descendent of the parable."[38] He makes this claim by means of pointing out that the poem,

> like the parable, does not look outside itself for the "point" of the poem, since the poem is the point[;] . . . its goal is not to tell a complete story, as a novel does, but to use a life episode—often one that is seemingly unimportant or that other, less perceptive eyes would have overlooked—to inspire or even prod the reader to look at life in a different way.[39]

This movement, a poetic prodding toward looking at life in a different way, is also key to the vision of the pastoral encounter as envisioned by Phil Zylla, Professor of Pastoral Theology at McMaster Divinity College.

Whereas Capps is certainly an advocate for the use of a poetic sensibility in cultivating an invitational—but not spineless!—stance for pastoral caregiving, Zylla goes even further, claiming that theopoetics should be a key component of all pastoral theology and seminary training. With Capps, Zylla also closely associates the work of poet and pastor, suggesting that both are charged with ferreting out means of expressing "the complex reality of concrete situations."[40] To this I would add that the task of a minister is to encourage others to do the same as well, not to teach that a reliance upon the ordained to do it for them. The charge of Christian leaders is to engender environments in which people can learn to articulate, explore, and enter into the reality of God's movement, not become gatekeepers who mete out wisdom in due proportions as they see fit.

37. Ibid., 2.
38. Ibid.
39. Ibid.
40. Zylla, "What Language Can I Borrow?" 130.

Through the development of an appreciation for the poetic, pastors and lay people alike can develop a greater ability to express themselves, communicate with one another, and to listen across personal differences and cultural boundaries. Zylla asserts that "if we are to speak meaningfully of the deeper experiences of God in our lives and in the lives of our congregations, we need to pay careful attention to how language may express the depth dimension of our searching."[41] As the necessity to consider multi-cultural and minority perspectives continues to press on the church, Zylla offers that theopoetics ought to be more seriously considered by pastoral theologians. For Zylla, poetically engaging the Divine moves toward the depth. He suggests that a theopoetic approach to the pastoral care encounter would have three distinct core components, and lays each out succinctly.

First would be the reestablishment of "contact with the complex and concrete world of human experience, what William James called "primary reality." Zylla terms this transition an "acceptance of Numinous Silence," and lifts up the human longing to name the Mystery as a marker of this stage.[42] In a near echo of MacKendrick, he warns against the abandonment of naming, even though God cannot be named in entirety, whether through prose or poetry. He advocates for the attempt regardless, as long as there is an acceptance of an eventual turn—or oscillation—to silence and the realization that words will eventually fail. In the failing though, there are gifts. "Grace. Advent. Mystery. Small, diminutive, vulnerable we stand before our Creator. Discerning. Waiting. Prayerful. . . . God meets us in these moments of contrition, light and opening of the eyes."[43] The pastoral care giver and the congregant can pause in the mystery, accepting that sometimes it is the stillness and silence that best communicates God's motion.

Following this first phase would come the grounding of "pastoral responses and pastoral reflection in concrete realities and not general abstractions."[44] Rather than rely on an entirely rational or formulaic modeling to guide pastoral care, Zylla reminds us that ministry is not as predictable as some may like, and counsels yielding to "the complexity, all the while opening ourselves to the prompting of God who invites

41. Ibid., 131.
42. Ibid.
43. Ibid., 135.
44. Ibid., 131.

our courage and our expectant participation."[45] While this section of his work is not a focus for him, he seems to allude to a deeper level of acceptance than that expounded in his first movement. Beyond the "numinous silence" is a period of confusion that must also be embraced. Zylla acknowledges that while the mystery of his first movement is powerful, sometimes the needs of the congregation are anything but mysterious. People cry out for pastoral care for a variety of reasons, and what is encountered in the particulars of each person's life may not be full of mystery at all, but rather confusion and contradiction. In those tortuous times, Zylla cautions against abstracting the situation in an attempt to meet some externally imposed model, urging caregivers to "move with the Spirit into the ambiguity" toward "Ministry as Disorientation."[46] When someone is providing pastoral care, they may be of greater service than they think merely by reflecting back the concrete aspects of a situation without trying to untangle them, accepting the sense of disorientation as necessary for moving on toward the third movement.

In the close of his proposed framework, which Zylla terms the "Ministry as Reorientation" movement, the care giver re-articulates not only concrete details, but her sense of how those details bear the mark of the Divine.[47] In these types of "reorientation" conversations, Zylla suggests that rather than just providing psychologically-based support, the minister can offer the petitioner an opportunity to re-calibrate, to understand how the presence of God in their life is there, waiting to be seen. While at first this can seem like somewhat of a "grin and bear it" approach, what is being proposed is decidedly not an ascetic pietism, but rather an infusion of faithful theopoetic vision into sessions often grounded in models of rational psychology.

While Zylla has every intention of providing the emotional and social support desired in pastoral care encounters, he also is challenging the field to move beyond the discursive, maintaining compassion while plunging more deeply into the mystery. He posits that "the lived transforming Word guides the sensitive articulation of authentic pastoral conversation," and urges the field of pastoral theology to take up the charge of poetically delivering God's Word in a way reminiscent of 1 Peter 4:11: "If

45. Ibid., 137.
46. Ibid.
47. Ibid., 138.

anyone speaks, he should do it as one speaking the very words of God."[48] This kind of speaking not only serves the listener, but the speaker as well, inviting them both into deepening opportunities to reorient their lives. What is shared in a theopoetic space is not prescriptive, but descriptive: the articulation of a perceived presence of the Divine and an acknowledgement that "the deepest strivings of our hearts end in God's presence. The deepest longings of our souls require God's touch."[49]

While Capps and Zylla are the most explicit advocates for an integration of the poetic with the pastoral care encounter, a conversation about the relationship between pastoral care and poetic perspectives cannot come to a close without at least addressing two other therapeutic modalities that are quite resonant with theopoetics: poetry therapy and logotherapy. As such, though a fuller assessment of the utility and efficacy of these methods would eventually necessitate clinical research and consequent theological reflection, here my hope is merely to point to counseling practices and perspectives that may readily become part of the repertoire of a pastor or pastoral caregiver looking to develop more theopoetic tools.

Resonant Therapeutic Modalities

Poetry therapy was codified as an expressive therapy during the 1980s and "Certified Poetry Therapists" are trained through the National Federation for Biblio/Poetry Therapy much as are other creative arts therapists. Although even poetry therapists acknowledge that the field is a "nontraditional form of therapy," it does hold affiliate status with the National Coalition for Creative Arts Therapies, and as such, is a standardized field of training, practice, assessment, and licensure. Poetry therapy consists of "a trained facilitator [who] uses guided discussion to help the clinical or developmental participants integrate both feelings and cognitive responses to a selected work."[50] Primarily, it is a group therapy model wherein the facilitating therapist leads a number of people into a reflection on a text, so that they can come to practice the skills of interpretation and shifting their understanding without having to address their own

48. Ibid., 137.
49. Ibid., 132.
50. Hynes, *Biblio/Poetry Therapy*, 17.

psychological states head-on. In time, as skills of reflection and interpretation are strengthened, they are turned inward as well.

> The steps in the bibliotherapeutic process are fourfold: after a participant's attention is caught by something in the reading (recognition), he or she goes on to look at the issues and the personal feeling-response to them (examination). The process then moves to a deeper level of understanding in light of any new feelings or ideas that emerge in the dialogue (juxtaposition). Finally the individual evaluates the impression and insights and integrates them into his or her inner-self (self-application). The whole process culminates in a new, deeply personal meaning that will inform future attitudes and actions.[51]

One of the characteristic facets of poetry therapy is that it is primarily focused on encouraging the development of healthy tools of self-awareness and "feeling-responses," rather than treating the symptoms of mental illness as such. Poetry therapy is not designed for acute intercessory therapeutic situations, but for the support and growth of healthy mechanisms for interacting, assessing, and coping with the world. This is precisely the kind of activity in which I believe a Christian leader may well serve to help his or her congregants. It seems as though poetry therapy may be able to be adapted for use in events like Bible studies and small group discussion. Moreover, in some of the more recent literature in the field there are articulations of poetry therapy practice that would be almost immediately able to be implemented in congregational settings, with—I presume—the same documented mental health and wellness benefits poetry therapy has in secular settings.

For example, Nicholas Mazza, editor of the *Journal of Poetry Therapy*, and a leading scholar in the field, offers that in addition to the fourfold process addressed above, poetry therapy can be conceived of as a three-component model.

> The first component, receptive/prescriptive, involves the introduction of already existing poetry (or other forms of literature) in a therapeutic context. The purpose could include validating a feeling, promoting self-disclosure, and advancing group discussion.
>
> The second component, expressive/creative, encourages client expression through a number of writing methods (e.g., poetry, letters, journals, and stories). Various individual and

51. Hynes, *Biblio-Therapy*, 43.

group exercises can be used for clinical/health purposes. They might act as a safety valve to express feelings, provide a sense of order and control, or promote group process variables such as cohesion.

The third, the symbolic/ceremonial component, uses metaphors, rituals, symbols, storytelling, and performance (for example, dance or movement) as a means to deal with life transitions; for example, a ritual to deal with death and loss.[52]

Using poetry therapy techniques as a model, I can readily imagine integrating creative practices into church settings such that the group could read together, write together, and then mutually co-create and enact liturgy together as well. Even the way that poetry therapists talk about poetry is in resonance with much of the literature regarding the value of theopoetics. Mazza writes that "poetic language [has proved] the most adequate medium for responding to modernity. It has the kind of variety and indeterminacy, richness, and flexibility that make it privileged ground for experimenting with human potentialities and responses, redeeming the past, assimilating the present, and projecting the future."[53] This is nearly an exact echo of Capps's claims regarding the utility of the poetic in individual pastoral care encounters.

Finally, the last indicator that there is fertile ground for future work on the intersection of theopoetics, pastoral care, and poetry therapy is because of the emphasis and technique of "interactive listening," practiced by facilitators of poetry therapy. Entailing an active encouragement of the patients rather than the typically more passive, non-directive, patient-centered Rogerian types of interaction,[54] poetry therapy training involves the development of techniques that may well address Capps's desire to "know our listening is very important . . . yet continue to wish that those with whom we have caring exchanges might know more deeply the robust faith of which they are capable."[55] Ultimately, there would need to be some adaptation and contextualization to fully employ the insights of poetry therapy, but I think that it could be a significant resource for the development of a theopoetic approach to the pastoral care encounter, especially in group settings. For exploration of therapeutic models resonant

52. Mazza, *Poetry Therapy*, 53.

53. Ibid., 4.

54. Hynes, *Biblio-Therapy*, 17–19.

55. Capps, *The Poet's Gift*, 39.

with theopoetic perspectives that more readily address one-on-one pastoral care encounters, I turn to Viktor Frankl's work with logotherapy.

Frankl was an Austrian Jew, psychiatrist, and the founder of logotherapy, a form of psychoanalysis akin to Freud's methods, but with an enormous shift in emphasis. Whereas Freud and the "First Viennese School of Psychotherapy" grounded their theories of human action in the subconscious machinations of "the will to pleasure," and Alfred Adler's "Second Viennese School" based theirs in a reading of Nietzsche's "will to *power*," Frankl and his "Third School" presumed that the foundational drive was not for sex or power, but for meaning. A survivor of the Shoah, Frankl developed logotherapy as a result of his reflection upon how he managed to survive and maintain his sanity in that most heinous of situations.[56]

James Ellor, pastoral theologian and Professor of Social Work at Baylor University, believes that Frankl is a key mediating thinker to connect theological insight to healthy, psychological practice. He writes that linkages need "to be developed between theology and psychology that will afford a more complete dialogue toward viable explanations of human nature," and that "the work of Viktor Frankl offers important first steps toward developing the necessary bridges between theology and psychology."[57] The guiding principles of logotherapy are interesting to consider, and this section primarily addresses that aspect of the practice. More important for caregivers though—and something beyond the intent of this chapter—would be to take that interest and fold it into a thorough exploration of the *techniques* of logotherapy applicable in practice.

First published in summary form in his text *Man's Search for Meaning*, Frankl explicitly differentiated logotherapy from psychoanalysis, emphasizing a Kierkegaardian stance on existential anxiety.

> Logotherapy regards its assignment as that of assisting the patient to find meaning in his life. Inasmuch as logotherapy makes him aware of the hidden logos of his existence, it is an analytical process. . . . In logotherapy's attempt to make something conscious again it does not restrict its activity to instinctual facts within the individual's unconscious but also cares for existential realities, such as the potential meaning of his existence to be fulfilled as well as his will to meaning. . . . Logotherapy deviates from psychoanalysis insofar as it considers man a being

56. Marshall, *Logotherapy Revisited*, 4.

57. Ellor, "Bridging Pscychology and Theology," 90.

whose main concern consists in fulfilling a meaning, rather than in the mere gratification and satisfaction of drives and instincts, or in merely reconciling the conflicting claims of id, ego and superego, or in the mere adaptation and adjustment to society and environment.[58]

As a resource for pastoral care, logotherapy appears to have much to offer. Take, for example, the assertion that logotherapy "does not restrict its activity to instinctual facts within the individual's unconscious but also cares for existential realities, such as the potential meaning of his existence." This seems to open the way for intentional conversations regarding issues of vocation and discernment of God's will, topics that are less like "instinctual facts," and more similar to categories of ultimacy and "existential reality," areas of overlap with conversations grounded in faith as well. Marianne Marshall summarizes the core insights of logotherapy as three basic pillars or assumptions, which undergird the practice.

1. All human life has meaning under every circumstance, even those which are most painful and full of suffering.

2. Each person's main motivation for living is a will to find that meaning in life which is universally available.

3. Each person has the freedom to find meaning in what she does and experiences, and this includes the outlook one takes when confronted with a situation of grievous suffering and loss.[59]

This has resonance with classic Christian perspectives, which assert that the world provides means for God's ever-deepening revelation to us. Take, for example, Ignatius of Loyola's "First Principle and Foundation," a key text in his spiritual exercises, paraphrased below:

1. Everything in the world has the potential of calling forth in us a deeper response to our life in God.

2. Our only desire and our one choice should be to want and choose whatever better leads to the deepening of God's life in me.

---

58. Frankl, *Man's Search For Meaning*, 125.

59. Marshall, *Logotherapy Revisited*, 8–12.

3. All the things in this world are gifts of God, presented to us
so that we can know God more easily.[60]

While not an exact parallel to confessional Christian proclamation, that the precepts of logotherapy explicitly presume a movement toward meaning and intention beyond mere caprice is likely to prove beneficial for anyone attempting to develop techniques for a theopoetically-oriented concept of pastoral care. There are a number of resonant assumptions that overlap between Frankl's methods and the meaning-making that is inherent in theo-*poeisis*. Beyond the basic assumptions of logotherapy, an important factor in its compatibility with a theopoetic perspective is that rather than religion being construed as a mask or an obstacle to human flourishing—such as it is within Freudian psychiatry—faith is discussed as "something that spontaneously wells up from inside a person."[61] While logotherapy does not demand a set type of religious belief from those receiving counseling, it suggests that such a thing may well be useful for healthy growth.

Conclusion

Having considered how theopoetics might emerge through the sermon and in pastoral care, it is now important to remember the tension and motion indicative of a theopoetic stance. The danger with too much of a focus on the individual and on singular sites of meaning-making is that articulations of faith will slide toward the solipsistic and shallow. While the role of the pastor or priest is an important one, theopoetics is not only applicable to those who preach and provide pastoral care. Therefore, in the next chapter I consider some of the literature pertaining to the possible influence of theopoetics upon situations in communal settings. How is it that theopoetics might inform our practices of congregational worship? Are there ways in which we can explore the poetic corporately so as to include the community in the formation of the individual? What are ways that we might reframe activism and service to incorporate theopoetic insights? These questions inform the main thrust of the next chapter.

60. Fleming, *The Spiritual Exercises of Saint Ignatius*, 17.
61. Jefford, "An Evaluation," 4.

8

Theopoetics through Worship, Formation, and Service

Church services are poetry from beginning to end; they just are poetry.
... Religion is serious poetry—which is not to say religion cannot be light-
hearted. But at its highest it turns important; and important involvement with
language, use of language for significant human experiences,
merges inevitably into poetry.

—WILLIAM STAFFORD[1]

CONCEIVED OF AS "THE church's response to God's action within
our daily lives,"[2] worship is a ripe opportunity to explore how we
might communally respond in a poetic way to God's action. While simultaneously engaging in sacramental actions and prayers with long,
rich histories, it is nevertheless the case that our time together can be
a place of exploration and new-naming how God is seen and felt to be
moving in the world. Indeed, it may well be that worship is one of the
best places to encounter new ideas, grappling with them not only communally, but temporally and spatially as well.

As determined as theopoetic perspectives might be in affirming the
flesh, actual experiences *in* the flesh are not the same as discussions about

1. Stafford, *You Must Revise Your Life*, 71.
2. Poling, "Poetic Worship," 1.

them. As such, worship provides a chance to explore meaning in ways that are not the same as cognitive exercises, regardless of how poetic and imaginative they might be. In the words of liturgical theologian Richard McCall, "however useful the application of verbal analogies to bodily experience, the body, as the primal experience of space and time through its ability to move and touch, may be said to embody categories which are *a priori* even to language."[3] By entering into a liturgical space we enter into an opportunity to learn anew about God not merely as concept, but as communally-witnessed experience. Especially if a congregation is trying to develop entire services that are more theopoetically oriented, the songs, recitations, prayers, and environment can be developed to deepen experiences that hopefully resonate with the invitation of the sermon as well. Participating in liturgy is a fundamental way in which we can express and explore how we are made in *imago dei*.

> If human beings are made in the image of God, it is our ability to act in time and space and not some state of being which defines that likeness. Or rather, our being-in-time, our becoming, is the only symbol of our being; and it is a real symbol because it reveals the procession of love which is the act symbolized in every moment, every occasion, every event which we name self and world and other.[4]

While McCall does not outrightly deny the possibility that God can be encountered in direct thought, he clearly emphasizes action and the presentation of symbolic namings as a privileged opportunity to do so. It is our ability to respond *to* God that McCall wants focus upon, not our ability to think *about* God.[5] It is precisely from this perspective that Travis Poling has written, "Poetic Worship: The Renewal of Liturgical Language."

Poling works within a framework resonant with McCall, and also with liturgist Don Sailiers, who claims that liturgy is "the poetic fusion of word and act,"[6] allowing for an enacted, embodied exploration of the Christian tradition via physical practices in the church. Where Poling goes further than Sailiers, though, is in asserting that "anywhere that language is used to communicate our conceptualizations of the world

3. McCall, "Liturgical Theopoetic," 401–2.

4. Ibid., 411.

5. The (perceived) tension between contemplation and action is specifically addressed in the next section of this chapter.

6. Saliers, "The Travail of Christian Worship," 187.

we inhabit—the very same world in which God's presence fully dwells—poetry and poetics can find a natural home."[7] Rather than merely an intersection of word and act, Poling understands the poetic to be the native register of liturgy: worship *is* the poetic exploration of God at work.

> Adam, in naming the animals with words, takes part in the creation of the earth. He did not make the creatures themselves, but created their names, one of the primary ways of knowing and identifying them in relationship to the rest of the world. To create through language is one of our highest callings, because at their best, words manifest the mystery of the divine among us. When humans gather to call on and encounter this mystery through poetic imagery and imagination, we are coming together in the act of worship.[8]

One of the consequences of Poling's position is a rethinking of how we conceive of the nature and flow of a church service. Whereas liturgy has often been traditionally taught using a relatively linear model, a theopoetic conceptualization of worship first begins in rethinking *how* we think about liturgy, only moving to develop new liturgy after first "unlearning our symbolic forms."[9] Citing Robert Webber's articulation of the traditional model, Poling says that worship is generally broken into "the four movements of worship: gathering, proclaiming, responding, and sending."[10]

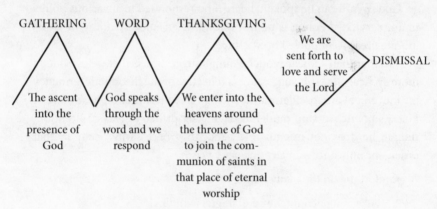

GATHERING WORD THANKSGIVING

The ascent into the presence of God

God speaks through the word and we respond

We enter into the heavens around the throne of God to join the communion of saints in that place of eternal worship

We are sent forth to love and serve the Lord

DISMISSAL

The Four Classical Movements of Worship.

7. Poling, "Poetic Worship," 11.
8. Ibid., 18.
9. Hopper, "The Literary Imagination," 220.
10. Poling, "Poetic Worship," 32.

While Poling agrees that there is value in these categories as a beginning place by which to come to understand how it is that worship functions, he proposes that poetic worship ought first begin with a wholly other model, one "more attentive to the dynamics of language and the presence of God in and for the world."[11] In the development of his liturgical model, one of the main criticisms that emerges is that the design of the traditional model seems to posit that worship is a linear, forward-moving, series of discrete actions that "suggest that we sit quietly and listen while God speaks to us, and when it is our turn to speak, God sits quietly and listens to us. The gathering and dismissal appear to be bookends; we walk in the door, then walk back out. We have heard God and God has heard us, but little else has occurred."[12] In contrast to this, Poling's poetic worship model raises up the reminder that the encounter with the strange Other of God may happen at any point in the designated time of gatherings.

While humans may desire to have God speak at a certain point during an hour, Poling reminds us that God is actually speaking as Poet of the World throughout and *in* the very existence of the service itself. Poetic worship "is not linear or sequential, but more fluid in the ways the four classical movements relate to public worship. For instance, . . . we are gathered not only at the beginning but all throughout worship, and . . . God's Word can be spoken, heard, and responded to at various points in any service."[13] Poling is pointing towards an understanding of God's infinite presence modeled in worship.

Rather than a linear model, Poling's suggestion is that we consider a more cyclical one. This suggestion is reflective of the theopoetic tendency for movement and oscillation rather than fixed terms and phases. I read Poling's poetic worship model as having six primary areas of attention, though he does not intend to say that they necessarily occur in that order—or only once—in any given service.

1. Calling on the many names of God

2. A sacred encounter and dialogue with God

3. A naming of the world anew

4. Seeing the world anew through naming

11. Ibid., 33.
12. Ibid., 34.
13. Ibid., 40.

5. Engaging with the world differently through new sight

6. The discontiguousness of *kairos* (God's time) and *chronos* (clock time)

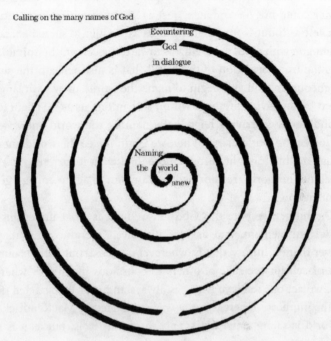

Poling's Movements of Poetic Worship.

Of initial importance for Poling is that the diagram and model exist in a visual state of openness and interconnectedness, a demonstration of "the eternal nature of God's presence," and "the interrelatedness of Creator and creation through God's eternal presence in and for the world."[14] The circular shape of the entire diagram reminds us that public worship need not be viewed as a linear series of events, but that each element (calling, dialogue, naming anew) can take place at various points in the service. We recognize God's presence through the language of the call to worship as much as in the Eucharistic words of institution. Likewise, God can respond to our speaking through the sermon just as well as a closing hymn. And we can rename our world in an offertory invitation just as we can in the benediction. Language brings us into closer relationship with

14. Ibid., 43.

God and the world in many ways. Through poetry and metaphor, we can begin to re-imagine how language moves through worship for the sake of God's reign.[15]

Also important to the diagram is the fact that the inner layer of two half circles face each other such that "without one half of the circle, the other could not be complete," just as "the worshiping community is incomplete without God present with us as we join in sacred encounter and dialogue with God."[16] Moving in toward the center, the spiral "symbolizes the transformation of the world that is just beneath the surface as we encounter God and begin to name the world anew with language renewed by the divine presence within and among us as we begin to live into God's always-arriving reign."[17] By naming the world anew we can begin to see the world anew. When we begin to see the world anew we can imagine that it might become more than what it currently is. When we imagine the world transformed we can plan to act to encourage that transformation.

The human response to God's movement is what underpins sacramental engagement, and as McCall notes, "sacrament can happen wherever there is liturgy, that is, wherever . . . the Trinity brings our acts of loss-of-self for the sake of others to conscious intention—wherever, that is, we act out the love which is always and ever being acted out in us."[18] The implication here is just as was articulated by MacKendrick, that "the world is sacramental not simply insofar as it 'is,' but as it is read; in the voice of praise we not only hear, but echo, in paying attention."[19] Theopoetics encourages the development of a practice of listening, and theopoetic worship would be the communal form of that practice in worship services.

By using his poetic worship model instead of the traditional one, Poling hopes to encourage liturgists to feel freer to explore in a fuller way how it is that communal space and action might be employed to engage with the possibility of God. A theopoetic perspective on liturgy does not deny the possibility of presiding over a service, but it does suggest that the primary action of the leader is an invitational one, not a performative one. In service to this idea, Poling closes his text with an index of

15. Ibid., 45.

16. Ibid.

17. Ibid., 46.

18. McCall, "Liturgical Theopoetic," 413.

19. MacKendrick, "The Hospitality of Listening," 105.

"12 Poetic Practices for Liturgists" to use as they consider how to craft services that inspire and draw people into conversations that begin more conversations rather than closing them down with rigid proclamation. Among his suggestions in that index are "place the psalms at the center of your worship preparation"; "support and encourage poets . . . in your congregation community to . . . compose poems and liturgical prayers and to present them in public worship"; and "hold a workshop with other liturgists, preachers, writers and artists in your congregation and wider church community, [exploring] together the theological and poetic nature of human and divine language."[20] Very concrete, these suggestions, and the others in Poling's contributions, are not radical departures from traditional preparation, however they do suggest some of the ways in which we might practice poetics together in congregational settings.

Throughout Poling's work there is a consistent echo of the idea that theopoetics is a language of resonance, movement, and mutuality, a way to call us all forth toward God as poets and readers of this world *and* to send us back out into the world with new eyes to see how it is that God is ever at work in creation. "God calls us to act as co-creators for the reign of God," writes Poling, "and we respond with words of commitment."[21] This engagement with the tangible actions of worship should then encourage tangible action with the world beyond the church walls as well: drawing the congregation into God's word should simultaneously ask them to bring their experience forward, and point them toward ways in which they can more fully participate in God's action. This is not to say that human action is ultimately what worship is about, but if McCall and Poling are correct, the movement and action of worship certainly are part of coming to know God more fully and to accept more readily that we might live sacramental lives. In Poling's words, "while God is greater than all our human efforts, the work on behalf of God's reign would be significantly different without human communities bound to God through the gift of language and *our participation* in God's re-naming."[22] The human capacity for language and reverence for God informs how we engage with the divine and how that engagement influences our continued participation in God's call in the world. Following this, I now move to consider the consequences of that participation, of communal worship, and of

20. Poling, "Poetic Worship," 87–90.

21. Ibid., 44.

22. Ibid., 45. Emphasis added.

the ways in which our corporate engagement with the Divine can lead toward individual commitment, transformation, and action.

Spiritual Formation and Service

The one who attempts to act and do things for others or for the world without deepening their own self-understanding, freedom, integrity and capacity to love Christ, will not have anything to give others. They will communicate to others nothing but the contagion of their own obsessions, their aggressiveness, their ego-centered ambitions, their delusions about ends and means, their doctrinaire prejudices and ideas . . . .

—THOMAS MERTON[23]

I believe that authentic and lasting changes in the inward landscape of the soul result in observable and concrete changes in outward action. Put in ecclesiastical terms, Christian engagement with sermons, Scripture reading, pastoral care, or worship ought to lead to life being lived differently than it would were it not for those interactions. In this section I want to consider how it is that theopoetics might help to reveal that individual spiritual formation and outward service are two facets of the same kind of discipleship that might be nurtured within a theopoetic sensibility.

Theopoetics offers an understanding that *how* we articulate our expression of the Divine can change *what* we experience, and as such, it can serve as a helpful mediator between inward and outward, between what we see, what we say, and what we do. This section begins by taking up a discussion on the nature of spiritual formation, offering that the development of the Christian imagination is a primary tactic for the encouragement of theopoetically-oriented spiritual formation practices. I then move on to consider how theopoetic social action can be seen as spiritually formational, and close with a brief exploration of the work of Roberto Goizueta, who argues that developing a theopoetic worldview necessitates a grounding in praxis and a tangible engagement with the material world.

Whether it is through Catholic and Ignatian channels, the work of Protestants like Dallas Willard and Richard Foster, or organizations like the United Methodists' The Upper Room, "spiritual formation" has

23. Merton, *Contemplation in a World of Action*, 179.

found its way into many churches and is an area of regular consideration for many pastors. Those concerned with developing spiritual formation programs are those interested in encouraging practices that support the inward life. The Renovaré Institute, Richard Foster's organization for encouraging spiritual disciplines, writes as follows, offering a concise articulation of the work of spiritual formation.

> We are all spiritual beings. We have physical bodies, but our lives are largely driven by an unseen part of us. There is an immaterial center in us that shapes the way we see the world and ourselves, directs the choices we make, and guides our actions. Our spirit is the most important part of who we are. And yet we rarely spend time developing our inner life. That's what Spiritual Formation is all about.[24]

To the extent that formation is about tending to that which "shapes the way we see the world and ourselves," theopoetics is explicitly relevant and applicable in its encouragement of new sight, and "strange" articulation of the type imagined by MacKendrick. Thus, while it is common to see lists of formation practices that include prayer, reading Scripture, fasting, and worship—among others—I want to suggest that the development of a theopoetic approach to spiritual formation will also include work intended to nurture the Christian imagination.

> Imagining is an act of hope, a challenge to fate, an effort to take matters in hand and to accept our unique role as human beings, "in the world but not of it." It is the weaver of culture. . . . To all this there is a frightful corollary. Free to play with the givens, to reject or distort input, at the interface between our senses and ourselves, our imagination has a terrible power over our inner life, over the decisions we make. . . . For the imagination always totters between that Wisdom, which played at the feet of the Creator before the stars sang together, and madness. Educating the imagination is thus of primordial importance.[25]

Just as theopoetics is not about theology done in verse, I am not suggesting that whole congregations begin to pray in couplets—or just imagine going to church. I am instead interested in cultivating that Aristotelian mark of poetic genius: seeing the unfamiliar in the familiar and the familiar in that which is not. Whether through outreach and ministry

24. Renovaré, "What is Spiritual Formation?"
25. Langan, "The Christian Imagination," 65–66.

practices, the art and texts selected for personal reflection, the type of prayer undertaken, or any number of other possible spiritual disciplines, the theopoetic approach will be that which allows for newness and inspiration to inch in, slowly transforming our limited ways and sight. To begin, let us consider how a public witness ministry might be developed theopoetically so as to serve not only as witness, but also as an opportunity to be greeted by the great strange Other of the Holy Spirit and given new sight. Matt Guynn, a Church of the Brethren minister and social activist trainer, is also a scholar of theopoetics, and he has operationalized at least one practice that I think is a useful example of the kind of possibilities available.

Consider a congregation—or a group of members from a congregation—that has decided to participate in a public witness involving protest signs. Regardless of the topic or social stance of the group, Guynn suggests that the theopoetic gesture is to create signs that invite dialogue, a take on Holland's articulation that theopoetics is "writing that inspires more writing." A simple move perhaps, but then again, theopoetics seeks revelation in the theophonies of the everyday as well as the thunderous crash of the veil tearing apart.

> Something concerns me about the widely used yard signs that the Friends Committee for National Legislation has distributed before and during the occupation of Iraq: "WAR IS NOT THE ANSWER." No, it's not the answer—I don't dispute that. But these kinds of statements don't help foment the process of social ferment and imagination. They help people who already have tendencies toward one camp or the other to line up with and against each other. They are a fine way to make one's moral witness. But how can we actually help present an alternative vision, or better yet, engage folks in the process of seeking that vision?
>
> Imagine [instead] signs with questions—genuine, not sarcastic—not answers. Imagine activists who see their role as one of helping societal consciousness to change, and who believe this needs to happen by helping people connect the dots, while resisting the urge to connect the dots for them—which precludes the invitation into engagement.[26]

There are at least two things to note in this small practice that seem to be reflections of a theopoetic stance. First, that the congregants are *not* being asked to back away from their position or deny that they believe

26. Guynn, "Theopoetics and Social Change," 104.

what they believe. They are, however, being asked to consider how they might best invite others into engagement, and not merely parade about a "moral witness." Secondly, there is an acceptance that they cannot "connect the dots" for anyone: that is something that must happen between that person, their reason, prayer, imagination, and God. The theopoetically-inspired activist "wants not just words—but enfleshed initiative. . . . The theopoet change-maker seeks new re-engagements of faith stories. Not only community change, but individual regeneration. And not only individual salvation, but full-bodied wholeness, for the person, the faith community, the neighborhood."[27] Argumentation and proof rarely changes minds where religion and tradition are concerned, but stories, engagement, and the experience of life encountering the Spirit can. In some aspects, a theopoetically-inspired piece of social action may well resemble a practice of spiritual formation.

> Spiritual formation is not a toolkit for "fixing" our culture or our churches or even our individual lives. . . . So we stoutly refuse to engage in formation work to "save America from its moral decline" or to restore churches to their days of past glory or even to rescue folk from their destructive behaviors. No! We do spiritual formation work because it is kingdom work. Spiritual formation work is smack in the center of the map of the kingdom of God.[28]

Spiritual formation and its "stout refusal" to be co-opted into other causes and theopoetics and its invitational stance of hermeneutic humility both skate on thin ice: each can become mere exercises in quietist navel-gazing, unwilling to take a stand. Beautiful, enriching, and well-crafted exercises perhaps, but something less than an encounter with the revelatory and prophetic in-breaking of the kingdom of God. While theopoetics is not about understanding—or mastering—God, it *is* about evoking some sense of the Spirit. That is, "as a form of revelation, theopoetics always points *beyond* itself; by definition, theopoetics points beyond mere aesthetics to a God who is made manifest in life itself."[29] Were it otherwise, and theopoetics was solely focused on doing "justice . . . to the pre-rational in the way we deal with experience,"[30] then it would indeed lose its power to bring vibrancy and "purge Christianity of its own

27. Ibid., 106.
28. Foster, "Spiritual Formation Agenda," 2.
29. Goizueta, "U.S. Hispanic Popular Catholicism as Theopoetics," 266.
30. Wilder, *Theopoetic*, 2.

complacencies."[31] The imagination is to be cultivated both for its own sake *and* for its capacity to allow us to envision a world that has not yet come. Here once again is that resonant libration and oscillation: neither wholly focused on the particulars of expression and experience nor upon rational externalities and utility.

Nurturing our personal spiritual life is done in the context of the world around us: we must search inwardly *and* outwardly, seeking to see more closely what shifts in our inward life are calling us to do in the physical present. Functionally, this is about developing nuanced skills of discernment and perception such that the creative articulation and exploration we do continues to point beyond and not back at ourselves. It is precisely because the "imagination always totters between Wisdom . . . and madness,"[32] that we ought to tend to it, place it in prayer, and explore how it might be used to encounter our seductive God.

Books like Dave Harrity's *Making Manifest* and Troy Bronsink's *Drawn In* are part of a rising tide of artistically inspired texts written for use in spiritual formation, and each contain good examples of activities that might help a person of faith to cultivate "a disposition to receive" what is around us, helping us to articulate what we perceive in new ways. None of these texts necessitate *a priori* faith commitments or academic theological literacy, but instead are full of exercises that can be done individually—or with a congregation—that invite people to discover their own voice and how it reflects God, God's movement, and God's nature. Consider for example, the following reflection exercise from Bronsink's book.

Exercise 13

Before we go on, look at the stuff around you. What is it made of? Is the counter or sofa near you made of wood? If so, do you know what kind of wood? Ash, oak, mahogany? Can you imagine the mountain that held the granite under your feet, or the great tree from which the beams and rafters around you were hewn? How many different textures can you identify around you? Are there coarse as well as supple things nearby? Look around you for something that you regard as holy. Why is it holy? What marks something as holy to you?[33]

31. Ibid., 23.
32. Langan, "The Christian Imagination," 66.
33. Bronsink, *Drawn In*, 68.

Beginning with small noticings of particular sensations and closing with a reflection upon that which is holy, Bronsink is encouraging us to consider how our sense of the divine is inherently bound up in "the stuff around" us. Bound up in, but not equivalent to. Here we do well to remember Catherine Keller's reflection that what is announced by things is not that they *are* God, but that "God is somehow somewhere in this all, every ripple and all, every bite, flight, scramble, or stillness of it."[34] Our task is not to become consumed in the materiality of the world, but to understand that it calls us forth like an icon, asking for our full attention and then thrusting that attention out beyond our recall, granting us a moment of Zylla's disorientation and a chance to recalibrate so that we might more faithfully live with knowledge of the possibility of the in-breaking kingdom of God. Harrity's work in *Making Manifest* suggests a similar approach.

Harrity writes that his book is a "devotional book grounded in the acts of writing, solitude, and community . . . meant to incline your heart and mind toward mystery, wandering, seeking, exploring, and contemplation."[35] It is composed of one month of meditations and writing prompts intended to help cultivate the creative and imaginative in those who work through it. While Harrity is a fine poet himself and the book does serve as a means to practice the craft of writing, he notes that it is equally written to "give you and your faith community the tools you'll need to create art, to live intentionally, and explore the mysteries of your faith through acts of writing."[36] He envisions his book as a kind of catalytic compound meant to help us together come to an awareness of Spirit through creative practices.

> We have the chance, as believers, to grow together in unwavering awareness of the reality of our belief by way of our imaginations. Wisdom, faith, and peace are all acts that reach their fullest potential in community, and as Christians, we'll need those ingredients to rouse and realize the Kingdom of God within and around us.[37]

By opening ourselves up to quiet reflection and God's Spirit, and then *creating* from that space Harrity believes that we participate and

34. Keller, "The Flesh of God," 97.
35. Harrity, *Making Manifest*, 1.
36. Ibid., 3.
37. Ibid., 6.

manifest the movement of God in the world. By inviting others to engage in these practices with us, we engender the possibility that by hearing from one another about how God is manifesting we all come to a greater sense of how we are being called out into the world to serve and to be.

> Move through these pieces—poems, reflections, scriptures, and exercises—day by day, and expect something to change in you. Not because of anything that's been written in the pages by me, but because you're taking time to allow for quiet and creativity in a way that you hadn't before. Writing—much like the Kingdom of God—is a place where nothing is ever wasted, where all time spent is good time.[38]

Harrity asks us to trust in God's presence and our capacity to create language that helps us and others come more fully—even if never completely—into an understanding of God's work in our midst. In creating a space for reflection and the presence of God without trying to press God into a particular agenda, Harrity hopes to invite us into an environment that is both critically engaging and spiritually insightful. Consider the first pairing of reflective poem and writing exercise from the book:

Your Days Are Waiting

There's a sound like certainty a river makes,
the steady way leaves float the surface like paper boats.
Or the noise of hooves throbbing in the light.
There is a waking in the wilderness.

What is inside your mind
that waits to slip away?

Will you remember what it was like to stare
into the constant face of the moon?
To watch the jet stream's hand push the clouds through night?
And stars like ships on the ocean?

Your days are waiting to be left behind.
So tonight, before sleep helps you to forget,
etch in yourself
this moon,
this leaf,
this star.

---

38. Ibid., 7.

[Having read the above poem], take some time to think about the way you see the world—what's it like to live with your uniqueness? It's something we don't often think about. Your hairs are numbered and your being known. So, tell about it. Give some serious thought to what it's like being you.

Are you a glass-half-full or half-empty person? A black-and-white or gray person? Are there times when you only see what you want? Or do you consider yourself a diplomat—seeing the world from many angles? Why?

What do you want to see in the world? What do you hope for? Who has given you your vision? What informs it most? Dig deep.

What is it that you want to say to the world? What do you want your voice to be for?[39]

Note how Harrity's prompt readily lends itself for reflections on a number of traditional, doctrinal themes. Is our hope eschatological? Do we fear the materiality of the world? What do we understand our vocation to be? Who has God called *you* the reader to be? Harrity asks us each to consider these questions as a pastor's sermon might, but then he asks us to *actually answer* his questions. In so doing we may articulate a vision of the world or an articulation of hope we didn't even know we had. And some of those will not mesh well with traditional understandings, but that isn't the point at this stage of things: our task is to enter into the process trusting that our prayerful intentionality and God's grace will meet. Later we may want to talk to a pastor, priest, or theologian about what has come up for us, but if that happens it will be separate from this space which is cleared and open for new sight and language.

Resonant with this model of full attention to world and spirit, seeing them as bound together, theologian Roberto Goizueta suggests that one way to categorize theopoetics is as a mediating method that bridges and works simultaneously in theology, ethics, and aesthetics. Indeed, he writes that theopoetic sensibilities *must* engage each of these registers, or it has failed to live up to its potential.

> Unless a Christian theopoetics is itself grounded in historical praxis, or communal intersubjective action as an end in itself, the imagination, the affect, and their evocative, symbolic, or poetic expressions will not promote such intersubjectivity, but will, instead, serve the equally ahistorical ends of an instrumentalist

39. Ibid., 17.

ethics and a conceptualist theology, which will remain unin-
formed by a now disembodied theopoetics. When—rather than
historical praxis—aesthetic ambiguity, otherness, and "feelings"
become ends in themselves, praxis becomes paralyzed.[40]

For Goizueta it is essential that the particularity of the theopoetic
utterance not obscure its content. For example, he points to the difference between traditional representations of Jesus on the cross in "barrrio
churches" and "Anglo suburban" churches. He writes that the former are
more likely to have "bleeding, contorted images of the Crucified One,"
whereas the latter have more "pleasing images of the resurrected Christ,
with arms gloriously outstretched, superimposed on an all-but-invisible
cross."[41] He suggests that while both might be valid aesthetic choices, it
is the bleeding image that thrusts us out into the world and its suffering,
which we are all too inclined to forget.

While I think there is some truth in his bifurcated split in sanctuary
art choices between Anglo-Protestant and Latino-Catholic congregations, I think that the problem has less to do with direct connections to
racial, social, or class bias, and more to do with the momentum of patterns of thought within traditions. While the differences are represented
starkly by a racial divide, I believe they are present in other places as
well, regardless of race. What is at stake here is the fact that *whenever* we
encounter "an all-but-invisible cross," we are seeing a "Christ [that] is
not a person, but a type. A paradigm, an idea: the theopoetic image has
been displaced by the theological idea."[42] In his pressing insistence upon
the connectedness of the image to actual, historical flesh and context,
Goizueta reveals that his rationale is grounded in a fear for what happens
when theopoetics drifts into "mere aesthetics," and becomes preoccupied
with valorizing individual experience, forgetting that theopoetic movement is always in flux, never resting on the particular *or* the universal,
but pulsing between and through both. With the rise of a shallow—and
false—theopoetics of self-indulgence and solely personal sensation there
is a seizing suspension of movement beyond the self and a numbing
fixation upon silence and inaction. In Goizueta's words, "to absolutize
the preconceptual is to absolutize ambiguity, and absolute ambiguity is

40. Goizueta, "U.S. Hispanic Popular Catholicism as Theopoetics," 265–66.
41. Ibid., 276.
42. Ibid., 277.

the handmaiden of totalitarian domination."[43] He is entirely uneager to place so much emphasis on the pre-linguistic and intuitive that theology loses its capacity to call out and challenge oppression and systems of domination.

Here again is an echo of Keller and her insistence that "if, by either its discursive playfulness or philosophical mysticism, theopoetics dilutes the force of the process counter-orthodoxy, then we should stop now . . ."[44] What is crucial to understand is that whether the issues in sight are contemplation and prayer or action and witness, theopoetics affirms that the one will cyclically lead through to the other and back again. Reflection leads to service and vice versa, never coming to rest in a rigidity toward either direction, but both at once, as if some poetic parallel to the Chalcedonian definition: theopoetic formation as both contemplation *and* action, acknowledged in two natures, inconfusedly, unchangeably, indivisibly, and inseparably.

Flagstones in Fog

There is much to do for those who would help to encourage others to develop the expressive, invitational, hermeneutically humble, and yet nevertheless, socially-engaged stance that comes with theopoetics. This chapter and the previous one have barely scratched the surface of what might be possible, and none of it was even based on congregational experience or qualitative research! Moving forward, it is my hope that some of the tensions and exploratory work around *what* theopoetics is can diminish some, and more attention can be paid to its application and implementation in congregations and worshiping communities from a variety of different Christian traditions.

I believe that each of the approaches addressed in this section is reflective of how theopoetics might manifest itself in concrete practices within the church. Each affirms that the imagination is to be cultivated both for its own sake and for its capacity to allow us to envision a world that has not yet come. There is a resonance and oscillation: neither wholly focused on the particulars of expression and experience nor upon rational externalities and utility. They each show support for a kind of non-discursive theological approach that cannot help but be contextualized

43. Ibid., 266.
44. Keller, "Theopoetics and the Pluri-Verse," 180.

and affirm the legitimacy of individual bodies, experiences, and perspectives. By engendering environments in which space is made for voices to be heard speaking in registers that might not be dominantly normative, these practices help to support the discovery of how varied and polyphonic our faith(s) may be: even within a given community. Finally, none of the practices addressed suggest that the task of theological reflection is ever complete or fixed. To paraphrase Scott Holland, they are practices that invite more practice, conversations that invite more conversation.

My sincere hope is for the recognition that in theopoetics there exists a vision for guiding the development of practices that more fully engage the breadth of human experience in regards to theological discourse and Christian faith. I believe that theopoetics has the potential to be of great service to the church, but if that is to be the case it must overcome its own, painfully ironic and "long addiction to the discursive, the rationalistic, and the prosaic."[45] The intent for the establishment of the theological and academic category termed "theopoetics" has—for the entirety of its brief usage—been about embodiment and liberation. It is well past time that those of us interested in theopoetics make sure we use our time and energy to contribute in ways that honor that intent.

> My plea for a theopoetic means doing more justice to the symbolic and the pre-rational in the way we deal with experience. We should recognize that human nature and human societies are more deeply motivated by images and fabulations than by ideas. . . . This plea therefore means according a greater role to the imagination in all aspects of the religious life. . . . When imagination fails doctrines become ossified, witness and proclamation wooden, doxologies and litanies empty, consolations hollow, and ethics legalistic.[46]

I think that Wilder's plea still has power, calling out to us from 1976 and asking that we encourage the development of the Christian imagination. *My* plea, though, is that we recall that his supplication was for that development to occur in *all* aspects of religious life, not just in texts that academics read to one another at conferences.

That is not to say that all theologians interested in theopoetics must become pastors or church consultants working directly with congregations. However, I do believe that some move must be made such that the

45. Wilder, *Theopoetics*, 2.
46. Ibid., 3.

insights and affirmations of theopoetics are made available to those who are in a position to help concrete practices get developed. This might entail an increase in emphasis on collaborative work with those are not yet aware of theopoetics as a framing vision. For example, Heather Walton and Pam Couture co-chair the Practical Theology and Poetics Working Group of the International Academy of Practical Theology, and they have—as of 2012—explicitly voiced interest in "the way in which writing style interacts with research methodology enabling insights to be drawn from reflexivity, self examination and autoethnography," as well as the "impact of affective, mystical and imaginative approaches" on theology.[47] This suggests that those interested in theopoetics may have something interesting to add to developing conversations in the field of practical theology. Similarly, John Schluep, United Church of Christ pastor and co-director of Warrior's Journey Home, a veteran's healing group, believes that we need the aesthetic to more fully connect to human experiences of healing and grief.

> There are wounds that need to be cleaned that normal types of talking cannot get into. Sometimes the pains that war inflicts on people who were soldiers need a language of poetry to clean them out. . . . Every Wednesday night we have faculty from the Wick Poetry Center [at Kent State] who come to help the [veterans] at Warrior's Journey Home. . . . Poets and artists are needed for their power to allow Spirit to do Spirit's work and leave us with words that heal.[48]

Perhaps Schluep may be interested in how theopoetics might help him frame the healing ministry he is part of. Or perhaps theologians interested in trauma and healing might be interested in the ways in which "normal types of talking cannot get into" some types of wounds. However it is framed, the utility and transformative power of the aesthetic and poetic can serve to help heal, comfort, or critique, and theologians interested in theopoetics may well want to consider how they might generatively serve alongside pastors, filmmakers, poets, and artists of all stripes.

> We must begin to train scholars and interpreters of the text to have an aesthetic formation that prepares them for a controlled application of the creative imagination. Artists and poets have been ahead of us in this matter, and we may need to study more

47. International Academy of Practical Theology, "Practical Theology and Poetics."
48. Schluep, "Personal Interaction."

about how these persons have used their imaginations in disciplined ways. That study could help us to express the truths of the biblical texts in ways that would improve and vivify our own formation.[49]

Whether or not "theopoetics" as a term is used or not is irrelevant if what theopoetics represents isn't finding its way into our streets and sanctuaries or assisting to "vivify the formation" of people of faith. These last two chapters have pointed in the direction of possibilities I hope are nurtured toward such life. Theopoetics has primarily been a word and way of thinking confined to journals and academic texts: it has not yet been explored much in our churches and communities. And yet, in spite of this, I believe we can proceed forward, taking a blind step and hoping that, though we see through a glass but darkly, there will be moments, large and small, wherein theopoetics will be able to blossom forth, serving to usher in moments and experiences that are transformatively Christ-like.

John Woolman was an eighteenth-century, colonial, American itinerant minister in the Religious Society of Friends. He became famous for his widespread travel, and faithfulness in refusing to pay military taxes for war, his witness against the unjust treatment of workers, and as a proclaimed abolitionist as early as 1746. Sometimes referred to as the leading contender for the title of "Quaker Saint,"[50] though his service had enormous positive influence on those around him, and his life seemed to be a beacon by which others might guide themselves, Woolman himself said that his ministry was "like walking into a muddy ground with mist all around, . . . able to see only one flagstone forward at a time." Only when he took the next step "would the next step become clear."[51] I believe that the same is true for future exploration of, and practice with, theopoetics as well. More is to be discovered, and we will only find our way by walking.

---

49. Hoyt, "Interpreting Biblical Scholarship," 38.

50. Cady, *John Woolman: The Mind of the Quaker Saint.*

51. Packard, "Talk to 9th International Conference."

Epilogue

When I came upon the myth of objectivity in certain model thinkers, it made
me angry.... From my own experience I knew very well that it was enough
to take from a man a memory here, an association there, to deprive him of
hearing or sight, for the world to undergo immediate transformation, and for
another world, entirely different but entirely coherent, to be born. Another
world? Not really. The same world rather, but seen from another angle, and
counted in entirely new measures. When this happened, all the hierarchies
they called objective were turned upside down, scattered to the four winds ....

—Jacques Lusseyran[1]

Throughout this text I have regularly referenced the theopoetic
proclivity to approach theological discourse from more-than-slight-
ly off center. In particular, I have lifted up Rubem Alves as an author who
willfully and explicitly subverted the norms of formal theological method
so as to create literary spaces that honor fleshly experience. Thus, it is
with a bit of contrition that I note my own methods in this book are relatively staid: perhaps my prose has at times been more evocative than that
which might appear in the *Journal of the American Academy of Religion*,
but by and large I have trodden a path mostly rooted in formal academic
discourse. I have done this on purpose, hoping to collect the whole of the
history and practice of theopoetics in one place so that it might be com-
pactly available, comprehensible, and advocated for. I desire that *Way to
Water* itself might serve as a path, exposing theopoetic thought to those
who might not otherwise find it relevant or accessible. That being said, I
feel as if I must reveal that for all the ways in which I believe this project

1. Lusseyran, *And There Was Light*, 143–44.

has successfully met those goals, it is still less than complete. Or perhaps it has been *too* complete.

The author of the epigraph that opens this chapter is Jacques Lusseyran, a French resistance fighter within the Buchenwald concentration camp during World War II, a professor of French literature after the war, and blind since an accident when he was eight years old. He writes of his blindness as both a loss and an opening, a deprivation of sight *and* a transformation of the world, so that the myth of utter objectivity was scattered to the winds. In closing, I've framed this epilogue after Lusseyran: it is a conclusion from a new angle, and counted in new measures. It is an ending that has been deprived of any explicit argumentative arc and works instead only with hope and gestures toward the unveiling of a new world waiting to be born. A world, perhaps, in which the river of the water of life flows, bright as crystal.

This closing functions as a series of aphorisms, intended to be taken together as a verbal bricolage, a playing around without playing pretend. These short pieces explore how we see and speak, and I offer them to you as an invitation to more conversation, more writing, and an ever-deepening sense that the possible is a category without end. I hope that they are a way to water.

Radiological Gorillas

In a recent article in *Psychological Science*, scientist Trafton Drew details research in which subjects were asked to look closely at x-ray images of lungs like the one below, searching for white spots that might be cancerous. Some were trained as radiologists and some were untrained, with no affiliation to the medical profession.

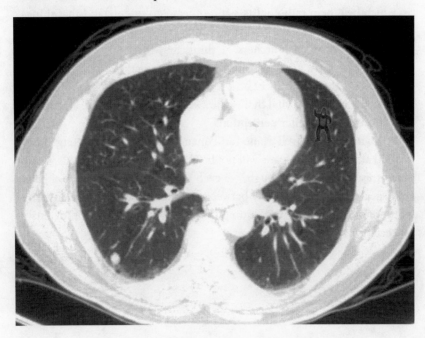

Test Image from "Sustained Inattentional."

While searching for the spots where cancer might be present, people became highly focused on the task at hand. So much so, in fact, that when they were later asked if they had seen the image of a gorilla pasted into the upper right hand quarter, 83 percent had not. The subjects, both trained and untrained, were so attentive to the hunt for possibly cancerous nodules that they cognitively filtered out the gorilla as irrelevant. Physically speaking, they *had* seen the gorilla: eye-tracking devices used during the study revealed that more than 60 percent of those who reported *not* seeing a gorilla had actually let their gaze linger upon the gorilla a statistically longer amount of time than on the rest of the image. They *saw* the gorilla, but they did not *perceive* the gorilla. In other words, our capacity to filter the world around us is so aggressive that it empirically changes what we do and do not see.

Drew, co-author of the study, says that in the wake of this experiment, "we need to think really carefully about the instructions that we give to professional searchers, like radiologists or people looking for terrorist activity. Because what we tell them to look for will in part determine what they see."[2] As he moves forward he is planning additional research in which he'll help radiologists—and others—to understand that things can hide in plain sight.

As "professional searchers," I think that theologians and pastors should take Drew's advice to heart. As the occupations to which many look for guidance in terms of how it is that we are to understand and see God in the world, it is vital that we be aware that the language and advice we disseminate can alter perception.

No matter how well trained and open to seeing the surprising Other of God at work, theologians will not be able to catch all the details. None one of us can. Luckily though, we each possess the means to see, hear, and speak truth, so hopefully between us all we'll be able to catch some glimpse of our gorilla God, hiding there the whole time but previously unseen.

2. Spiegal, "Why Even Radiologists."

Poem for the Poet

You gave me your child.
Have given me your children.
And with such faith and grace . . .

How could you know I would receive them?
That they would be welcomed
into my home and given a place
there by the hearth?

You bid them their leave regardless,
zippering up each in paper coverings
and tending to the ravenous needs of all
until each stood on its own well enough
to reach my ear and whisper to me
your urgent request.

And how audacious you must be
to let them go out into the world
knowing how cold it has been.

Such a great path they have traveled,
and you—you having gone before them
must have come even farther than that.
You must be so tired at times, so worn.

Thank you for your care, for daring
to hope that some would make it.
And so I would have you know this:

One at least has found a home,
has found his way to my door.
And I, having answered, though
it was the dead of the night,
find your invitation irresistible.

Yes.

Yes, I will.

Possible Apocrypha

In the halls of Colgate Rochester Crozer Divinity School it survives as lore that famed "Death-of-God" theologian Bill Hamilton once told a student there that he didn't have the right to proclaim God dead: the student had not worked hard enough on imagining God as being alive to reject the notion. Whether this is apocryphal is aside from the truth of its wisdom.

As wild as the jazz musician Miles Davis got in his later years, when he graduated from high school he went to the remarkably traditional Julliard School of Music, where he studied classical European technique and repertoire. This is also true of Picasso. While many associate him with the Cubism of famous paintings like his "Guernica," his earliest "academic" painting was completed while he was only fifteen years old, and it was unabashedly done in the Old Masters style of Classical Realism. "First Communion" more closely resembles a Rembrandt than what most of us imagine is a Picasso. This reminds us that the work we later see in "Guernica" neither sprang forth fully formed nor came about as result of an inability to portray things in other ways.

The craft of theology is no less demanding than art or music. Indeed, its roots are in an experience of the sort that engenders some of the greatest art known to humanity. And so we should remind ourselves that when we seek to practice it in its mature form, we must realize that there is a body of tradition and technique we would do well to know. It need not trap or deaden our imagination, but to proceed without acknowledging it would be a mark of hubris indeed.

My highest hopes for theopoetics do not involve the end of formal theological education. Rather, they involve the *re-invigoration* and re-direction of theology "proper." A movement toward exploration and new-naming, an encouragement to accept wisdom wherever it arises, and a willingness to admit things might be changing faster than we know how to understand.

For those who have been formally trained in theology, theopoetics is a call to be more attentive to personal experience and the voices of those who have insight but may not have the diction of the discipline fully developed. For those who have not been formally trained, theopoetics is an encouragement, an inciting push to speak, an affirmation that all of God's children may speak a wise word. For all of us, theopoetics is a reminder that God may well be at work all around us, in our words and in the world, in ways which we have never considered before.

Theopoetics accepts that there is a language and diction unique to theological discourse *and* it encourages us to play with that discourse, to ask how it limits us, and to consider what happens when we mix our own paints.

In Response to the Question "Are you a Poet?"

Sometimes I have been asked this.
And,
depending on my mood, the time of day,
or the degree to which I am, at that time,
struggling with my sense of self,
I have offered several responses.

I have said no.
I am not a poet.
How could I be something so frivolous
at a time when rights are being trampled,
children are starving,
and we still haven't figured out to all just get along?

I have said yes.
I am a poet.
How could I not be
at a time when rights are being trampled,
children are starving,
the beauty of the desert has been lost,
and everything deserves to be listened to?

I have said no because I want to write
poems which serve as soil.
Poems which are rich black loam that smells of song,
and hold heavy on the hands,
bearing the weight of possibility
from which might spring forth fountains of flowers
and the heady smell of spring hyacinth
and later, the summersweet.
I say no because I want to write poems like that,
poems that are dark and loved,
poems felt underfoot and walked upon,
poems that hold up houses and the witchhazel's March blooms.
I say no because that is what I want and all I've managed is this.

I have said yes because when I taught middle school English
one of my students used to stay in on Tuesdays
so that we could read together.
And one day I laid out Yeats's "The Second Coming"
so we spent 40 of his 14 year old minutes

wondering what revelation was at hand,
and what rough beast slouched toward Bethlehem to be born.
I say yes because in spite of the pressing weight and darkness
my young friend grew lighter as we read and left me with this:
>   *It's like there is a whole world in there. We just read it over*
>   *and over*
>   *and we could keep reading. I bet there are things in there*
>   *that even you haven't seen.*

He paused then,
and aware of his arriving peers,
the rush of rumor and hallwall hormone returning,
he finished quickly, breathing his words out:
>   *. . . and . . .*
>   *I think everyone could find things . . . but I bet they won't take*
>   *the time.*

When I say yes it is because of him.
Of wanting to find ways to help people to take the time.

I've said yes because I wanted to impress,
because I wanted to get signed on for a reading series,
because I needed to sell a couple chapbooks to break even,
because it always fascinates my storyteller friends,
because I love language and culture and the fact
that if I say "A picture is worth" I know some
of you will finish it for me by saying "_____."
I say yes because I feel it is right and has been for a long time.

I've said no because I worry what people will think,
because I haven't found a publisher to put my poems to page,
because I think that the word is loaded,
because I don't want to get caught up in the technique
when the mystery is profound,
because Mark Twain, that old fool Clemens,
wrote that once he had mastered the language
of the water and had come to know everything
a steamboat captain should know, all the grace,
beauty, and poetry went out of the majestic river.
I've said no because I'm afraid of losing language's majesty
and maybe
just maybe
I'm afraid that beyond such a loss is an introduction
and what I meet there will be too much for me.
I've heard Rilke wouldn't go to his daughter's wedding

because he thought he'd be better off staying home
in case the inspiration for a poem struck.
I say no because of that.

But sometimes I hold off answering so quickly,
one way or the other,
and share something else . . .

I have heard of a poet whose songs can ignite
piled oily garaging rags at thirty paces
so that their garage garbage light
passes through walls and watching faces,
making whole houses transparent with flame.

A poet who can touch the soft wings
of a word-powdered winding-powered
butterfly and still let it fly off,
subtle hints of assonance
and congruence
and all of that academic nonsense-ients,
found so naturally on its flittering path
that the nuts and bolts of the lyrical machine
are ground down
to little sparking jewels instead of ponderous similes
and pompous flow.

I know,
should this poet show soul, baring it all,
bringing full faculties to call
we'd all be knocked over solid,
the force of life funneled into flights
of words so torrential
and profoundly consequential
that we'd be lucky to ever get up again,

so content would we be to let searing solid jabs
of charred history and personal mystery
mix with thick honey words, turning the whole
of the world into an amber hued paradise,
heavy with perfumes and full of lotuses
nodding in agreement, sympathetic pollen tears
dusting everything with exotic saffron
till all of ours skins shine gold.

I've heard of this poet

but we have not yet met.

In response to the question "Are you a poet?"
I sometimes share that.

Ornithological Illustration

Fish-Hawk & Fish-Crow. Alexander Wilson, 1829.

In 1812, the American ornithologist John James Audubon painted a historic image of a bird in flight. It was a whippoorwill. The occasion of this painting is notable because in it Audubon broke with standards of period ornithological illustration. To more "properly" depict the nature and action of the bird in flight in three dimensional space, he used artistic techniques of foreshortening: the nearest parts of the bird were enlarged so that the rest of the form appeared to have depth and go back into the space of the painting. Alexander Wilson, one of the most famous painters of birds prior to Audubon, painted things in a flat perspective such that they could be measured more accurately. Audubon, however, painted to capture movement and aid in their identification in the wild. Because of this foreshortening, accurate measurements could not be taken from the illustration. As a result, his images were not valued as highly, even though they looked more life-like.[3]

I have come to believe that the issue is not so much that speaking of the Divine is impossible, but rather that it is impossible to speak about with objective certainty. At best, theology becomes less relevant the more the theologian employs solely the language of logic. At worst, it can become an exercise of tilting-at-windmills, attempting to enumerate the single way things are, were, and always will be.

3. Bierregaard, "John James Audubon."

Common Osprey, Fish Hawk, John James Audubon, 1840.

Many Christians struggle to find language to articulate their sense of the Divine. There are a variety of reasons why this can be the case; however, the end result is that there are a number of people in contemporary culture who are not fully comfortable with the formal dogmatic positions of their own denomination of origin, and do not feel as if the proposed theology of the tradition matches their experience of God in the world. Unfortunately, people also often feel equally uncomfortable questioning these positions from within the institution. Questioning is often discouraged and literalism and/or adherence to tradition becomes the order of the day. A regrettable consequence of this dynamic is that some choose to remain within their tradition, their own voice silenced, and others choose to leave, only voicing their concerns from without. In both situations, an opportunity for dialogue is missed, and in so missing, another possibility to enrich the conversation of the church has been lost.

Theopoetics is a way of perceiving and expressing so as to more directly articulate how the Divine manifests in human experience of the world. It presumes that there is a Divine source to creativity and creation, and that at times it is more noticed than others. I am not interested in attempting to do away with all of our formal dogmatic positions and traditional practices. That would be impossible! Instead, I am eager to open spaces in which we can honor the infinite-becoming of God, accept that our words are shallow reflections of God's Word, and ask how we might better pronounce our praises and laments.

Audubon did not seek to end the production of images from which measurements could be taken, *and* he knew that he could offer something more.

Parallel Lines Intersect

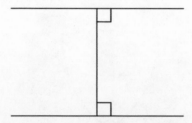

Two Parallel Lines. Wikimedia Commons.

If you ever studied geometry you were most likely taught that at least part of the definition of what "parallel" means includes the fact that, even as they extend into infinity, two parallel lines will never touch. For centuries this was accepted as an absolute and eternal *a priori* truth of mathematics and reality. In the early part of the nineteenth century, however, a number of people began to publish work that threatened the stability of this cornerstone premise.

What was being explored was the possibility of a type of geometry that did not presume to work upon a flat plane. Whereas geometric proofs had for centuries taken it for granted that the shapes being investigated only existed in—and on—two dimensions, by the mid-1800s, geometries of irregular, or non-Euclidean, surfaces were being considered. These explorations led, among other things, to the previously ludicrous statement that parallel lines could intersect. To see how this is possible, first look at the diagram above and imagine that the lines go off the edges of this page forever to the left and right. Because those two lines are both perpendicular to the same third line it means they will never touch. Or, at least, it *used* to mean that.

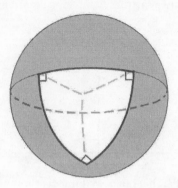

Triangle with Three Right Angles on Sphere. L. Callid Keefe-Perry, 2013.

What mathematicians were beginning to articulate was the possibility that we could begin to think of lines that were not on flat planes. Consider the sphere in this illustration. Note that it has a triangle drawn onto its surface with a very unusual quality: all three of its angles are 90°! Try and imagine those lines represented without first knowing that they were drawn on a sphere.

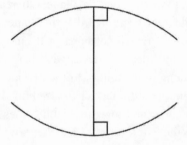

Two Parallel Lines on a Non-Euclidean Surface. Wikimedia Commons.

Now, consider that I had shown you the image at the on this page first, saying that they were parallel lines. You would have been well within reason to say, "No they're not. They're not even straight lines!"—and yet they *are* lines, just lines drawn upon a surface that is not flat, that is not the way in which we are accustomed to geometry being represented. As a result of this non-standard, elliptic geometry, we have a situation where it is accurate to say that parallel lines "curve toward" each other and intersect.

Sometime around 1830, the Hungarian mathematician János Bolyai published a treatise on this type of geometry, writing in his conclusion that "it is not possible to decide through mathematical reasoning alone if the geometry of the physical universe is Euclidean or non-Euclidean; it is a task for the physical sciences."[4] I want to say the same: it is not possible to decide through theology alone what the nature of God is; that is a task for thinking, for feeling, for talking about over hot coffee at a well-worn kitchen table, for considering in the moments before dreams catch our children after we've sung them to sleep.

"Ludicrous" statements like "parallel lines can intersect" become more sensible once we understand they come from a context foreign to our usual assumptions. Theopoetics asks what theology might sound like if it was done in three dimensions, not just on a flat plane.

---

4. Faber, *Foundations of Euclidean and Non-Euclidean Geometry*, 162.

Naming a Stream

for Nahar Nadi

They entered from the East and they came
with strength and Baptism on their breath.
Where property could not be claimed outright,
control was exerted by more subtle means:

    Muhhekunnetuk was unceremoniously stripped,
    generations of knowledge and name peeled off
    to be replaced by a new one: Hudson.

And while sensitive culturalists may grimace,
quite clear in their conviction of the crime,
it should be said that the river never voiced
a word of complaint on her own behalf,
bearing the new sounds back out to ocean
—same as the old, same as the older—
to slip into mixing there with deeper seas.

Likewise, Lord Krishna, in a verse of the Gita,
tells Arjuna that it is better to walk down the path
of your own life, struggling, than to set one step
on another's road, no matter how clear their way
seems to be:
            ours is to follow the route cut out
for us, unconcerned with the diversions provided
by other eager hands and lulling voices.

Considering then, my daughter's impending birth
and attempts to come upon precisely the right name,
I find myself poorly-suited to the task. Perhaps
we'll settle certainly and choose to call her Corinne,
condemning her to that life when in truth
she was meant to be someone else.

Who did they think they were? Who are we?
What we see as stream is gone after a glance,
slipping out to wider waters even as we think
to mark it on our maps.

Our true names carve into the earth: each day sites
are lifted away by rain and its restless wander and return.
Soil shaped while every instant it adds aspirations

and syllabants to stone until a day when, with an empty bed,
we can walk out, and up,
straight to the source.

Auto-Ionizing Water

For Christians who understand God to have been enfleshed in the person of Jesus of Nazareth, there exists a clarion call not only to discipleship, but to a model of God that is grounded in the spiritual and physical realities of this world. A world that is not philosophically divided into spirit and matter, but that is both in simultaneity. God's expression is—and has been—in the particulars of situations, communities, and collective sorrows and joy. And does articulating God by means of our human experience bring about its own challenges?

Absolutely. But what other choice is there? It is only through our brokenness and human sense that we experience anything. The acknowledgement that, in fact, our experience heavily influences discussions on the nature of God, opens up the possibilities of theological discourse. When this is accepted, theology moves from a scientistic discipline of proof and proposition toward a passionate exploration of how God is seen to be ever-renewing all that is, in our lives, our homes, communities, and all across this wounded world. In other words, a God out of context is not much God at all: it is a poor sort of articulation of God that is so far removed from life that it does not have bearing upon human actions and understanding.

If our explication of the nature of the Divine somehow places God fully beyond human access, then God becomes available only beyond humanity. If, conversely, it is the case that God's presence is at least somewhat experiential, then our models and articulations of the Divine ought to provide for this to be the case.

What we know of God is contextual, personal, and ever capable of change. As we study theology we immerse ourselves in a living stream of interpretive tradition. We study not a series of facts about God, but a series of interpretations and articulations developed by certain people at certain times in certain places. Human notions of God are ever-changing, even if God is not. So how then are we to understand our role as theologians? What is our task if we know that we too are grounded in our own context and can't get out of it to articulate God in a way that is fully and factually complete? I have an answer that I'll offer via analogy, of all things, to chemistry.

Asked what H_2O is, most people will answer water. They are correct, and there is more to the story than their response. Formed the other way around, "H$_2$O" as an answer to the question "What is water?" is not wholly correct.

$$2H_2O \qquad\qquad H_3O^+ \quad OH^-$$

Diagram of Water Auto-Ionizing. Wikimedia Commons.

Imagine two molecules of water, each with two atoms of hydrogen associated to a larger atom of oxygen. What we have discovered is that even in a container of "pure" water, the reality is that a collection of H$_2$O molecules do not remain simply a collection of H$_2$Os. Instead, they begin to interact with one another, resulting in one of the two oxygen atoms taking a hydrogen atom from the other, an event that chemists notate as 2 H$_2$O <—> H$_3$O$^+$ + OH$^-$ and refer to as the "self-ionization" of water. Even though water is H$_2$O, that is, two hydrogen atoms and one oxygen atom, water does not ever actually exist in a pure H2O form. Some portion of any water sample is constantly in a state of transition and relation, an oscillation in process between H$_2$O, H$_3$O$^+$, and OH$^-$.

So too is God: somewhere between transcendent and immanent; personal and eternal; and any number of other poles. By extension then, our task as theologians is not to name God as a fixed God that is and always will be, but to describe God in a such a way that it evokes some of the Divine nature as it is in the process of becoming something other than what we have named it.

This is not to say that God is becoming something ungodlike any more than it is to say that water is not water-like simply because we always thought it was "just H$_2$O." The function of our theology is to provide a sketch of how it is that God is at some middle point of becoming something more than we thought it was, but not so far afield that it is unrecognizable. Two molecules of water do not self-ionize into wombats: they stay water-related, just further from the idea of "pure" water than we first thought. There is a sense of continuity between H$_3$O$^+$ and OH$^-$ such that it makes sense to call a mixture of those things H$_2$O, even though what we have discovered challenges our sense of what exactly that wet stuff is. The study of theology should do this as well: push us beyond that which we had previously contemplated, enabling us to better name God in our context for our people in our place and time.

Understanding and/or relating to some aspect of the Divine does not entail understanding and/or relating to the entirety of God. If you ask my wife if she knows me, she is sure to say yes, and you would think nothing of it. Of course she knows me. And yet there are thoughts I think, things I see, and stories I have heard that she has no knowledge of. That doesn't mean she does not know me: it means than I am more than that which she knows. I see no reason why this should not be the case with God as well. We articulate God's qualities—and the nature of God's action—not to limit or ascribe finitude to that which we know is profound and immense, but as an offering and invitation to others that they might respond in kind, lending their voices to a conversation that is both the echo of ancient words and the renewal of current hope.

As we scientifically name water as H_2O because that is the state in between its two poles of existence, so too can we conceive of God. It's just that while water "self-ionizes" into two distinct parts, each of which is qualitatively identifiable, quantifiable, and fixed, God seems to be formed of more parts than we can name. Yes Father, yes Son, yes Holy Spirit, and yes Midwife and Shekhinah; also Alpha and Omega; Love and Light; and Living Water and Word. Yes, yes, and infinite-becoming yes.

Why theology? Because as people of faith and Christian leaders, lay and ordained, part of our work entails leading, and while we may have some vision of what we want to end up with, knowing how to get there—and how people have tried to get there before—certainly helps that effort. Put another way, a map isn't useful for getting you from "here" to "there" if you don't know where "here" is. Theology is the study of human reflection on God and it is our "here." How we go forward will be up to us, and theopoetics is a way that honors embodied experience, expects exploratory articulations of the Divine, and acknowledges that God can be perceived to be at work in unexpected ways all throughout this broken and joy-filled world.

Finding Thomas

For one summer after graduating college I spent occasional evenings at a local coffee shop performing walk-around magic, moving from table to table, when I caught someone's eye who looked like they might be interested. I mostly did card work and coin sleights, but every once in a while, if it felt like a table was on board, I would do some mentalism, or "mindreading." I worked for tips, having barely convinced the night manager it was worth having me around in the first place. I'd been performing as a magician publicly since my younger sister's eighth birthday party when I was twelve, and for various reasons that summer really needed to feel like magic was possible again.

After a few weeks of some of the most magic-dense days of my life I stopped performing there and ended up moving from that city shortly thereafter. Six months later I hadn't been practicing much and I distinctly remember the feeling one night when I did some minor disappearance for friends at some party: my hands themselves felt off. The illusion worked, the Queen vanished, and people were pleased, but *I* felt sloppy and uncommitted doing it. A microsecond here . . . a tiny bit less precision there . . . nothing that mattered to those who I was trying to entertain, but enough for me to be displeased with my own skills. And that was a breaking for me. I couldn't enjoy the excitement of a crowd caught up in the impossibility of matter disobeying the rules of the world when I knew the hands that helped that illusion take place were not up to snuff. I was distracted and worried that I'd botch something or let out a flash or clink, and in that slip or sound the whole illusion would come down for us all. That night was the last time I can remember doing any magic for a crowd.

Some days I regret it. I've spent hundreds of hours—probably thousands—practicing a very particular set of minute skills, movements, and mindsets and I will never get those minutes back. Sometimes when I'm playing cards with friends I feel the impulse to try something—mostly for the joy of trying—but I imagine I'll just disappoint myself. Oh sure, sometimes if I'm fiddling with a pack of cards by myself I play around, but performing for other people lost its joy. Until my daughter was born.

Now more than three, she has just begun to be able to possess a feeling of awe when something that clearly cannot happen happens regardless. I've begun to disappear things now and then and she's found that the empty air is capable of producing a number of objects. . . . What is interesting is that as far as I can tell she doesn't particularly associate the magic with me: it is something that is happening in the world and she assumes it is as amazing to me as it is to her. Maybe it is. There's a particular kind of joy in watching her gasp and laugh as she closes her hands on nothing only to open them to find bits of candy and families of foam rabbits.

I had about a month of this joy with her when something changed.

One January evening we were playing with her trains when one of them disappeared after I ran my hand over it. She laughed, squealing "Where did it go, Papa!?!," and began to charge around the room to see which chair or couch had snatched away her toy. And then she stopped. In a moment of inspiration she turned to me triumphantly and said "I know! I'll just *make* it come back!" Setting herself down deliberately she flourished her hands magically . . . and—in what I thought was a moment of paternal genius—the train appeared in my hands *exactly* as she finished her arcane, toddler gesticulation.

It was then she began to cry.

She hadn't seen the train reappear. "Papa . . ." she sobbed, "my magic doesn't work right . . ." I showed her that the train had reappeared but she wasn't interested. . . . She gestured again, and again whatever it was that she envisioned happening didn't happen.

"Sweetie," I said, "look here and see my hands. The train's right here."

My attempts to calm her failed as she built up to a shriek. "But it's not doing what I *want!!!*" As her tears and volume grew, all attempts to soothe her were worthless until my wife came in from the other room to see what damage I had done. As she walked past me I told her that our daughter had just discovered magic isn't real.

But that isn't quite right. It isn't that magic isn't real. It's that magic was never supposed to be the point in the first place: awe was. Awe, and the laugh that erupts when the impossible takes place right in front of you. In your own hands. It's about knowing it is impossible, and feeling it there in front of you regardless.

And so when Nahar is older—perhaps when she is grown—I'm going to tell her this story and then together we'll see if we can't find Thomas . . .

Bird Shadows

My God is the god in the next room,
cooking unseen feasts and humming;

the ache of the moment before the rain
when you're sure the whole June
cloud is ready to burst through
though you haven't felt a single drop;

the photographer's ironic smile
after her darkroom discovery
that in the background of a misfire
she has captured two lovers gazing
longingly at each other's meals;

the dandelion blade that insists
adamantly that it must reside directly
in the middle of your neighbor's
suburban blacktopped driveway;

the sight of the shadow of a bird flitting
by the sill near the bed of an aging Grace,
who can no longer move but counts herself
lucky because at least she can still see.

This is my God:

    expectant and grinning,
    wild and impossibly near.

Appendix of Definitions

Thomas Dailey

As a method of interpretation, theopoetics seeks to articulate the spiritual meaning that comes to us in, by, and through a symbolic experience. It affirms the transcendent significance of inspired texts or religious objects, and attempts to recognize that which God manifests to us in our encounter with the sacred symbol. As a form of religious thinking, theopoetics asserts the primacy of "invention" and "imaginative construction"; it is particularly appropriate for considering the experience of ritual and worship.[1]

Roland Faber

One moves into an "undefined land" in which one experiences differently, begins to think differently, and is encouraged nor just to adopt to, but to create new theological language.

Today, I think that not only can we not control this field or region in fact, but that it is of the essence of process theology to be an uncontrollable undertaking in the infinite adventure of God-talk, and consciously so, in modes that I came to name "theopoetics."[2]

Jeff Gundy

Theopoetics sort of exists in this gap between the spiritual and the religious. It has to do with the effort to articulate what it means to seek God in the present tense, in the hazardous and precious medium of language, informed by what has come before, but not bound to formulas and doctrines.[3]

1. Dailey, "Eucharist and the Theopoetics of Encounter," 3.
2. Faber, "Process Theology as Theopoetics."
3. Gundy, "Lecture: Songs from an Empty Cage."

Matt Guynn

[T]heopoetics, opens up a space for unanticipated dreaming in which the past, present, and future are re-shaped as we reorganize and even re-create our own stories and our relationships with others, the world, and the Divine. . . . [It] is a style of writing or a theological stance, an artful way of working with language and worldview. The theo-poet uses the occasion of the poem to creatively suggest, ambiguously hint, generously intimate in ways that create space for the reader or the public to face the unknown, engage Mystery, to dream and be transformed.[4]

Scott Holland

Good theology is a kind of transgression, a kind of excess, a kind of gift. It is not a smooth systematics, a dogmatics, or a metaphysics; as a theo-poetics it is a kind of writing. It is a kind of writing that invites more writing. Its narratives lead to other narratives, its metaphors encourages new metaphors, its confessions more confessions . . .[5]

Stanley Hopper

Theology tends to develop talk about God logically, where the logos is constrained within the model of Aristotelian propositional thinking; whereas theopoetics stresses the poem dimension, the creativity of God, his is-ness, if you wish to theologize it, so that I must move within his own creative nature and must construe him creatively, so that I would become co-creator with God, if you must speak theologically. If I am go-ing to talk about God, I must recognize this mythopoetic, metaphorical nature of the language I use.[6]

What . . . theopoiesis does is to effect disclosure [of Being] through the crucial nexus of event, thereby making the crux of knowing, both morally and aesthetically, radically decisive in time. . . . [Like Rilke] . . . we must learn, with trust, to be one with, a breathing with the inhale and exhale of Being, in order that "the god" may breathe through us, and we, through the translation of its breath into song, may be . . . the eyes of becoming and a tongue for Being's utterance.[7]

4. Guynn, "Theopoetics: That the Dead," 99.
5. Holland, *How do Stories Save Us?* 37.
6. Miller, "Stanley Hopper and Mythopoetics," 6.
7. Hopper, "Introduction," xix–xxi.

L. Callid Keefe-Perry

[Theopoetics is] an acceptance of cognitive uncertainty regarding the Divine, an unwillingness to attempt to unduly banish that uncertainty, and an emphasis on action and creative articulation regardless. It also suggests that when the dust has settled after things have been said and done in the name of God, the reflection and interpretation to be done ought to be grounded in dialogue and enacted with a hermeneutic of hospitality and humility, an acceptance of cognitive uncertainty regarding the Divine, an unwillingness to attempt to unduly banish that uncertainty . . .

Catherine Keller

There are four theopoetic oscillations or themes:

1. Theopoetics is not theology-as-usual nor is it "not theology." It rhythmically destabilizes the certainties of traditional theological inquiry

2. God-talk is mindful of its own edge, e.g., the unspeakable vs. the word, or between silence and language itself. Process theopoetics is the steady work of auto-deconstruction: the critique of abstractions in order to keep discourse vibrant and relevant.

3. This discourse occurs in a space between theopoetics and theopolitics. Poiesis is the making of something that previously did not exist, a creative practice. It is an action, a poem.

4. Theopoetics is not just involved with theology-as-method, but also with the Logos of Scripture. There is a multiplicity of oscillations waiting to be unleashed. Theopoetics is in one sense polyphilia: the love of and for multiplicity.[8]

Richard D. McCall

Theo-poetic would be a way of doing theology that would derive not only from the content but also from the structure of liturgy as act, work (*ergon*), event. The question which would need to be asked is: What sort of God is one who is active in these events? This, in turn, begs the anthropological

---

8. Hubert and Slettom, "Poetics, Post-Structuralism, and Process," 9.

question: Who are we who engage in such activities, who thus enact our relatedness to each other and to the One we call God?[9]

Sandra Schneiders

To begin with, we need to recognize that the discourse about "theopoetics" in general and particularly in relation to the interpretation of Scripture is a quite recent development arising at the intersection of theology and literary studies much like "biblical spirituality," which arises at the intersection of biblical studies and spirituality. The interactive meeting ground of literary biblical studies, theology, and spirituality is precisely theopoetics or a theory of the spiritually transformative power of biblical texts as texts, actualized through a certain kind of reading or interpretation. . . . It would probably be accurate to say that theopoetics is the literary or textual face of the wider concern with theological aesthetics as an approach to spirituality.[10]

J. Denny Weaver

A non-poet's definition of theopoetics might be that it is a hybrid of poetry and theology. But to call it that misses the mark. It is an entire way of thinking. From the side of poetry, it shows that ideas are more than abstractions. They have form—verbal, visual, sensual—and are thus experienced as least as much as they are thought. . . . What one learns from the theology side of theopoetics has at least as much importance. One observes that theology is more than an abstraction. It is a way of thinking, visualizing, and sensing images of God. And at that juncture, theologians should become aware that traditional theology . . . is a way to think about the divine but is only one of multiple ways to consider God. Thus for theologians, theopoetics will underscore their (sometimes reluctant) admission that theology is one form of truth but ought not be confused with TRUTH itself.[11]

9. McCall, "Liturgical Theopoetic," 402.
10. Schneiders, "Biblical Spirituality," 145.
11. Weaver, "Series Editor's Forward," 13.

Bibliography

Altizer, Thomas. *The Call to Radical Theology*. Albany, NY: State University of New York Press, 2012.

—. *Living the Death of God: A Theological Memoir*. Albany, NY: State University of New York Press, 2006.

—. "Review of Tomorrow's Child: Imagination, Creativity, and the Rebirth of Culture." *Journal of the American Academy of Religion* 42.2, (1974) 376–78.

Altizer, Thomas, and William Hamilton. *Radical Theology and The Death of God*. New York: Bobs–Merrill, 1966.

Alves, Rubem. *The Poet, The Warrior, The Prophet*. Philadelphia: Trinity, 1990.

—. "Theopoetics: Longing and Liberation." In *Struggles for Solidarity: Liberation Theologies in Tension*, edited by Lorine M. Getz and Ruy O. Costa, 159–71. Minneapolis: Fortress, 1992.

Bakhtin, M. M. *The Dialogic Imagination: Four Essays*. Austin, TX: University of Texas Press, 1981.

Balthasar, Hans Urs von. *Epilogue*. San Francisco: Ignatius, 2004.

—. *Explorations in Theology Vol. 1*. San Francisco: Ignatius, 1989.

Barnes, M. Craig. *The Pastor as Minor Poet: Texts and Subtexts in the Ministerial Life*. Grand Rapids: Eerdmans, 2009

Barth, Karl. "The Strange New World within the Bible." In *The Word of God and the Word of Man*, translated by Douglas Horton, 28–50. New York: Harper and Row, 1957.

Beardslee, William. "Amos Niven Wilder: Poet and Scholar." *Semeia* 12 (1978) 1–14.

Bierregaard, Richard O. "John James Audubon—A Bird's-eye View." The Department of Biology, University of North Carolina at Charlotte. Online: http://www.bioweb. uncc.edu/bierregaard/audubon.html. Accessed 8/24/2009.

Boer, Tjeerd de. *Hoe zullen wij over God spreken?: de poëtische theologie van het alledaagse van Rubem Alves*. MA Thesis. Proefschrift Vrije Universiteit Amsterdam, 2010.

Borchert, Gerald L. "Demythologization." In *Evangelical Dictionary of Theology*, edited by Walter Elwell, 334. Grand Rapids: Baker Academic, 2001.

Bent, Charles N. *The Death of God Movement*. New York: Paulist Press, 1967.

Bronsink, Troy. *Drawn In: A Creative Process for Artists, Activists and Jesus Followers*. Brewster, MA: Paraclete, 2013.

Brueggemann, Walter. *The Prophetic Imagination*. Minneapolis, MN: Augsburg Fortress, 2001.

Bruner, Jerome. "The Narrative Construction of Reality." *Critical Inquiry* 18.1 (1991) 1–21.

Cady, Edwin. *John Woolman: The Mind of the Quaker Saint*. New York: Washington Square, 1966.

Caeiro, Alberto. "The Essential." Translated by Rubem Alves. In *Transparencies of Eternity*, 28. Miami, FL: Convivium, 2010.

Cervantes-Ortiz, Leopoldo. *Teología ludo-erótica-poética de Rubem Alves*. Quito, Ecuador: Consejo Latinoamericano de Iglesias, 2003.

Conklin, William. Personal Correspondence. 11/1/2012. Email.

Crossan, John. *A Fragile Gift: The Work of Amos Niven Wilder*. Ann Arbor, MI: Scholars, 1981.

Capps, Donald. *The Poet's Gift: Toward the Renewal of Pastoral Care*. Louisville: Westminster/Knox, 1993.

Caputo, John. *Against Ethics: Contributions to a Poetics of Obligation with Constant Reference to Deconstruction*. Bloomington, IN: Indiana University Press, 1993.

———. "Jacques Derrida (1930–2004)." *Journal for Cultural and Religious Theory* 6.1 (2004) 6–9.

———. *Philosophy and Theology*. Nashville, TN: Abingdon, 2006.

———. *What Would Jesus Deconstruct?* Grand Rapids: Baker Academic, 2007.

———. *The Weakness of God: A Theology of the Event*. Indianapolis: Indiana University Press. 2006.

———. *The Insistence of God: A Theology of Perhaps*. Indianapolis: Indiana University Press. 2013.

Caputo, John, and Catherine Keller. "THEOPOETIC / THEOPOLITIC." *Cross Currents* 56.1 (2006–7) 105–11.

Carroll, Lewis. ""Poeta Fit, Non Nascitur." In *The Illustrated Lewis Carroll Collection*, 754–58. Oxford: Benediction Classics, 2009.

Chopp, Rebecca. "Reimagining Public Discourse." In *Black Faith and Public Talk: Critical Essays on James H. Cone's Black Theology and Black Power*, edited by Dwight N. Hopkins, 150–66. Maryknoll, NY: Orbis, 1999.

———. "Theology and the Poetics of Testimony." *Criterion* 37.1 (1998) 1–12.

Cohen, Leonard. "Anthem." From *The Future*. SBME Special Markets, B0012GMVDK, CD, 1992.

Dailey, Thomas F. "Eucharist & the Theopoetics of Encounter according to St. Francis de Sales." In *Human Encounter in the Salesian Tradition*, edited by Joseph Chorpenning, 63–76. Rome: International Commission on Salesian Studies, 2007.

Deleuze, Gilles. *Anti-Oedipus*. London: Continuum, 2004.

Derrida, Jacques. "Circumfession." In *Jacques Derrida*, edited by Geoffrey Bennington and Jacques Derrida, 3–315. Chicago: University of Chicago Press, 1993.

———. "Interview with Jean–Louis Houdebine and Guy Scarpetta." In *Positions*, 37–96. Chicago: University of Chicago Press, 1981.

———. "Interview with Julia Kristeva." In *Positions*, 15–36. Chicago: University of Chicago Press, 1981.

———. *On the Name*. Translated by David Wood. Stanford, CA: Stanford University Press, 1993.

———. *Positions*. Chicago: University of Chicago Press, 1982.

Drew, Trafton, Melissa Võ, and Jeremy Wolfe. "The Invisible Gorilla Strikes Again: Sustained Inattentional Blindness in Expert Observers." *Psychological Science* 24.9 (2013) 1848–53.

Eliot, T. S. "The Social Function of Poetry." In *On Poetry and Poets*, 3–16. New York: Farrar, Straus, and Giroux, 1957.

Ellor, James. "Bridging Psychology and Theology When Counseling Older Adults." In *Viktor Frankl's Contribution to Spirituality and Aging*, edited by Melvin Kimble, 87–102. New York: Haworth Pastoral, 2000.

Encyclopedia of World Biography. "Amos Niven Wilder." In Encyclopedia of World Biography. Thomson Gale, a part of the Thomson Corporation. 2006. Online: http://www.answers.com/topic/amos-niven-wilder. Accessed 12/9/2012.

Epperly, Bruce. "Process Theology and Lived Omnipresence: An Essay in Practical Theology." Lecture given at Claremont School of Theology at the Center for Process Studies. Online: http://www.ctr4process.org/publications/SeminarPapers/29_2%20Epperly.pdf. Accessed on 7/25/2006.

Faber, Richard L. *Foundations of Euclidean and Non-Euclidean Geometry*. New York: Dekker, 1983.

Faber, Roland. *God as Poet of the World: Exploring Process Theologies*. Louisville: WJK, 2008.

———. "Process Theology as Theopoetics." Lecture at Kresge Chapel, Claremont School of Theology, February 7, 2006

Faber, Roland, and Jeremy Fackenthal, eds. *Theopoetic Folds: Philosophizing Multifariousness*. New York, Fordham University Press, 2013.

Feuerbach, Ludwig. *The Essence of Christianity*. Translated by George Eliot. New York: Digireads.com, 2012.

Fish, Stanley, *Is There a Text in This Class? The Authority of Interpretive Communities*. Cambridge: Harvard University Press, 1980.

Fleming, David. *The Spiritual Exercises of Saint Ignatius: A Literal Translation and a Contemporary Reading*. Saint Louis, MO: Institute of Jesuit Sources, 1978.

Foster, Richard. "Spiritual Formation Agenda: Three Priorities for the Next 30 Years." *Christianity Today*, 4 Feb 2009. Online: http://www.christianitytoday.com/ct/2009/january/26.29.html. Accessed 2/20/2013.

Frame, John. "Death of God Theology." In *New Dictionary of Theology*, edited by David F. Wright and Sinclair B. Ferguson, 188–89. Downers Grove, IL: InterVarsity Academic, 1988.

Frankl, Viktor. *Man's Search For Meaning*. New York: Washingtion Square, 1984.

Gadamer, Hans-Georg. *Truth and Method*. London: Sheed and Ward, 1975.

George, Archimandrite. *Theosis: The True Purpose of Human Life*. Mount Athos, Greece: Holy Monastery of St. Gregorios, 2006.

Goizueta, Roberto. "U.S. Hispanic Popular Catholicism as Theopoetics." In *Hispanic/Latino Theology: Challenge and Promise*, edited by Ada María Isasi-Díaz, 261–88. Minneapolis: Fortress, 1996.

Gundy, Jeffrey. "Songs from an Empty Cage: Some Notes on Theopoetics." Lecture at Hillsdale College 2/13/12. In John Rasche's "Gundy speaks at Hillsdale College." Online: http://www.hillsdale.net/article/20120216/NEWS/302169939.

Guynn, Matthew. "Theopoetics and Social Change." *Cross Currents* 60.1 (2010) 105–14.

———. "Theopoetics: That the Dead May Become Gardeners Again." *Cross Currents* 56.1 (2006) 98–109.

Harrity, Dave. *Making Manifest: On Faith, Creativity, and the Kingdom at Hand*. Wilmore, KY: Seedbed, 2013.

Heidegger, Martin. *The Piety of Thinking: Essays by Martin Heidegger.* Translated by James G. Hart and John C. Maraldo. Bloomington, IN: Indiana University Press, 1976.

――――. *Poetry, Language, Thought.* Translated by Albert Hofstadter. New York: Perennial Classics, 2001.

Hemming, Laurence P. "Are We Still in Time to Know God?" In *Religious Experience and Contemporary Theological Epistemology*, edited by Boeve De Maeseneer and Van den Bossche, 159–76. Louvain, Belgium: Peeters, 2005.

Hocking, Jeffery. "Risking Idolatry? Theopoetics and the Promise of Embodiment." *THEOPOETICS*, 1.1 (2014) 125–54.

Holland, Scott. "The Anabaptist's Will, The Pietist's Heart and The Lover's Gaze." *Brethren Life and Thought*, April 2012. Online: http://www.brethrenlifeandthought. org/2012/04/10/the-anabaptists-will-the-pietists-heart-the-lovers-gaze/.

――――. "Damn the Absolute! Or Why We Still Need William James." Lecture. Leuven Encounters in Systematic Theology VII: To Discern Creation in a Scattering World, 10/29/2009.

――――. "Editorial." *Cross Currents* 56.4 (2007) 4–5.

――――. "Foreword." In *Songs from an Empty Cage: Poetry, Mystery, Anabaptism, and Peace*, by Jeffrey Gene Gundy, 11–12. Telford, PA: Cascadia, 2013.

――――. *How Do Stories Save Us?* Grand Rapids: Eerdmans, 2006.

――――. "Theology Is a Kind of Writing: The Emergence of Theopoetics." *Cross Currents* 47.3 (1997) 317–31.

Hopper, Stanley. Interview. Dan Noel interviewing at Drew University, 1977. Online: http://www.sarcc.org/Hopper.htm. Accessed 11/11/2012.

――――. "Introduction." In *Interpretation: The Poetry of Meaning*, edited by David L. Miller, ix–xxii. New York: Harcourt Brace, 1967.

――――. "The Literary Imagination and the Doing of Theology." In *The Way of Transfiguration: Religious Imagination as Theopoiesis*, edited by R. Melvin Keiser and Tony Stoneburner, 207–29. Louisville: Westminster John Knox, 1992.

Hoyt, Thomas. "Interpreting Biblical Scholarship for the Black Church Tradition." In *Stony the Road We Trod: African American Biblical Interpretation*, edited by Cain Hope Felder, 17–39. Minneapolis: Fortress, 1991.

Huggins, J. Blake. "Writing on the Boundary Line: Theopoetics as the Eschatological Breaking of Form." Paper delivered at the Theopoetics Working Group 11/16/2011. Online: http://theopoetics.net/wp-content/uploads/2011/11/Writing-on-the-Boundary-Line-Updated.pdf

Hulbert, Steve & Jeanyne Slettom. "Poetics, Post–Structuralism, and Process." *Process Perspectives: Newsmagazine of the Center for Process Studies* 29.1 (2006) 9–10.

Hunt, Stephen. "'Inhabiting a Space on the Outer Edges of Religious Life': The Radical Emergent Christian Community of Ikon." *Marburg Journal of Religion* 15 (2010) 1–20.

Hynes, Arleen, and Mary Hynes-Berry, eds. *Biblio/poetry Therapy, A Resource Bibliography: A Selected Multidisciplinary Bibliography of Reference Materials Related to Poetry Therapy*, St. Joseph, MN: Bibliotheraphy Round Table, 1992.

――――. *Biblio-Therapy: The Interactive Process Handbook.* Boulder, CO: Westview, 1986.

International Academcy of Practical Theology. "Practical Theology and Poetics." Online: http://www.ia-pt.org/practical-theology-and-poetics/. Accessed 10/12/2013.

Jefford, Russel. "An Evaluation of the Importance of Viktor Frankl for the Psychology of Religion." *Early Church.co.uk*. Online: http://www.earlychurch.co.uk/pdfs/The%20 Importance%20of%20Viktor%20Frankl%20for%20the%20Psychology%20of%20 Religion.pdf. Accessed 2/20/13.

Johnson, Mark. *The Meaning of the Body: Aesthetics of Human Understanding*. Chicago: University of Chicago Press, 2007.

Jones, Kathleen. "On Authority: Or, Why Women Are Not Entitled to Speak." In *Feminism and Foucault: Reflections on Resistance*, edited by Irene Diamond and Lee Quimby, 119–33. Boston: Northeastern University, 1988.

Kaiser, Melvin. "Introduction: The Artistry of Theopoesis." In *The Way of Trans-figuration: Religious Imagination as Theopoiesis*, edited by R. Melvin Keiser and Tony Stoneburner, 1–18. Louisville: Westminster John Knox, 1992.

Kant, Immanuel. *Critique of Pure Reason*. Translated by Marcus Weigelt. New York: Penguin, 2007.

Kaufman, Gordon. *God the Problem*. Cambridge: Harvard University Press, 1972.

Kearney, Richard. *Anatheism*. New York: Columbia University Press, 2010.

———. "Epiphanies of the Everyday: Toward a Micro–Eschatology." In *After God*, edited by John P. Manoussakis, 3–20. New York: Fordham University Press, 2006.

———. "The God Who May Be: A Phenomenological Study." *Modern Theology* 181 (2002) 75–85.

———. *Poetics of Imagining*. New York: Fordham University Press, 1998.

———. *The Wake of Imagination*. London and New York: Routledge, 1988.

Keefe-Perry, L. Callid. "Divine Exploration and Invitation." *Cross Currents* 60.1 (2010) 89–104.

———. "Theopoetics: Process and Perspective." *Christianity and Literature* 58.4 (2009) 579–601.

———. "Toward the Heraldic: A Theopoetic Response to Monorthodoxy." In *Theopoetic Folds: Philosophizing Multifariousness*, edited by Roland Faber and Jeremy Feckanthal, 142–58. New York, Fordham University Press, 2013.

Keller, Catherine. "The Flesh of God: A Metaphor in the Wild." In *Theology That Matters: Ecology, Economy, and God*, edited by Kathleen R. Darby, 91–108. Minneapolis: Fortress, 2006.

———. "Goddess, Ear, and Metaphor: On the Journey of Nelle Morton." *Journal of Feminist Studies in Religion* 4.2 (1988) 51–67.

———. "Poetics, Post-Structuralism, and Process." *Process Perspective* 29.1 (2006) 1, 10.

———. "The Pluri-verse." In *Theopoetic Folds: Philosophizing Multifariousness*, edited by Roland Faber and Jeremy Feckanthal, 179–94. New York: Fordham University Press, 2013.

———. "Richard Kearney's Endless Morning." In *Philosophy and Social Criticism* 30.7 (2004) 890–96.

Klemm, David. "Foreword." In *The Call to Radical Theology*, by Thomas J. J. Altizer and edited by Lissa McCullough, ix–xiii. Albany, NY: State University of New York Press, 2012.

Kraybill, Donald. *The Upside-Down Kingdom*. Harrisonburg, VA: Herald, 2011.

Langan, Janine. "The Christian Imagination." In *The Christian Imagination: The Practice of Faith in Literature and Writing*, edited by Leland Ryken, 63–80. Colorado Springs, CO: Waterbrook, 2002.

Laurent, Samuel. "Incarnational Creativity: A Pneumatology of Improvisation." PhD diss., Drew University, 2012.

Levinas, Emmanuel. *Totality and Infinity*. Pittsburgh: Duquesne University Press, 1969.

Lindbeck, George. *The Nature of Doctrine: Religion and Theology in a Postliberal Age*. Louisville, KY: Westminster John Knox. 1984.

Linhares, Bruno. "Nevertheless I Am Continually with You: A Cosmopolitan and Theopoetic Reframing of Pastoral Theology." PhD diss., Princeton University, 2008.

Lorde, Audre. "Poems are Not Luxuries." In *Claims for Poetry*, edited by Donald Hall, 282–85. Ann Arbor, MI: University of Michigan Press, 1982.

Luphor, David. "Language Surprised." *Interviews and Encounters with Stanley Kunitz*, edited by Stanley Moss, 1–9. Riverdale-on-Hudson, NY: Sheep Meadow, 1993.

Lusseyran, Jacques. *And There Was Light: The Autobiography of a Blind Hero of the French Resistance*. Sandpoint, ID: Morning Light Press, 1998.

Lyotard, Jean François. *The Postmodern Condition*. Translated by Geoff Bennington and Brian Massumi. Minneapolis, MN: University of Minnesota Press, 1984.

MacKendrick, Karmen. *Divine Enticement: Theological Seductions*. New York: Fordham University Press, 2013.

———. *Fragmentation and Memory: Meditations on Christian Doctrine*. New York: Fordham University Press, 2008.

———. "The Hospitality of Listening: A Note on Sacramental Strange-ness." In *Phenomenologies of the Stranger: Between Hostility and Hospitality*, edited by Richard Kearney and Kascha Semonovitch, 98–108. New York: Fordham University Press, 2011.

———. *Word Made Skin: Figuring Language at the Surface of Flesh*. New York: Fordham University Press, 2004.

Marshall, Marie, and Edward Marshall. *Logotherapy Revisited: Review of the Tenets of Viktor E. Frankl's Logotherapy*. Ottawa, ON: Ottawa Institute of Logotherapy, 2012.

Martin, Daniel. "Charles Hartshorne, Theologian, Is Dead; Proponent of an Activist God Was 103." Obituary. *New York Times* October 13, 2000. Online: https://www.nytimes.com/2000/10/13/us/charles-hartshorne-theologian-is-dead-proponent-of-an-activist-god-was-103.html.

May, Melanie. *A Body Knows: A Theopoetics of Death and Resurrection*. New York: Continuum, 1995.

———. *Bonds of Unity: Women, Theology and the Worldwide Church*. Atlanta: Scholars, 1989.

Mazza, Nicholas. *Poetry Therapy: Theory and Practice*. New York: Brunner-Routledge, 2003.

Mazza, Nicholas, and Charles Hayton. "Poetry Therapy: An Investigation of a Multidimensional Clinical Model." *The Arts in Psychotherapy* 40 (2013) 53–60.

McCall, Richard. "Liturgical Theopoetic: The Acts of God in the Act of Liturgy." *Worship*, 71 (1997) 399–414.

McCullough, Lissa, and Brian Schroeder, eds. *Thinking through the Death of God*. Albany, NY: State University of New York Press, 2004.

McFague, Sallie. Review of *Theopoetic: Theology and the Religious Imagination* by Amos Niven Wilder. *Journal of Biblical Literature* 96.4 (1977) 592–93.

McLuhan, Eric. "Marshall McLuhan's Theory of Communication: The Yegg." *Global Media Journal* 1.1 (2008) 25–43.

Mead, James. *Biblical Theology: Issues, Methods, and Themes.* Louisville: Westminster John Knox, 2007.

Merton, Thomas. *Contemplation in a World of Action.* Garden City, NY: Image, 1973.

Meyer, Betty. *The ARC Story: A Narrative Account of the Society for the Arts, Religion and Contemporary Culture.* New York: Association for Religion and Intellectual Life, 2003.

Miller, David. "Introduction." In *Why Persimmons? and Other Poems: Transformations of Theology in Poetry,* by Stanley R. Hopper. Atlanta: Scholars, 1987.

———. "Stanley Hopper and Mythopoetics." Speech delivered 2/5/2000. For the 40th anniversary meeting of The Society for the Arts Religion and Contemporary Culture. Online: http://www.sarcc.org/Hopper.htm. Accessed. 11/9/2012.

———. "Theopoetry or Theopoetics?" *Cross Currents* 60.1 (2010) 6–23.

Miller-McLemore, Bonnie. "Revisiting the Living Human Web: Theological Education and the Role of Clinical Pastoral Education." *Journal of Pastoral Care and Counseling* 62.2 (2008) 3–18.

Minear, Paul. "An Early Christian Theopoetic?" *Semeia* 12 (1978) 201–13.

Moltmann, Jürgen. *The Crucified God: The Cross of Christ as the Foundation and Criticism of Christian Theology.* Minneapolis, MN: Fortress, 1993.

Mongrain, Kevin. "Von Balthasar's Way from Doxology to Theology." *Theology Today* 64.1 (2007) 58–70.

Moore, Marianne. *Complete Poems.* London: Rowe, 2003.

Moore, Zöe. *Introducing Feminist Perspectives on Pastoral Theology.* Continuum, 2002.

Murchland, Bernard, ed. *The Meaning of the Death of God.* New York: Random House, 1967.

Neuhaus, Richard. *Death on a Friday Afternoon.* New York: Basic, 2000.

Nicholas of Cusa. "Trialogus De Possest." In *A Concise Introduction to the Philosophy of Nicholas of Cusa,* edited by Jasper Hopkins, 62. Minneapolis, MN: University of Minnesota Press, 1978.

Ostling, Richard, and Joseph J. Kane. "Religion: Jim Bakker's Crumbling World." *TIME Magazine* December 19, 1988.

Packard, Rosa C. "Talk to 9th International Conference of War Tax Resisters and Peace Tax Campaigns." 9/13/2002. Hirschlau, Germany. Online: http://www.rosapackard.org/ptw/9thinternational.html. Accessed 3/9/13.

Poling, Travis. "Poetic Worship: The Renewal of Liturgical Language." MA Thesis. Richmond, IN: Bethany Theological Seminary, 2011.

Puleo, Mev. "Rubem Alves." In *The Struggle is One: Voices and Visions of Liberation,* 185–202. Albany, NY: State University of New York Press, 1994.

Pronger, Brian. *Body Fascism: Salvation in the Technology of Physical Fitness.* Toronto: University of Toronto Press, 2002.

Renovaré, "What is Spiritual Formation?" Online: https://www.renovare.org/formation/spiritual-formation. Accessed 1–10–14.

Rich, Adrienne. *Poetry and Commitment.* New York: Norton, 2011.

Ricœur, Paul. *The Symbolism of Evil.* Boston: Beacon, 1986.

Rilke, Rainer M. *Book of Hours: Love Poems to God.* Translated by Anita Barrows and Joanna Marie Macy. New York, Penguin: 1997.

Rollins, Peter. "Christian A/Theism." *Movement: Termly Magazine of the Student Christian Movement* 122 (2006) 12–18.

———. *How (Not) to Speak of God.* Brewster, MA: Paraclete, 2006.

————. *The Idolatry of God: Breaking Our Addiction to Certainty and Satisfaction.* New York: Howard, 2013.

————. *Insurrection: To Believe Is Human, To Doubt, Divine.* New York: Books, 2011.

————. "MatterCon '09: Keynote seminars." Posted 2/9/2009. Online: http://peterrollins.net/?p=455. Accessed 9/14/12.

————. "What is Pyrotheology?" Posted 8/3/11. Online: http://peterrollins.net/?p=2390. Accessed 8/9/2012.

Roszack, Theodore. *Where the Wasteland Ends.* Garden City, NY: Doubleday, 1972.

Saliers, Don. "The Travail of Christian Worship." In *Arts, Theology and the Church: New Intersections,* edited by Kimberly Vrundy and Wilson Yates, 178–91. Cleveland, OH: Pilgrim, 2006.

Saxon, William. "Amos N. Wilder, a Bible Scholar, Literary Critic and Educator, 97." Obituary. *New York Times.* May 4, 1993. Online: https://www.nytimes.com/1993/05/04/obituaries/amos-n-wilder-a-bible-scholar-literary-critic-and-educator-97.html.

Schluep, John. Personal Interaction. 11/12/13. Boston University.

Schneiders, Sandra. *The Revelatory Text.* San Francisco: Harper Collins, 1991.

————. "Biblical Spirituality." In *The Bible and Spirituality: Exploratory Essays in Reading Scripture Spiritually,* edited by Andrew T. Lincoln, 128–50. Eugene, OR: Cascade, 2013.

Sedgewick, Eve. *Touching Feeling: Affect, Pedagogy, Performativity.* Durham, NC: Duke University Press, 2003.

Skidmore, Thomas. *Politics of Military Rule in Brazil, 1964–1985.* New York: Oxford University Press, 1988.

Small, Christopher. *Musicking: The Meanings of Performing and Listening.* Middletown, CT: Wesleyan University Press, 1998.

Spiegel, Alix. Narrator of "Why Even Radiologists Can Miss a Gorilla Hiding in Plain Sight." Morning Edition. National Public Radio, Feb 11, 2013. Online: http://www.npr.org/templates/transcript/transcript.php?storyId=171409656.

Stafford, William. "Ultimate Concerns." In *The Darkness Around Us Is Deep,* 61. New York: HarperCollins, 1993.

————. *You Must Revise Your Life.* Ann Arbor, MI: University of Michigan Press, 1987.

Taylor, George H. "Ricoeur's Philosophy of Imagination." *Journal of French Philosophy* 16.1 (2006) 93–104.

Theuring, Ashley Elizabeth. "Expressing the Ineffable: Theopoetics of Abraham Joshua Heschel and Dorothee Sölle." MA thesis, Xavier University. 2011.

Tillich, Paul. *My Search For Absolutes.* New York: Touchstone, 1969.

Tripp, Andrew. "Pastoral Theopoetics." Paper delivered at the Theopoetics Working Group 11/19/2012. Online: http://theopoetics.net/wp-content/uploads/2012/11/Tripp-Pastoral-Theopoetics.pdf.

Vandermeersch, Patrick. "The Failure of Second Naïveté." In *Aspects in Contexts: Studies in the History of Psychology of Religion,* edited by Jacob A. Belzen, 235–80. Amsterdam: Rodopi B.V., 2000.

Victorin-Vangerud, Nancy M. "From Metaphors and Models to Maps." In *Theology That Matters: Ecology, Economy, and God,* edited by Kathleen R. Darby, 91–108. Minneapolis: Fortress, 2006.

Viney, Donald. "Process Theism." *Stanford Encyclopedia of Philosophy,* edited by Edward N. Zalta. Stanford University, 2008. Online: http://plato.stanford.edu/archives/win2008/ entries/process-theism. Accessed 5/8/2012.

Weaver, J. Denny. *The Nonviolent Atonement*. Grand Rapids: Eerdmans, 2011.

———. "Series Editor's Foreword." In *Songs from an Empty Cage: Poetry, Mystery, Anabaptism, and Peace*, by Jeffrey Gene Gundry, 13–14. Telford, PA: Cascadia, 2013.

Whitney, Barry. "Hartshorne and Theodicy." In *Hartshorne, Process Philosophy, and Theology*, edited by Robert Kane and Stephen H. Phillips, 59–60. Albany, NY: SUNYs, 1989.

Wilder, Amos. *Early Christian Rhetoric*. Cambridge: Harvard University Press, 1971.

———. "Kerygma, Eschatology and Social Ethics." In *The Background of the New Testament and Its Eschatology: Studies in Honor of C. H. Dodd*, edited by W. D. Davies and D. Daube, 509–36. Cambridge: Cambridge University Press, 1956.

———. *New Testament Faith for Today*. New York: Harper, 1955.

———. "The Relation of Eschatology to Ethics in the Teaching of Jesus as Represented in Matthew." PhD diss., Yale University, 1933.

———. "Scholars, Theologians, and Ancient Rhetoric." SBL Presidential Address. *Journal of Biblical Literature* 75 (1955) 1–11.

———. *Theopoetic: Theology and the Religious Imagination*. Philadelphia: Fortress, 1976.

Yoder, John. *The Politics of Jesus*. Grand Rapids: Eerdmans, 1994.

Zylla, Phillip. "What Language Can I Borrow?" *McMaster Journal of Theology and Ministry* 9 (2007–8) 129–43.

Index